DATE DUE

DATE DUE			
DEC 12 '86			

ZOLA

ZOLA

———❖———

JOANNA RICHARDSON

ST. MARTIN'S PRESS
NEW YORK

CONTENTS

ILLUSTRATIONS

The publishers would like to thank Paul Elek Ltd for the loan of the photographs.

INTRODUCTION

Zola was the most contentious novelist. He was contentious of his own free will. His obscure provincial childhood, his impoverished years in Paris, his awareness of his humble origins: all made him eager to assert himself. His training as a journalist reminded him of the need to create sensations. 'One has,' he said, 'to be execrated in order to be loved.' He chose to impose himself on literature not only by his talent, and by a life of unremitting work, but by a shrewd use of publicity; and the author of *L'Assommoir* and *Nana*, the early defender of Manet, the writer of *J'accuse* . . . , was a publicist of unusual distinction. He had a flair for sensing a theme of general interest, and for exploiting it. He knew how to attract and hold attention. Descended from a family of soldiers, he was always militant. Zola, explained Fernand Xau at the height of the novelist's career, 'is all of a piece. He is a soldier who is going straight to his goal, where his duty and his orders call him.'

Zola's goal remained the truth, and this search for truth was the unifying factor in his life. It informed nearly everything he wrote in his maturity, and it inspired much of his behaviour. Yet Zola saw existence, and art itself, through the prism of his own personality. 'A work of art is a corner of creation seen through a temperament.' So he insisted; and, again: 'A work of art is like a window open on creation; set in the embrasure of the window, there is a sort of transparent screen through which we see things more or less distorted.' If Naturalism meant a rigorous concern for the truth, this truth remained the truth as he saw it. He had no time for taste or decorum; in his fiction he recorded facts. But the facts were chosen for a reason, coloured by his own preoccupations. In the twenty Rougon-Macquart novels there are some twelve hundred characters, but there are very few good human beings. For all his documentation, Zola presents only a facet of the truth. He gives a biassed and incomplete likeness of an age.

It may also be argued that, in his monumental series of novels, breadth and energy take the place of penetration. Zola does not

seriously consider the subtleties of the human mind, the compli-
cations of the human heart. Indeed, it has been said that he
lived on scientific materialism, that is to say in a spiritual void.
It is, perhaps, unwise to be too intellectual about him. Zola was
not an intellectual writer.

Whatever his methods and whatever his weaknesses, he remains the author of *La Curée, Nana, Germinal, La Bête Humaine*:
of novels which, as Mallarmé said, satisfy the general public and
give something new to men of letters. The Rougon-Macquart
novels have been confirmed by time among the outstanding
works of fiction of the Third Republic. Perhaps we should dis-
count the books that followed. For Zola's art was largely the art
of compensation and sublimation; and, with the advent of
Jeanne Rozerot, his creative need had been satisfied. The
Rougon-Macquart had been fraught with his own frustration,
his search for the ideal relationship, his profound longing for
posterity. In *Les Trois Villes* he can only repeat, at inordinate
length, what he had so often proclaimed: that man's salvation
lies in his natural fulfilment. The creed had been implied in *La
Faute de l'Abbé Mouret*; it had been affirmed in many other
Rougon-Macquart novels. It gains nothing from this cumbersome repetition, or from still further repetition in the first two
of Les Quatre Évangiles. The message of *Fécondité* is implicit in
its title, and it is repeated in *Travail*; but the interest of these
two books lies in their political content. In his last works, the
angry young journalist has become the prophet of socialism.
Some might call him the herald of Utopia. Zola's belief in
socialism – and in the United States of Europe – make him immediately modern. They bring the one-time admirer of Hugo
and the friend of Flaubert into the last decades of the twentieth century.

I should like to acknowledge my debt to Professor F. W. J.
Hemmings and Dr Colin Burns and, in America, to Martin
Kanes and R. J. Niess. Among French scholars I must of course
mention Henri Guillemin, Henri Mitterand, Guy Robert and
René Ternois. All students of Zola are indebted to his son-in-law,
Maurice Le Blond, for his patient editing of the works, and to
Denise Le Blond-Zola for her biographical records of her father.
Jean-Claude Le Blond assures me that he has no unpublished
correspondence in his possession. Dr François Émile-Zola refuses

to allow the publication of Zola's intimate letters. One can only regret this serious and avoidable loss to Zola studies. It is sad that the decision should still be made three-quarters of a century after Zola's death.

I gladly record my gratitude to the President and Fellows of Wolfson College, who enabled me to begin this book in Oxford; and, once again, I am grateful to the Librarian and staff of the Taylor Institution for their understanding help. I must thank the staff of the British Library, and those of the Library, University College London, who let me use Zola's unpublished correspondence with Marius Roux. I am very grateful to Mrs Norah Smallwood, who allowed me to examine the letter-books of Zola's English publishers, Messrs Chatto & Windus. I much appreciate the assistance I received at the Bibliothèque Nationale, where I studied Zola's papers. I am happily indebted to the Rockefeller Foundation, who invited me to work on this book at the Bellagio Study and Conference Center, and to Dr and Mrs William C. Olson, who gave me hospitality at the Villa Serbelloni. I owe much to the late Dr W. G. Moore, who gave me years of encouragement and criticism. I am glad to thank Dr Richard Fargher and Dr Alan Raitt for their continued help.

Oxford – London   JOANNA RICHARDSON
Paris – Bellagio
1976 – 1978

PART ONE

PLASSANS AND PARIS
1840-1861

Émile Zola was born in France, and during a lifetime of sixty-two years he rarely left its shores. He earned his literary renown for a series of novels on the Second Empire. He was profoundly involved in an affair which touched the heart and honour of the French nation. He lies, now, in the Panthéon. It is something of a paradox that he was French by naturalisation.

The Zollas – to use their native surname – were a Venetian family.[1] Tradition says that Antonio Zolla, great-grandfather of Émile, was born in Brescia in about 1727. From an early age he served in the Levantine provinces of the Venetian Republic. In 1771 he became a captain of infantry. He married Antonia Palatiano, who was thought to come from Padua, and he died in 1787, leaving three sons. Carlo, the second, had been born in 1752 at Zara, in Dalmatia, where Antonio had then been garrisoned. He followed his father's career, and went to the military college at Verona. He became a captain in the engineers, and he married Nicoletta Bondioli, a sergeant-major's daughter.

The youngest of their four children, Francesco Antonio Giuseppe Maria, was born in Venice on 7 August 1795. In 1810, when he was still a boy, he went to the military school at Pavia. Two years later he was commissioned. He stayed in an Italian regiment in the Austrian service, but in 1817 he was allowed to complete his studies at Padua University, where he became a doctor of mathematics. In 1820 he made his choice, and set up as a civil engineer. Since there was little future for him in Italy, he went to Austria. Here, in 1823, he helped to plan the first railway line in Europe. Four years later he proposed to the Austrian government that they should permit him to build another; he asked for the concession for the company which he wanted to found. His grandiose ambitions were thwarted. The French Revolution of 1830 ruined the bank on which he depended; and for financial (and perhaps political) reasons Francesco left for Paris.

In 1831 he sent the French Ministry of War a plan for the fortifications of the capital. His plan was rejected, and he remained unemployed. The Foreign Legion had just been created. Resilient as ever, he set off to join it in Algeria. His life with it was brief. A sergeant's wife, Mme Fischer, fleeced him of 1500 francs. He had borrowed the money from the clothing store, but expected to replace it unobserved. The authorities were indulgent, and dismissed the charges against him, but he resigned his commission. Early in 1833 he landed at Marseilles, and set up, once again, as an engineer.

His determination was unflagging. In the next few years he conceived a series of projects. He went to Paris, where he was received by Louis-Philippe, and presented him with his plan for the port of Marseilles. The King allowed him to name the proposed dock after his third son, the Prince de Joinville. Perhaps it was this encouragement which led Francesco Zolla to stay in Paris. 'In four years,' he remembered, 'I spent everything I had earned in Marseilles, and I lived for three years in Paris without earning a sou.'

It was in Paris that François Zola, as he now called himself, fell in love with a girl as she came out of mass at Saint-Eustache. She was vital, well-built and brown-haired. She was twenty-four years younger than he was, and her name was Émilie-Aurélie Aubert. She was the daughter of Louis-Auguste Aubert, a house-painter. She and François Zola were married at the *mairie* of the first arrondissement on 16 March 1839.

The alliance was hardly grand, but it brought some northern French solidity to a Mediterranean family. For Émilie – born in 1819 – came from Dourdan (the birthplace of La Bruyère, and of the critic Francisque Sarcey); it lay between the forest of Dourdan and the vast grain-producing plain of the Beauce – one day to be the setting of *La Terre*.[2]

It was, however, in Paris that Émilie gave birth to her son. Émile-Édouard-Charles-Antoine Zola was born at 10 *bis*, rue Saint-Joseph, on 2 April 1840.

Émile Zola's Parisian birth was to mean little to him. In October his father submitted another plan for the fortifications of Paris. It was rejected. François Zola took his family back to Provence, and settled in Aix. Undaunted by experience, he determined to supply the city with water. A society was established, with a capital of 600,000 francs. He signed contracts with the civic authorities for the aqueduct and the canal. The work was begun. A dam near Aix was one day to bear his name.

At last the Zolas had a hope of prosperity, and Émile's future seemed to be assured. However, two events in his early childhood were to mark him ineffaceably. Almost exactly on his fifth birthday he was brutally made aware of sex. On 3–4 April 1845, the local superintendent of police reported: 'We have sent to the Palais de Justice a certain Mustapha, aged twelve, a native of Algiers, a servant of M. Zola, civil engineer . . . He is accused of assaulting the young Émile Zola.'[3] This police report, discovered many years afterwards in the municipal archives in Marseilles, may help to explain Zola's lifelong horror of homosexuality and his timid, often guilty attitude towards sex. As Professor Hemmings suggests, it was probably Mme Zola who had discovered the *jeux interdits*. The fact would largely explain Zola's later attitude towards her: an ambivalent attitude of suppressed guilt and emotional dependence. The episode might also help to explain his eventual coldness to his wife, his happiness with a mistress who was too young and timid to remind him of the masterful older boy.

Two years after this assault, his happy childhood ended. On 28 March 1847 François Zola died, suddenly, at Marseilles. He was said to have died of pleurisy. He was fifty-one.

Émile had grown up in a large house in the impasse Sylvacanne in Aix. When his father died, the house became too expensive to maintain. The family moves from lodging to lodging reflected their sad descent in society. From the impasse Sylvacanne they moved to the pont de Béraud, in the outskirts of Aix, then to the rue Bellegarde, the rue Roux-Alphéran, the cours des Minimes, and finally to a workman's lodging in the rue Mazarine. This childhood of increasing and oppressive poverty was to shape Zola's mind and, to some extent, his career. He was one of those *déclassés* so numerous in the nineteenth century, and the characters in his Rougon-Macquart novels were frequently to be aggressive outsiders like himself.

At home, he lived the lonely life of an only child. He was surrounded by adults: a doting mother and her two ageing parents. 'My mother was very kind and weak where I was concerned,' Zola recalled, 'and so I grew up without discipline. At the age of seven or eight I still couldn't read . . . I developed on my own, and I think that's the best way.' He added, pugnaciously: 'I don't believe in education.'[4]

However, he went to the Pension Notre-Dame and, at the age of twelve, to the Collège Bourbon in Aix. There are conflicting accounts of his schooldays. Marius Topin, who sat next to him in class, maintained that Zola won prizes every year for his work in classics. Seillière, in his life of Zola, says that he was far from precocious, and that he chose to try for the *baccalauréat ès sciences* because he felt an aversion for Greek and Latin.[5] Whatever the truth, he was drawn to literature. One day he escaped from the classroom and slipped into a poetry festival at the Hôtel de Ville. They were reading Provençal poems, and Mistral was there.[6]

Édouard Rod also noted that Zola joined the school orchestra. At sixteen, he played the clarinet in the Aix theatre, 'and took his modest share of the applause.'[7] Years later, the billiard-room at Médan was adorned with a panoply of musical instruments, a clarinet among them. There was also an upright piano. But only towards the end of his life, when he was working on an opera with Alfred Bruneau, did Zola buy a harmonium; only then did he go to concerts. He was not naturally musical.

It was at the Collège Bourbon that he came to know Paul Cézanne, a banker's son, and Jean-Baptistin Baille, one day to be a civil engineer. Cézanne was older than Zola, and took him under his protection. The three boys became inseparable. They fished, they swam, and they explored Aix and the countryside around it. They climbed the foothills of Mont Sainte-Victoire, through thickets of oak and holly, pine trees and wild roses. They wandered along the goat paths by the ravines, and across the plains which were sometimes watered by the Arc or the Torse, and sometimes by the canal which François Zola had planned.[8] Zola was one day to be a lover of animals; but, as a boy, he went out early on November mornings, bent on catching thrushes in cages. In warmer weather he used to take a volume of Musset's poems in his game-bag, and read them, stretched out on the grass, with the smell of sage and lavender in the air.

Émile Zola had been born in Paris, but he was a Southerner by nature. It was in the old abandoned capital of Provence that he began to develop his mind and his emotional responses. He

loved the Provençal landscape. He loved Aix itself: the court-
yards planted with plane trees, the gently flowing fountains,
the tortuous streets, lined with splendid *hôtels*, whose massive
carved wooden doors remained closed, heavily, on the life of the
inhabitants.[9] At the age of fifty-two, he confessed:

Even now, when I close my eyes, there is not a street corner in
Aix, a stretch of old wall, a bit of sunlit pavement, which does not
come to mind with striking relief. I can recall the most obscure
paths in the neighbourhood, the little greyish olive-trees, the meagre
almond trees vibrating with the chatter of the crickets, the stream
which was always dried up, the white road where the dust cracked
underfoot, like a snowfall. It was Greece, with its pure sun on the
stark majesty of the horizons.[10]

At the age of fifty-six, thanking an Aixois friend for some olives,
he wrote gratefully: 'They brought me back a little of that South,
so distant to-day, yet so living in my heart. Some fruit or drink
or even smell will call it up with singular intensity.'[11]

In November 1857, Mme Aubert died. It was time to leave
Provence, and Mme Zola set off for Paris, ahead of her father
and son, to settle her late husband's claims and financial
affairs. 'My mother, a worthy and excellent woman, was led
by the best intentions,' Zola was to tell Fernand Xau, 'but she
hardly had any idea of business, and her inexperience led us to
ruin.'[12] In February 1858, when he and Monsieur Aubert
reached Paris, the family were obliged to take sordid furnished
lodgings at 63, rue Monsieur-le-Prince.

On 1 March, on the eve of his eighteenth birthday, Zola
entered the Lycée Saint-Louis as a day-boy. He felt miserable
and imprisoned.[13] He was in the second class, in the science section, but he was out of his element, and he did badly. He continued to long for Provence. He spent the summer holidays at
Aix, but autumn brought the dreaded return to Paris. He was
not only homesick; in November he fell ill with typhoid fever.
When he was convalescent, he wrote an account of his experience. It was to serve him, many years later, when he
described the illness and delirium of Serge Mouret.[14]

On 3 August 1859, he sat for his *baccalauréat ès sciences*, but he
failed the oral examination. He was found inadequate in

German, history and literature. In November he sat for the examination again, this time at Aix, and once more he failed.

This failure barred him from nearly all the liberal professions, and no doubt it helped to decide his future.

2

Late in November he returned from Aix to Paris. He was nineteen, and he had no qualification or profession.[1] He did not think immediately of living by his pen. Writing seemed to him an outlet for his emotions. 'I'm planning to describe the birth of love, and to take it up to marriage,' he told Cézanne. 'I have never loved except in dream, and no-one has ever loved me, even in a dream! Never mind, as I feel I am capable of a great love, I shall consult my heart, I shall create myself some fine ideal, and *perhaps* I shall carry out my plan.'[2]

The ideal did not need to be created. At the turn of the year, Zola discovered it.

The other day, at a friend's, I came across an old, discoloured engraving [this to Cézanne on 16 January 1860] ... I was not surprised by my admiration when I saw it signed with the name Greuze. It showed a young peasant girl, tall, of uncommon beauty of face: one would have said a goddess from Olympus, but she had an expression so simple and so tender that her beauty almost turned into sweetness ... I looked for a long while at that engraving, and vowed that I should love the original, if such a portrait – doubtless an artist's dream – can have one.[3]

Years later he was to realise the dream of *La Cruche cassée*. In these early months of 1860, reality in Paris was all too distant from divine Olympus. He was overwhelmed by self-doubt and solitude.[4] He recognised that he must earn his living, no matter how, and spend his nights in working for his future. 'The struggle will be long,' he wrote, 'but it doesn't frighten me. I feel something within me, and, if this something really exists, sooner or later it must appear.'[5]

He was aware, already, of his literary gifts, but he needed the recognition of the world. 'If you are always unknown,' he told

Baille, 'you come to doubt yourself. Nothing enlarges an author's ideas like success. No matter, if I am to be known I must go on working; I am young, and, if the last months . . . have harmed me, they cannot have stifled all poetry in me. I can feel it trembling within me.'[6] He was remarkably mature when he assessed himself, but his vision was still coloured by his readings of Musset in Provence. He saw himself as a Romantic poet. Cézanne wrote to him about realism. 'What do you mean,' asked Zola, 'by the word realism? You boast that you paint only things devoid of poetry. But everything has its poetry, the dunghill as well as the flowers . . . In other words, art is one, and spiritualist and realist are only words, and poetry is a great thing, and without poetry there is no salvation.'[7] It was a lyrical confession for the Naturalist-to-be.

The conversation of Provence continued by letter between Provence and Paris; and now, at last, his future seemed to be plain. He dreamed of literary glory.[8] He already had the determination of the self-aware – and that of the bitter young man who meant to compensate himself for his wretched youth. He took a job as a Customs clerk at 60 francs a month. He kept his persistent resolve to be a poet.

The world is rushing down the path of the future, eager to see what is waiting at the end of its journey. What then [he asked Baille] will the poet do? . . .

Science is not my affair . . . My whole ambition, as I have said, is to know grammar and history. What should I do with the rest? I'd rather draw everything from within myself than draw it from other people . . .

You accuse me of systems, and you are wrong; nothing is less systematic than my mind.[9]

It was, again, a remarkable statement from the future author of the Rougon-Macquart; but, if Zola continued to dream of a literary career, he still considered himself to be a creative Romantic. As yet he saw no relation between science and literature.

The summer of 1860 continued, and so did his introspection. Writing to Baille in July, he revealed his unceasing love of the ideal. He was touchingly innocent, disarmingly hopeful; and his beliefs and hopes may be recorded. For, whatever he maintained in his middle years, his fundamental needs were not to change. His romanticism was always to remain a significant element in his nature.

I turn my eyes away from the dunghill to look at the roses [he wrote, now, to Baille]. I do not deny the usefulness of the dunghill, for it makes my fine flowers bloom, but I prefer the roses, though they have so little use. That is my position in regard to reality and the ideal . . .

I don't deny love in the least, and I don't despair of anything; I only await some good angel . . . I am quite aware that perhaps my wish may never be realised. But there is a perhaps, and that is my salvation.[10]

Zola was becoming increasingly absorbed by the thought of his literary future. In his own phrase, he felt the wings beating behind him. He was already militant. 'Make no mistake, the artist is a soldier: he fights in the name of God for all that is great [this to Baille on 10 August] . . . In our age of materialism, . . . the poet has a sacred mission. At every moment, and everywhere, he must show the soul to those who think of nothing but the body, and God to those whose faith has been strained by science.'[11] Zola did not yet deny religion. Like Hugo, now in exile in Guernsey, he had a poetic mission, and his mission seemed evident.

His existence remained all too wretched. He was unsettled by poverty, by boredom, and by his first, bitter love affair.[12] His sexual urges were strong, but no doubt he recalled his experience with Mustapha; and, as the only son of a widowed mother, whose emotional life was centred in him, he was probably immature in his attitude to women. As for marriage, he considered it with youthful self-esteem. 'Every woman,' he told Cézanne, 'has the stuff of a good wife in her, it's for the husband to arrange this stuff as well as possible.'[13] Such brutality concealed his nervousness. In fact he was timid with women; and, while he dreamed of the Greuze peasant girl, he could only aspire, in reality, to a passing affair with a prostitute. He was disillusioned by the experience. He was also determined, once again, to turn experience to literary advantage. On 5 February 1861, he announced to Cézanne: 'I am emerging from a harsh school, that of real love . . . I have new views on love. They will be extremely useful to me in the work that I hope to write.'[14]

At about the end of April, Cézanne arrived in Paris; but the old intimate friendship could not be resumed. Cézanne was melancholy, and he returned to Aix in September. From his belvedere at 24, rue Neuve-Saint-Étienne-du-Mont – where Bernardin de Saint-Pierre had written much of his work – Zola was forced by poverty to move to an indescribable *hôtel garni* used by students and prostitutes: 11, rue Soufflot. Edmond Lepelletier, one of his biographers, was later to chart his moves to 7, impasse Saint-Dominique; to the rue de la Pépinière, Montrouge; 7, rue des Feuillantines; 278, rue Saint-Jacques; 142, boulevard Montparnasse. When Zola could afford a candle, he was happy, for it meant that he could write at night. Already he had the religion of efficiency. 'I have no pity,' he was to say,' for the fate of the vanquished, when it is their weakness which is to blame . . . You achieve nothing without determination.'[15]

PART TWO

APPRENTICESHIP
1862-1869

3

In February 1862 his apprenticeship began. That month, through one of his father's friends, he became a clerk at the Librairie Hachette. He was paid 100 francs a month. For the first few weeks he did nothing but pack books for delivery. Soon after he began, he had a letter from the critic who was largely to form his literary theories. Taine sent him a complaint.

My dear Sir,
    Yesterday I received a letter from *Mr Matthew Arnold, 2, Chester Square, London*, to whom I had written when I sent my book. He had received the letter, but not the book. Would you give orders in London about this, as soon as possible, and have the book sent to him?[1]

Zola later became the head of the publicity department. His salary was doubled. He came to know publishers, authors and critics. In this literary atmosphere, his personal ambitions became intense. On 5 June 1863 he sent Jules Claretie two stories for *L'Univers illustré*. 'I beg you, with all the fervour of a beginner, not to condemn me without reading me . . . Think that for me it is almost a question of literary life or death.'[2] Unsophisticated but resolute, he also confronted the publisher Albert Lacroix, and begged him to read his *Contes à Ninon*. 'Just read one of them, at random. I assure you that I have talent.' He spoke with such conviction that Lacroix published the book at his own expense.[3] It appeared on 24 October 1864.

Contes à Ninon reveals the romanticism which, for most of his career, Zola was to struggle to repress. Ninon is the ethereal love of the adolescent in Provence. She is the dream which had haunted him among the vines and olive-trees: a mistress who owed more to his imagination, to his reading of romantic poets, than she did to any living figure. She is now the voice of memory, an insistent voice urging him to re-tell the tales he had told her in Provence. There is a suggestion of Perrault in 'Simplice', the story of the prince who died for love of a water-sprite. There is a touch of him, again, in 'La Fée amoureuse', where the lovers are turned into sprigs of marjoram, and yet again in 'Sœur-des-pauvres', the tale of a child with a magic fortune who tries to cure the ills of the world. Yet in this collection of innocent, idealistic tales, we find the humanitarian instincts, the search for the Utopian society, which we shall find again in Les Quatre Évangiles at the end of Zola's career. Other features will remain constant: among them the belief in pathetic fallacy. The forest in 'Simplice' anticipates the conservatory in *La Curée*, the garden in *La Faute de l'Abbé Mouret*. We recognise, too, in Sœur-des-Pauvres, an embryo of Denise Baudu and Pauline Quenu. Zola dreams persistently of the perfect woman. The theme of 'Celle qui m'aime' is one which he was soon to develop in *La Confession de Claude*: the disillusionment of romantic love. He has his vision of a smiling girl, white-robed and wreathed with flowers; but it is a transient vision, bought at a fair. The dream is mere commercial enterprise.

His literary dreams remained, and they were now becoming realities.

Every day my position becomes clearer; every day I take a step forward [this on 6 February 1865]. Where are the evenings of peaceful application, when I found myself alone in front of my work, not knowing if it would ever see the day? Then I debated with myself. I hesitated. Now I must go on, go on whatever happens. Whether the written page is good or bad, it must appear. I am really delighted to find myself emerging, little by little, from the crowd. I also feel a sort of anguish when I wonder if I shall have the strength I need ... I impatiently await the day when I shall feel strong and powerful enough to leave everything, and to devote myself to literature.[4]

Journalism might bring him an income. It was also a means of reaching a large public. Zola took it into account in his search for fame. On 11 April he wrote to Alphonse Duchêne, on *Le Figaro*: 'I know that you like to try people out, to discover new contributors. Try me, discover me.'[5] Already he was learning the importance of intrigue; and already his politics were bearing fruit. On 7 December he thanked the Goncourts for inviting him to the first performance of *Henriette Maréchal*.[6]

On 15 November the *Bibliographie de la France* had registered

Zola's second work. *La Confession de Claude* recalls his own recent experience. Claude is twenty, and a poet. An instinctive pride has kept him chaste. One evening he meets a prostitute, and sleeps with her. Next day he is ashamed, and wants to dismiss her, but she is destitute and, out of pity, he decides to keep her. He tries to redeem her, but instead it is she who degrades him. He is abandoned by his friends, and reduced to poverty. His pride is roused at last. He leaves Paris and returns to his family in the country.

    La Confession de Claude is youthful and earnest; it is also shrill and unmoving. Surprisingly enough, it drew the attention of the public prosecutor. Louis Hachette, disturbed by such *réclame*, asked Zola to leave his firm or abandon literature. On 27 January 1866 Zola wrote to a friend from Aix, Marius Roux:

    I'm leaving the Librairie on Wednesday; and every hour that I still have to spend there has its work marked out.

    Give me until the end of next week, and I will come and greet you at your restaurant, or else I will write to you to arrange a meeting.[7]

On 31 January, after four years at Hachette's, Zola left the firm and became a contributor to *L'Événement*. Henri de Villemessant, the editor, maintained that a journalist must surprise the public every day. Zola was to remember the lesson.[8]

    He began by using his contacts, his journalistic flair, to introduce 'Livres d'aujourd'hui et de demain'. This feature combined book reviews with gossip and news of work in preparation. On 2 February the first of these articles was published. On 14 March he reviewed Victor Hugo's latest novel, *Les Travailleurs de la mer*. 'My whole being is violently shaken by these strange and powerful pages.'[9] Next day Mme Hugo told her husband: 'The review in *L'Événement* is perhaps the best. It is better than praise, it is glorification. Apparently Mr Zola is a young man of talent who is still unknown.'[10] He was rapidly becoming known, and learning how to make friends. Among his papers is a note dated only 18 March. 'Insult rarely touches me, sympathy always touches me. You have written a fine and noble page on my book, which goes to my heart. I thank you. I am moved. Victor Hugo.'[11]

Zola was already outspoken and original. Even now, in 1866, his combative support of Taine earned him the critic's interest and gratitude. On 2 March Taine wrote to thank him for an article. He expounded the theory which Zola was to use in his Rougon-Macquart novels.

Dear Sir,

... There are five or six pages at the beginning which I am really proud to have occasioned. Thank you very much ...

When a man is born he brings into the world his own soul, his distinct personality, and the more intensely, the more completely this soul and personality reveal themselves, the greater in proportion his work will be. But (1) Since he belongs to a race, the characteristic features of his soul are also found in the other men of this race ... (2) In the long run, the sum of physiological forces develops the constituent qualities in this race. It produces ... a high proportion of the men whom they call great men ... Therefore the Individuality is itself produced according to certain rules; this is Darwin's law ... The external milieu, education, the surrounding pressure finally develop the great individuals in this direction ...

As you see, I'm arguing; accept my scribble as a proof of the great interest of your article, and of the lively pleasure it has given me.[12]

Zola now earned 500 francs a month on *L'Événement*: two and a half times his final salary at Hachette's. He was learning the art of self-advertisement. On 8 June he asked Roux: 'Did you get the brochure and the book that I've just published? I count on you for an article in the *Mémorial* [*d'Aix*]. Thank you in advance.'[13] The article was duly written.

The inventive literary critic was also an audacious writer on art. At the Salon of 1866 the young, progressive artists had had their work rejected. There was no painting by Manet, Renoir or Cézanne. Zola wrote an unsparing criticism of the Salon. On 7 May he was taken by Antoine Guillemet, the landscape painter, to Manet's studio, where the artist had organised a private exhibition. This visit marked the beginning of a friendship which was to last until Manet's death. From 27 April to 20 May, Zola published a series of articles on him in *L'Événement*. His enthusiasm for Manet aroused such a protest that he was obliged to leave the paper.

Zola, it must be emphasised, was not a professional critic of art. He himself admitted from the first that he could not discuss technique or style. The beauty of a work of art was, for him, the life it contained, the sign of the creator's temperament. He admired Manet's realism, simplicity and strength. In 1884, introducing a posthumous exhibition of Manet's work, he was still to praise his uncompromising realism. Such praise was not dispassionate. Zola defended Manet all the more warmly because he saw the artist, like himself, as 'a determined fighter, an unpopular man who did not tremble before the public, . . . but tried to control it, to impose his temperament upon it'. He identified Manet's struggle with his own.

He appreciated Monet, too, for Monet painted with passionate truthfulness. Years before he wrote *La Terre*, he admired the poetry of Millet's countryside, 'a poetry which is pure reality'. He respected Pissarro's 'bitter quest for truth'. Much of Zola's criticism suggests the espousal of causes rather than the expression of an artistic nature. It is a statement of solidarity with his co-religionists in art.

Much of it was naturally given to attacks on academic painting. Zola constantly attacked the artistic Establishment: the École des Beaux-Arts, the Salon, the jury system, the influence of cliques, the award of medals and decorations. He derided public taste, the witless following of fashion. He scorned the microscopic detail of Meissonier, the highly polished portraits of Dubufe. He deplored the pretentions of Doré, when the illustrator tried his hand at large-scale historical painting.

Zola was, perhaps, more concerned with creeds and personalities than he was with the canvases at the Salon. His views were limited. He was sadly grudging in his admiration of Moreau. He might have shown more appreciation of Boudin. Nor did his opinions broaden or mature. Indeed, certain passages were repeated almost verbatim over the years: a fact which suggests both the pressures of journalism and the limits of his own appreciation. Yet, whatever his shortcomings, he had artistic sense; and the artists whom he admired have also been acclaimed by posterity.

In 1866 the romantic in his nature was submerged; Zola was increasingly identified with the current movement of Realism. He did not intend to be labelled; he meant to move with his age. On 11 May, in 'Les Réalistes du Salon', he insisted that he was no Realist, that he simply believed in life and truth. Then, echoing his recent letter from Taine, he explained:

> The wind is in the direction of science; we are driven, despite ourselves, towards the exact study of facts and things. All the strong new characters which appear therefore affirm themselves in the direction of truth . . .
> The definition of a work of art could only be this: *A work of art is a corner of creation seen through a temperament.*[14]

And again: 'I am more concerned with life than with art.'[15]

On 23 June a collection of his articles was announced under the title of *Mes Haines*. The title was misleading, for there was only one severe attack in the book; on the other hand, Zola made himself the militant apologist for controversial artists and writers. Among them was Courbet. 'Personally,' wrote Zola, 'I affirm it as a principle that a work lives only by its originality. I must rediscover a man in each work, or the work leaves me cold.' And then, again, almost quoting his letter from Taine:

> Do you not understand that art is the free expression of a heart and mind, and that it is all the greater the more personal it is? . . .
> If you ask me what I come to do in this world, myself, I shall answer: 'I come to live aloud.' . . .
> I have been enabled to see some of Courbet's first pictures, in the master's studio . . . Courbet is the only artist of our age; he belongs to the family of the makers of flesh.[16]

In his appreciation of *Germinie Lacerteux*, by the Goncourts, Zola returned again to the principles of Taine:

> There is, no doubt, an intimate relationship between modern man, such as he has been made by an advanced civilization, and this novel of the gutter . . .
> For me the work is great, in this sense that it is . . . the manifestation of a strong personality, and that it lives largely with the life of our age. I am not concerned with any other merit in literature.[17]

Whatever his denials, Zola had accepted Realism.

4

On three occasions in his life, Zola belonged to a kind of brotherhood. He had been one of the close-knit group of Provençal friends, and in time he was to preside over the École de Médan. Now, in the late 1860s, he frequented the Café Guerbois, near the place de Clichy, where he met the pleiad of artists known as the École des Batignolles. Perhaps, as Lepelletier suggests, his Venetian heredity gave him a taste for pacts and private understandings. He had, as it were, the tradition of the secret societies and the Council of Ten.[1]

The 1860s were difficult years for young painters in France. The Salon juries deprived them of their only means of reaching the general public. Few critics chose to notice them; few buyers were prepared to invest in pictures by unknown artists who did not satisfy their penchant for prettiness. At the Café Guerbois, the reactionary judgment of the juries was discussed as eagerly as the recent 'discovery' of Japanese prints, the rôle of shadows or the use of bright colours. Manet came to the café with Renoir, Monet and Bazille, Sisley, Pissarro and, occasionally, Cézanne, *l'éternel refusé*. There, too, was Degas, who had recently discovered his true *genre*: painting the world of Longchamp and Chantilly. Some of the habitués of the Café Guerbois were recorded by Fantin-Latour. *Un Atelier aux Batignolles* was shown in 1870, in the last Salon of the Second Empire.

The café meetings had been chance meetings when they began in 1866; gradually they had become regular gatherings. In the final years of the Empire, the Café Guerbois was established as a centre of intellectual life. During the Franco-Prussian War it was abandoned, and the meetings were not resumed in the post-war years.

Armand Silvestre, the man of letters, had sometimes spent an hour in the café; he had observed that Zola was still fighting for fame, 'but the sense of imminent victory was visible in the serenity of his glance, and in the calm assurance of his conversation. You would have had to be blind . . . not to sense a power in this man, just from looking at him.'[2] No-one could have failed to notice Zola's determination. From the beginning of his career he devoted himself, inexorably, to work. Apart from the books and documents essential to his task, he hardly read at all. He informed himself only in passing of current events. He saw a few friends, but with them the conversation returned to the sole object of his thoughts. He chose to be single-minded, and he needed isolation for his purpose. There was, he wrote, no solitary except the writer who had wanted solitude, in the freely chosen confines of his work.

Zola had once been led by a Greuze engraving to dream of love, and the dream of an ideal was not to leave him. But, whatever his later boasts, he seems to have been neither a philanderer nor a passionate lover in his youth. As for marriage, he still thought of it from a coolly practical point of view. His idea of the perfect wife was, however, remarkably advanced. It anticipates the more progressive views of the 1970s to a quite extraordinary degree.

The mission of woman, Zola said, was to be the collaborator of man,

the faithful companion, the conciliatory and devoted equal. And so, first and foremost, woman must be liberated: we must liberate her body, heart and mind.

She must be educated, and made our sister in her thinking . . . The married woman must be more than a housewife and a re-producing machine, she must be a soul who understands the husband's soul, a thought which has communion with the thought of the man who is chosen and loved . . . I want all the young ladies' boarding-schools in existence to be demolished, and, on their ruins, I want us to build colleges where our daughters will be brought up like our sons . . .

Having liberated the mind, we must liberate the heart and body. We must give women equality before the law, and we must re-establish divorce. The question of children is secondary [Zola was rightly to change this opinion]; a law will be found to safeguard their interests. But what is quite essential to break is this bond of iron, which eternally unites two beings one to the other. It is absolutely vital that the man and woman should be free in their union, and that it should not be an article in the Code which makes them faithful.

Thenceforth, the couple will go forward with a sure step. It will be united, body and soul, by the very liberty of marriage. The union will be worthier, nobler, deeper, and the couple will be a single being.[3]

Zola himself, at twenty-five, was not ready for marriage, but the year 1865 seems to have set the pattern for his private life. About a year earlier, Cézanne had introduced him to Gabrielle-Éléonore-Alexandrine Meley. Gabrielle – known as Coco – was handsome and Junoesque. She herself would never speak about her origins and early years, and they are still somewhat mysterious. According to Armand Lanoux, she had been born in Paris on 23 March 1839, the daughter of a compositor, Edmond-Jacques Meley. Her mother had died when the child was ten.[4] According to Guy Robert, Gabrielle was born on 26 March 1839; she was the natural daughter of a hosier and a saleswoman.[5]

Albert Laborde, her biographer, was to give the most complete account of the facts; and he had the advantage of being her godson and, indeed, the son of her cousin, Émile Laborde.[6] Jacques-Alexandre Meley, so Laborde recorded, was a cotton merchant in the Seine-Inférieure. He and his wife, the former Marie-Rose-Bibienne Baudet, had three children: Bibienne-Alexandre (grandmother of Laborde), Narcisse, and Edmond-Jacques, who was born in 1820. Edmond-Jacques was eighteen when his daughter, Gabrielle, was born; and Caroline-Louise Wadoux, her mother, was seventeen. Laborde assumes that both families helped to bring up the child.

Nine years after his daughter's birth, Edmond-Jacques finally married, but he did not marry Caroline-Louise, and his wife proved to be an unkind stepmother. In 1849 Caroline-Louise married a certain Louis-Charles Deschamps. According to her marriage certificate, she was then a florist, and lived at 123, rue Saint-Honoré. A few months after her marriage, she died; and Laborde surmises that perhaps a sister of Deschamps, herself a florist, took care of the child. Gabrielle was to show an unusual knowledge of flowers.

Some said that, when Zola met her, she was a laundress. Whatever her profession, his family were to keep a copy of *La Confession de Claude*, inscribed: 'To my dear Gabrielle, in memory of 24 December 1865.' That was presumably the date when she became Zola's mistress. He was probably not her first lover;

indeed, it has been suggested that her feelings for an earlier lover inspired Zola with the plot of *Madeleine Férat*. It is possible that she had been intimate with Cézanne.[7]

However, it was with Gabrielle that Zola moved to his last address on the Left Bank. In 1866 they settled at 10, rue de Vaugirard, near the Théâtre de l'Odéon.[8]

5

On 17 November 1866, the *Bibliographie de la France* announced Zola's forthcoming novel, *Le Vœu d'une morte*. It was duly published by Achille Faure, and then it was very properly forgotten. It is a sugary, improbable morality: a strikingly poor work for the young man who was already making himself a name. For it was this year, by invitation, that Zola sent a paper to the Congrès scientifique de France. Here, for the first time, he defined the novel. Even now, his opinions were revolutionary. 'The drama is dead,' insisted Zola, 'and science has just been born ... The framework of the novel itself has changed ... It is simply a question of recording human facts, and of showing the bare mechanism of the body and soul.'[1]

There is a constant aggressive tone in Zola's criticism. It is the tone of a would-be leader, but one may also detect in it the assertiveness of the insecure. Zola came of a family of soldiers; he was also a provincial in Paris, he had known the bitterness of the poor and declassed. He was not to forget his experience. 'I am only a fighting critic,' he wrote, 'who clears his path before him, since there is nobody else to clear it.'[2] 'You lead too contemplative a life,' he reproached a friend. 'I should like to see you with a more militant spirit.'[3] And again: 'I like difficulties and impossibilities. Above all I love life, and I think that production, of any kind, is always preferable to rest. Such thoughts will make me accept all the struggles that present themselves, struggles with myself and struggles with the public.'[4]

On 29 May 1867, writing once again to the same correspondent, Zola told him:

I am very pleased with the psychological and physiological novel which I am going to publish ... This novel is almost completely finished, and it will certainly be my best work. I think I have put myself into it, body and heart. Indeed I'm afraid I've put in a little too much of my body, and I shall rouse the Public Prosecutor. It's true that [the thought of] a few months in prison doesn't alarm me.[5]

Le Figaro had recently published a novel by Adolphe Belot and Ernest Daudet, La Vénus de Gordes, in which a husband was murdered by his wife's lover. Zola had recognised the dramatic potential of the subject. He had gone further, and imagined how, bound to each other by lust and remorse, the lovers could escape their torment only by suicide. He had treated this theme in a story which had appeared in Le Figaro on 24 December 1866.

In Zola's mind, this story seemed material enough for a novel, and he suggested it to Arsène Houssaye, who was then the editor of L'Artiste. 'I may never write Un Mariage d'amour unless I find an intelligent man who agrees to accept this novel on trust and to publish it in six parts, as fast as it is written . . . Say yes, and I shall start to write. I feel that this will be the great work of my youth.'[6]

Houssaye accepted the offer, and paid 600 francs for the serial rights. Zola submitted the first instalment on 4 March 1867, but publication was delayed till August, for Houssaye did not want to compromise his good relationship with the Tuileries. He told Zola that the Empress Eugénie read the review, and that he must therefore omit certain strongly worded passages from the serial. Zola agreed (so legend says), but he objected when Houssaye added a moral at the end. This was deleted.[7] Zola then took his novel to the publisher Albert Lacroix, who brought it out in December as Thérèse Raquin.

Thérèse Raquin gains its power from its squalid setting, the amorality of its central characters, but above all from the precision of the narrative. It follows the precepts which Zola had set out to the Congrès scientifique de France. It is not so much the story of a murder and its aftermath as a cool analysis of the couple who commit it. Zola studies their motives and their calculations, their immediate and delayed reactions to the event. He shows how in death, even more than in life, the figure of their victim comes to haunt them. This theme of the first lover, the unforgotten past, will recur more than once in his novels: in Madeleine Férat, in L'Assommoir, and – a closer analogy

– in *Germinal*. In Zola's work the past does not return unless it brings back guilt or disaster. This fear of the past seems to lie deep in his nature. Perhaps it owes something to Gabrielle's past rather than his own. It appears a strange recurrent personal motif in his so-called impersonal work.

Zola's years of apprenticeship had begun with his appointment to Hachette's, and they ended with *Thérèse Raquin*. He continued to provoke strong reactions from the critics. The Goncourts acclaimed this 'admirable autopsy of remorse'. *Le Figaro* denounced the book as 'putrid literature'.[8] Zola did not miss an occasion to advertise himself. He published a reply in the same paper.

He had already tried to enlist the support of Sainte-Beuve. When the book appeared, he had sent him a copy. On 15 December Jules Troubat, the critic's secretary, had answered: 'For some time, now, M. Sainte-Beuve has been much more unwell . . . He begs you to forgive him if he cannot have the honour of acknowledging your letter and the presentation of your book.'[9] In time, however, Sainte-Beuve recovered enough to write to Zola. 'You have done a bold deed,' he assured him. '. . . You have braved the public and the critics, too. Don't be surprised at certain displays of anger. The fight is on. Your name is known through it.'[10] Zola remained determined that his name should be known. He seems to have asked Taine himself to enter the fray as his supporter. In a letter among Zola's papers, presumably dated 1868, Taine explained to him:

I should find it rather difficult at the moment to write a note on *Thérèse Raquin* in the *Débats*. Polemic isn't really my strong point, and besides I think that the attacks which are being made on you are rather to your advantage. A criticised book is a noticed book. Th. Gautier and the Goncourts think that yours is good, and I consider it your best work . . . In my opinion, the work is solidly built on a sound idea; it is very well knit, very well composed; it indicates a real artist, a serious observer who is not seeking amusement, but the truth . . .

There, my dear Sir, is my very frank impression. If I dared to give advice, I should tell you that you needed to enlarge your scope and balance your effects. Balzac and Shakespeare are the great masters here. There is in the accomplished artist a sort of philosophical encyclopedist with grand and complex views. Today people specialise too much, they too often take a microscope and go deep into a fraction of the whole. You have written a powerful work, full of imagination and logic, and very moral. Now you must write another which embraces more things and opens more horizons . . .[11]

Taine wrote to Zola with respect. Lacroix showed touching confidence in him. *Contes à Ninon* had been a failure, but Zola had begged him to reprint it – with illustrations by Manet.[12] Lacroix was persuaded, but Manet did not deliver the promised illustrations. However, if he failed Zola as an illustrator, he did not fail him as a portrait painter. His portrait of Zola – begun in November 1866 – was shown at the Salon of 1868.[13]

The militant writer portrayed by Manet already proclaimed a literary cause of his own. It was in 1866, in an article on Taine, that Zola had first applied the word *naturaliste* to a fellow writer. The second edition of *Thérèse Raquin* appeared in April 1868. Its preface echoed his words to the Congrès scientifique de France, and it may be considered as a first Naturalist manifesto. 'I have simply performed on two living bodies the analytical process which surgeons perform on corpses.' So Zola explained. '. . . The scientific analysis which I have tried to apply . . . [is] the modern method, the universal means of research which the century uses so feverishly in order to break through into the future.'[14]

Naturalism owed much to Taine's determinist theory of the influence of race, environment and time on human character; it also owed much to his theory that the novel should be a kind of human case-history. Naturalism was little more than an exaggerated form of Realism. The difference between the two movements was to lie in the 'scientific' character which Zola imposed on the novel. Naturalism meant, to him, not only the faithful reproduction of nature, but the application of the methods recently advocated by Claude Bernard in his *Introduction à l'étude de la médecine expérimentale*. The art of the novel, like that of medicine, was – in Zola's hands – to be a matter of observation and experiment, leading to the proof or disproof of hypotheses. *Thérèse Raquin*, like *Madeleine Férat*, might well have fitted the framework of the Rougon-Macquart novels.

By the late 1860s Zola had a circle of distinguished acquaintances. He had called on Émile Littré in the rue d'Assas, where

Littré (published by Hachette) was working on his dictionary of the French language. Littré's neighbour, Jules Michelet, another Hachette author, was finishing his *Histoire de France*. Zola attended his soirées. He also claimed to have called on Sainte-Beuve. 'I went one day to take him a few documents. He was working on a notice on M. Littré . . . I stayed for five minutes at most, but I have never forgotten that white face, with the strong, thick features . . .'[15] The impressions were recorded after Sainte-Beuve had died, and they seem to have been pure invention. In an article on the critic, reprinted in *Documents littéraires*, Zola confessed: 'I must admit that I never saw Sainte-Beuve.'[16]

He did, however, meet Paul Meurice in the Cité Frochot, behind the place Pigalle. There, on Mondays, the devoted friend of Hugo used to receive artists and men of letters. Meurice was to found *Le Rappel*. Not long before it was launched, Manet introduced 'a young man of sombre expression, silent and short-sighted, who was presented as a bold and mordant critic'. It was Zola, who was accepted as literary critic on the new paper.[17] At the Cité Frochot he also met François Coppée. Their friendship was to last until the Dreyfus Affair.

Zola had already earned the Goncourts' approval by his support of *Germinie Lacerteux*; the brothers professed to admire *Thérèse Raquin*. On 14 December 1868 Zola cemented this cordial acquaintance and presented himself at Auteuil.

An indecipherable, deep and complex creature [so the diarists recorded] . . .; sorrowful, anxious, troubled, uncertain.

He talks about the problems of his life, of his desire and need for a publisher who would . . . [assure him] 6000 francs a year. [This would give him] enough for him and his mother to live on, and the chance to write *L'Histoire d'une famille*, a novel in ten volumes.[18]

6

Madeleine Férat is a novel in the realistic style of *Thérèse Raquin*. Zola had written it first as a play, but he had been unable to place it, and he had expanded it into a book. Like *Thérèse*

Raquin, the new novel is patently an early work; and it is also a violent romance.

Thérèse Raquin had been the analysis of remorse, considered apart from all moral or religious feeling. *Madeleine Férat* is the illustration of a physiological hypothesis. Zola had been struck by Michelet's statement in *La Femme*: 'The fertilised woman, once impregnated, will always bear her husband within her.' In *Madeleine Férat* he pursues this theory. He maintains that a woman belongs, body and soul, to her first lover: that she bears his mark ineffaceably. Even her child by another man may resemble the man she had first loved – especially if she had thought of him at the moment of conception. The theory is extraordinary; but Zola does not interpret his theories and documents as a scholar would interpret them. As Martino emphasises in *Le Naturalisme français*, Zola does not mind whether or not the basic fact is true.

The science is spurious, and the tale lacks conviction. *Madeleine Férat* is much less plausible than *Thérèse Raquin*. The characters are merely the protagonists in an intellectual exercise; their problems are academic, their moves are calculated, and their conversation is contrived.

Yet with this novel, once again, Zola offended the law. When *Madeleine Férat* was serialised, the public prosecutor summoned the editor of the paper. He warned him that, although he would only caution him, there might be legal proceedings when the work appeared as a book, and that he would then be compromised. The editor hastened to Lacroix. Lacroix refused to publish the book unless the offending passage was removed. Zola refused to make any changes; he discussed his case in an opposition paper, *La Tribune*.

He had also shown his vigour in his dealings with the municipal council of Aix. He had been determined that his father's achievement should be recognised. In September 1868 Marius Roux had handed a letter from Zola to the mayor of Aix, asking that a street should be named after François Zola. Zola was never to hesitate in asking favours of his friends. He always assumed that they would do research for his novels, publish favourable reviews, and help him to solve his personal problems. Marius Roux was a journalist, dramatist and novelist. Zola now turned to Roux, in Aix, with unquestioning confidence.

My dear Roux [this from Paris on 4 December],

... I should be grateful if you would first find out why I have
not yet received the copy of the resolution of the Municipal Council.
You know that I am only waiting for this document to send the
Council my official thanks. Would you be kind enough to see the
mayor and tell him that I am waiting for the resolution with legitimate impatience? ...

If you see Arnaud again, tell him that I am quite ready to sell
him *Les Mystères de Marseille* a second time. But the conditions of
payment which you mention hardly seem acceptable. I agree not
to sell him the novel *en bloc*, but I want to be paid for everything that
appears ...

All the papers are concerned about *Madeleine Férat* ... It may
be that I shall appeal to the Tribunal de commerce to prove to
Lacroix that daylight will not kill this poor lady.[1]

Zola's tough, aggressive behaviour proved to be rewarding. A
fortnight after this letter was written, on 19 December, the
municipal council of Aix re-named the boulevard du Chemin
Neuf the boulevard François Zola. Lacroix published *Madeleine
Férat* before the year had ended.

As for *Les Mystères de Marseille*, Zola himself was later to recall
its history. In 1867 he had just left *L'Événement*, and he had
found himself in financial straits. At this opportune moment he
had been approached by Alfred Arnaud, proprietor of l'Imprimerie nouvelle at Marseilles, and editor of *Le Messager de Provence*. Arnaud wanted to launch his paper with a novel, *Les
Mystères de Marseille*. It was to be based on facts which he himself would provide from the court reports of Marseilles and Aix
over the last fifty years. Zola accepted. The work would bring
him some two hundred francs a month, for nine months. As
soon as he had the dossiers, he settled down to his task.[2]

Les Mystères de Marseille is an unhappy piece of hackwork. It
had, however, been imposed on Zola when he was still seeking
himself; for the first time he developed a theme which was dictated by documents. This was the method he was to use in all
his later novels.

By the end of the 1860s, Zola's income from journalism was
assured. Like his father, he was drawn to grand enterprises. He
decided, as he had told the Goncourts, to write a series of ten

novels (there were eventually to be twenty) under the general title of *Histoire naturelle et sociale d'une famille sous le Second Empire*.

He had once said that science was not his affair; he was now absorbed by physiology and by natural history. In 1868–9 he became an assiduous reader in the Bibliothèque Impériale (now the Bibliothèque Nationale). He turned to Dr Lucas' *Traité de l'hérédité naturelle*. He was much impressed by the translation of Darwin's book, *The Origin of Species*, and by Claude Bernard's *Introduction à l'étude de la médecine expérimentale*. He felt that the new biological theories might contribute something original to literature – in particular that they might explain the forces of heredity. He was still, above all, influenced by Taine.

[Monsieur Taine] declares that he has found a universal law which rules all the manifestations of the human spirit . . . This theory sets down as a principle that intellectual facts are only the results of the influence of race, milieu and moment on man. Given a man, the nation to which he belongs, the epoch and the milieu he lives in, we can deduce the work which this man will give us. This is a simple problem, and one to be resolved with mathematical exactitude . . . Such a law, if it is valid, is clearly among the most marvellous instruments which we can use in criticism.[3]

It was also a marvellous instrument for the novelist. It was modern and original, and Zola recognised the poetry which a creative artist could draw from it. Early in 1869 he submitted a plan for his series of novels to Lacroix. He also sent him the genealogical tree of the Rougon-Macquart.

From the time he embarked on his Rougon-Macquart cycle, Zola's method of writing was not to change. It owed something, perhaps, to his father, who had been a doctor of mathematics and an engineer. It owed much to his own unremitting determination. As he said himself, he built his books like a mason. In his years of fame he advised a young author 'not to be impatient. No effort is wasted. Do your job, the masterpieces have only been built that way.'[4]

The genealogical tree of the Rougon-Macquart gave Zola the range of characters for his novels. The Second Empire imposed a time-scale. More than once he was to be compelled to ignore the time-scale, to graft new shoots on the family tree. What remains remarkable is Zola's consistency of purpose, his

fidelity to his vision, his punctual execution of his plan over a
quarter of a century.

Zola always began by preparing an *ébauche*. One cannot call
this a draft, or sketch. It was his record of his thoughts. He began
by thinking aloud on paper.

> His ideas only come to him when he is writing [explained R. H.
> Sherard]. He declared to me that he could never evolve a single
> idea by sitting still in his chair, and thinking . . . His *ébauche* is a
> sort of chatty letter addressed to himself . . . He then draws out a
> plan of the book, a list of the characters, and a most elaborate and
> detailed *scenario*. Each character and scene is then studied in detail,
> and wherever possible *de visu*. Incidents are then prepared for
> insertion in the story wherever available. It is only then, having
> actually written much more than the novel itself, that he sets to
> work to write it. The text of the sketch is rarely used at all . . .
> He writes very slowly and methodically . . . His daily task, as far
> as his novel-writing is concerned, has been four pages of print of the
> Charpentier form of volume daily, and he has never done more
> nor less . . . His plan is so clear in his head that he can resume
> his work on the following morning without having to read over
> anything of what precedes.[5]

Talking to Sherard towards the end of his career, Zola made
a further point. He considered the author's choice of names a
science in itself. He used to spend hours with the Guide Bottin,
making lists of potential names. 'I am', he said, 'quite a fatalist
in this matter, believing firmly that a mysterious correlation
exists between the man and the name he bears.'[6] The names he
kept for his first plan for the Rougon-Macquart cycle were
those of authentic Provençal families. Rougon was the name of
a schoolfriend at the Collège Bourbon.[7] Plassans was only a
pseudonym for Aix-en-Provence.[8]

In May 1869 Zola began the first novel in his series. He set out
to be a scientist in literature. Perhaps he founded his massive
work on an untenable premise; but Henry James was later to
decide: 'No finer act of courage and confidence, I think, is
recorded in the history of letters.'[9]

PART THREE

FOUNDATIONS
1870-1875

7

'If by love you mean wild passion, marriage certainly doesn't give it . . . But if you are not too demanding, if the love to which you aspire is deep and serene, if by happiness you mean days of sunshine and days of rain, then get married, *mes enfants*, get married!'[1] So Zola had written at the age of twenty; one wonders how, already, he had become so sober, so mature in his views. Perhaps his mother had enlightened him. For four and a half years, now, he had been living with Gabrielle. They had come to share an apartment with Mme Zola at 14, rue de La Condamine, in Les Batignolles. No doubt the arrangement was partly dictated by financial needs. It also suggests a par- ticularly close relationship between mother and son. Yet it may have been Mme Zola, with middle-class ambitions, who finally persuaded him to marry. Or perhaps, as he embarked on the Rougon-Macquart novels, Zola himself, like Sandoz in *L'Œuvre*, decided that marriage was vital 'for the great modern creators . . . Personally, he needed a guardian angel for his tranquillity, a centre of affection in which he could cloister himself, so as to consecrate all his life to the enormous work the dream of which he carried within him.'[2]

It has been suggested that, just as Gabrielle could not forget her earlier lover, so Zola had been haunted by his undeclared and unrequited passion for Louise Solari, the sister of his friend Philippe, the sculptor. In 1887, Jules Hoche was to publish an account of Zola's love for the girl who had, he said, been the Ninon of the *Contes* (and, according to others, Miette Chantegreil in *La Fortune des Rougon*). Hoche described how, in 1879, when Zola was in Aix, he had chanced to see a funeral passing. It was the funeral of Louise, long since married to another, but now dead. In fact Zola did not visit Aix in 1879, and Louise Solari had died, unmarried, in 1870. Marcel Girard made these points, and destroyed the legend of Zola's passion. He also ob- served that when Zola left Aix in February 1858, he was nearly eighteen, and Louise was just twelve.

It therefore seems unlikely that her death precipitated Zola's marriage; but, within a fortnight, at ten o'clock on the morning of Tuesday, 31 May 1870, he and Gabrielle were married at the *mairie* of the seventeenth arrondissement in Paris. Four of Zola's friends from Aix: Roux and Cézanne, Paul Alexis and Solari (the brother of Louise), witnessed this marriage which was to be so solid and so deeply disturbed. Zola's mother, sending cards to announce the event, discarded the bride's plebeian first name. Whatever relatives and friends might decide to call her, Gabrielle-Éléonore-Alexandrine Meley was now officially Alexandrine Zola.

Six weeks after Zola's wedding, on 15 July, France declared war on Prussia. She was belligerent and unprepared. This conflict was all the more tragic since it was unnecessary. 'This fearful war has made the pen drop from my hands,' Zola lamented to Edmond de Goncourt. 'I am like a soul in misery.'[3] Yet, as the Second Empire hastened to its end, his literary enterprise was taking shape. On 27 August he had *déjeuner* with Goncourt at Auteuil, and once again he discussed his epic. 'It is only by the quantity of volumes, the power of the creation,' Zola said, 'that one can talk to the public.'[4]

The time-scale of the Rougon-Macquart cycle was now unexpectedly imposed on him. On 2 September, seven weeks after hostilities began, Napoleon III surrendered with his army at Sedan; on 4 September the fall of the Bonaparte dynasty was decreed, and the Republic was proclaimed. Meanwhile the war continued, the Prussians marched on Paris, and the capital prepared for a siege. 'My wife is so terrified that I've decided to take her away,' Zola told Goncourt on 7 September. 'I'm going with her. But if I can come back in a few days, I shall return to my post.'[5] As a widow's son, he had been exempted from military service; and, as he was short-sighted, he had been rejected by the Garde Nationale. No doubt there were some who dismissed domestic obligations, forgot their disabilities, and thought only of the national salvation. Zola left Paris; his absence did not prevent him, twenty years later, from giving his impressions of the Siege in a collection of essays, *Bagatelles*.

Naturally enough he chose to escape to Provence. After a few days at L'Estaque, he settled with his wife and mother at 15, rue Haxo, in Marseilles. If he had ever considered returning to Paris, he now brushed the thought aside. In Marseilles he met Alfred Arnaud, who offered to launch a newspaper for him. For a short while Zola and Marius Roux ran *La Marseillaise*; but Zola soon foresaw that it would not last, and he felt that his future lay elsewhere. From 1 November he and Roux ceded their rights in the paper to Gustave Naquet, J.-A. Chappuis and J. Doucet, the director, administrator and printer of *Le Peuple*.

On 7 December, from a new address, 12, rue Moustier, Zola wrote to Alexandre Glais-Bizoin. This elderly acquaintance had been a founder of *La Tribune*, and a Deputy until the fall of the Empire. He was now a member of the Government of National Defence. Zola recalled his own collaboration on *La Tribune*, and he blandly asked Glais-Bizoin to help him become a préfet or sous-préfet. Soon afterwards he left his wife and mother in Marseilles, and set off for Bordeaux. The Government of National Defence had recently moved there; and there he met Glais-Bizoin, who promised him a préfecture.

Zola's letters to Marius Roux have, until now, been largely unpublished; they illuminate his wartime activities. While he waited to be made a préfet, it occurred to him that he might gain experience if he became sous-préfet of Aix-en-Provence; and since the post was already held by a Monsieur Martin, Zola indulged in some unprincipled and aggressive scheming. Alphonse Gent was the préfet of the Bouches-du-Rhône; if he chose to dismiss M. Martin, Zola might replace him (and continue his work for *La Marseillaise*). The préfet's chief administrative officer was Auguste Cabrol, an ex-journalist, and his former electoral agent. Zola sent Cabrol a letter and a telegram. On 12 December he asked Roux to call on Cabrol and repeat that M. Martin might be dismissed, since 'they ask no better than to appoint me at Aix'. Zola's tone must have offended the most benevolent authority. Nor did he content himself with letters to Cabrol and to Roux. Among his correspondence with Roux is a page from a letter presumably addressed to his wife or mother:

If Roux has any difficulty in sending me a telegram, after he's seen Cabrol, he should go back to Cabrol and have his message endorsed. An endorsement from Cabrol will remove any problems. He must tell him bluntly: 'We can't keep Zola in suspense in

Bordeaux. He must either be satisfied or told to come back, if there's nothing to be done.'

I've just had Roux's letter [added Zola], and I'm *very pleased*. The *Marseillaise* may be an excellent last resource. I am more set than ever on the Aix affair. In Aix, I am still on the *Marseillaise*. Roux must be firm with Naquet. The paper must survive, now. I am waiting for a definite answer. And if necessary vive *La Marseillaise*![6]

Within the next few days, it seems, the matter was settled. The last issue of *La Marseillaise* was published on 16 December. On 22 December Zola wrote from Bordeaux:

My dear Roux,

My wife must have told you that I was staying here, and that I have asked her to come. I have agreed to be secretary to Glais-Bizoin. The situation will allow me to study the people here, and to draw from them what suits me best – unless this post of secretary is exactly what I want.

As I was saying to my wife, Marseilles is finished. It was time to move, if one didn't want to play an embarrassing part there. I should have taken anything here rather than leave the place . . .

Here, at the Café de Bordeaux and on the pavement of the Comédie, you would think yourself on the boulevard des Italiens. I have met dozens of young colleagues. I think it is very good to be seen. With a little skill, we are going to make a triumphal return.[7]

In the meanwhile, the obliging Glais-Bizoin introduced Zola to Clément Laurier, director of staff at the Ministry of the Interior. Laurier promised to give him the first préfecture to fall vacant. On Christmas Day Zola wrote to Roux:

I am beginning to get very *cunning*. I see that I did well to accept this post as secretary, it will let me in on the secrets behind the scenes. I have seen some rather nice ones already in the correspondence . . .

Thank you for all your kindness to my wife and mother. I still don't know if I'll see them this evening. I must admit I'm beginning to be diabolically weary.[8]

The weariness no doubt continued. Alexandrine and Mme Zola were held up in the snow, and did not reach Bordeaux till the following evening. They brought financial problems with them, for Zola's salary was not yet due, and Alexandrine had virtually no money. Zola urged Roux to hasten the payment from Chappuis.

> We are still [he added] in all the fever of settling in. It is miserably cold. But at last I've managed to find a place where we shan't be too badly off, ourselves and the dog.
> I am still feeling my way . . . As I see it, at this moment, Bordeaux must be the way to Paris for us. It would be a good idea if you came.
> If you decide to join me, I suggest you come and stay with me . . . You could sleep in our dining-room for a few days. There are also rooms to let in our house . . .
> I await the *moneyed* reply with impatience. Let's hope that the snow doesn't hold up the courier.[9]

Marius Roux did not, it seems, sleep in the dining-room at 48, rue de Lalande. On 2 January Zola reminded him: 'Give me your address if you leave Marseilles. I shall certainly not stay long in Bordeaux. I have a more militant post in view.'[10]

He was still in Bordeaux when, on 17 February, he wrote to Paul Alexis, then in Paris. Manet had reported that the house in the rue de La Condamine had been requisitioned. Zola wondered if it had been ransacked. 'What a state it must be in, my poor study, where I began, so fervently, to write my Rougon-Macquart!' Finally a belated letter arrived from Alexis.

> Batignolles has not been shelled [this on 9 February], but part of your house has been requisitioned by the mairie of Bat^les to shelter a refugee family during the siege . . . I hasten to add that only the ground floor has been left at their disposal. Thanks to me, the Manet painting, your silver, and various other things which you left spread out on the tables have been taken up to the first floor. I have several times had a look round as I passed; so I hope you won't find too much damage.[11]

On 27 February Alexis added:

> Your house has been completely evacuated for the past ten days . . .
> Oh! I was forgetting: the pruning of your trees! I've seen a gardener. He asked 5 francs for pruning them and the vine and removing the caterpillars. Is this the price?[12]

Zola sent a five-franc order and a reminder: 'Don't let them touch the soil, there are peony and dahlia roots which would be massacred . . . I'm longing to see my Batignolles again, but I'm tied to Bordeaux by my duties as a journalist.'[13]

La Cloche had been founded by Louis Ulbach in 1868. It had been a weekly pamphlet directed against the Empire, in the style of Rochefort's *La Lanterne*. At the end of 1869, it had become a daily. Early in 1871, when the Government of France sat at Bordeaux, Zola found his militant post as a parliamentary correspondent. He sent Ulbach a series of letters on events.[14]

His dreams of prefectural office had now been abandoned. He had been offered a sous-préfecture – a considerable good fortune since he was not even a *bachelier*, and he had had no training or experience for the post. However, Clément Laurier had explained that the government needed a sous-préfet at Castelsarrasin (Tarn-et-Garonne). When Zola had held this appointment, Laurier continued, he would be rewarded with an important préfecture. The nomination had been signed when Zola learned of the armistice with Prussia. He then refused the sous-préfecture. Paris was open, and he felt the writer stirring within him. 'Remember that our reign has come,' he reminded Alexis. 'Peace is made. We are the writers of tomorrow.'[15] Armed with the manuscript of *La Curée*, the second of the Rougon-Macquart novels, he returned to Paris in the train which brought the Government back from Bordeaux.

Léon Deffoux records that Zola followed the sessions of the Assemblée nationale when it moved from Bordeaux to Versailles; but he had some trouble in fulfilling his task. The Commune had seized control of Paris. 'Pale, shabby, silent and observant,' Zola was arrested as a suspect by the Gardes nationaux. He was duly identified and freed, and went to Versailles, where the legitimate authorities arrested him again. He was kept in the Orangerie until Gustave Simon, son of the Minister of the Interior, had him released. But for this intervention, he might have been shot.[16] 'I wonder if I shouldn't be wise to pack my bags,' wrote Zola. 'What consoles me is that no third government can arrest me tomorrow.'[17] Some weeks later he went to Gloton, a hamlet near Bennecourt on the Seine, to await the end of the turmoil.

On 28 May 1871, the Commune was overthrown. On 30 June, from Paris, Zola told Alexis: 'They are printing *La Fortune des Rougon*. I shall get the first proofs any day.'[18]

8

The Rougon-Macquart novels, as we have seen, owed much to Dr Lucas' *Traité de l'hérédité naturelle*. They were also largely inspired by the theory which Taine had formulated on the influence of race, environment and time. They were to be based on the laboratory methods laid down by Claude Bernard in his study of experimental medicine. A novelist, Zola insisted, must be of his age, or, indeed, in advance of his era. In an age of scientific progress, he himself intended to give his fiction scientific authenticity. Through the microcosm of a family, he intended to explain the rise, corruption and fall of the Second Empire.

La Fortune des Rougon was published on 21 October 1871. It was to be the base for the whole edifice, and – rather clumsily – Zola prepared his ground. Adélaïde Fouque – Tante Dide – was born in Plassans. Her father died insane. She herself was eccentric. Soon after his death, she married Rougon, a gardener's boy who had worked for him. In time she gave birth to a son, Pierre. Then her husband died, and she became the mistress of Macquart, a drunken, furtive vagabond; by him she had a son and daughter, Antoine and Ursule. So, from *la grande ancêtre*, there sprang the Rougons and the Macquarts, the legitimate and illegitimate heirs, the middle class and working class, inheriting the strengths and weaknesses of their parents, influenced by marriage and money, by ambition and resentment, by personal vendettas and political events.

The Rougons and Macquarts are, from the first, almost entirely deplorable. Pierre Rougon cheats his mother and his Macquart brother and sister of their inheritance in order to finance his own career. He calculates a useful marriage. His wife, Félicité, is possibly the illegitimate daughter of a marquis; and, driven by her contempt for provincial life, she in turn takes Rougon as an accomplice to fight her destiny. Tante Dide had made Pierre a man of moderate ambition; Félicité brings up her sons to be capable of great vices and great virtues. 'Since you weren't rich, you had to make us workers,' so her eldest son explains to her. 'We are declassed, we suffer

more than you.' Eugène Rougon's bitterness is the bitterness
of Zola, left poor and declassed by his father's death. 'In the
provinces, they are implacable to families in decline.' The
observation echoes an experience. Desperate to rise in life, to
dominate, to make themselves amends, the Rougons reflect
their creator's own ambitions. They also distort them. They
wait like birds of prey for events; they are not concerned with
principles or with morality. The Macquarts have more lowly
ambitions, and they are flawed by their lack of education, their
poverty, their alcoholism and neurotic natures. They are condemned, from the first, to be criminals or victims.

   La Fortune des Rougon begins on the eve of the Second Empire.
The Rougons, in their apartment in Plassans, corroded by
frustration and ambition, see the coming change of régime as
the chance to escape from mediocrity. Félicité covets the house
of the tax-collector. The mirrors, the gilded furniture which she
can glimpse through her window urge her on towards a world
in which luxury and power will efface the past. She shrewdly
manages her husband; and her salon becomes a centre for an
intrigue in which political creeds are less consistent than the
belief in self-advancement. The Rougons plot with their dis-
solute half-brother, Antoine Macquart, and they so exploit
events that they secure power and status. Their eldest son,
Eugène, has immersed himself in politics in Paris; he obtains
the Légion-d'honneur for his father. Rougon becomes the
tax-collector; Félicité duly enters her Tuileries.

   Silvère Mouret, the orphaned son of Ursule Macquart, is
uncorrupt and enamoured of freedom. He is innocently in love
with Miette Chantegreil, a poacher's daughter. Miette is shot
in a demonstration against the *coup d'état*; Silvère is shot by a
gendarme in the closing passages of the novel. The death of
these children symbolises the death of idealism and integrity,
and the victory of corruption. If justice is to be done, the
Rougons must now be punished, and the Second Empire must
fall. *La Débâcle* must be written. Meanwhile, the reign of
Napoleon III and the triumph of the Rougons are established
together in blood.

In the autumn of 1871, accompanied by Alexandrine, Zola
found himself back in Provence. It was an unhappy visit. On

14 September, from L'Estaque, he explained to Roux: 'My wife has just lost her father. She left by the express train yesterday evening, and no doubt you will see her on Saturday. However, she is only staying in Paris for two or three days.'[1]

He himself was busy working on the second novel in his series. 'I presume that you must be plunged in the end of your *Curée*,' wrote Alexis on 28 September. 'I have not forgotten what you read me of it. In my mind's eye, I have often recalled your exotic and luxuriant conservatory, with the bizarre plants and the ardent vegetation [*sic*] . . . And your Phèdre chewing the poisonous flower. Coming back from the Bois with her tomorrow will be the greatest pleasure in my day.'[2]

Next day, 29 September, before *La Fortune des Rougon* had even appeared, *La Cloche* began to serialise *La Curée*. Such were Zola's working methods that the novel was not finished when its publication began. The author of *La Confession de Claude* and *Madeleine Férat* was once again involved with the law. Some weeks later, the Public Prosecutor sent for Zola, and advised him to break off his serial, which had offended the modesty of its readers. A court case would have given him resounding notoriety; but he did not want to cause trouble for the editor of *La Cloche*. He also wanted to save the book itself. The serial version ended with the twenty-seventh instalment.

The novel was published on 17 February 1872. It is much superior to its predecessor. It is set in Second Empire Paris, in a world of feverish intrigue, a world which is opulent, superficial and incurably corrupt. Its glitter and its emptiness are brilliantly implied.

La Curée is a satire on the men-about-town, financiers and politicians whose fortunes were linked with those of the régime. Zola had not known them personally. He judged them by the works of opposition journalists. 'My dear friend,' he had written to an unidentified correspondent, 'would you be kind enough to send me a copy of the *Paris-Journal* which gives Me Nicolet's speech against the Péreires? . . . I need to consult it for the business side of my novel.'[3] The Rougon-Macquart series was to be dominated by this cynical vision of the Second Empire. It was also to be informed by Zola's own contributions to the opposition Press. Its material and style had been partly suggested by journalism.

As *La Curée* begins, Eugène Rougon is a Minister in the Emperor's government. His younger brother, Aristide, comes to Paris to make his fortune. He, too, is hunting *la curée* – the quarry. He changes his name to Saccard to assert his independence. He earns millions by methods which are questionable in law and, by any moral standards, indefensible. As his wife lies dying he is planning a second, highly advantageous marriage. It is suggested by his sister Sidonie, a procuress and arranger of louche transactions. Renée is the daughter of a retired magistrate, M. Béraud Du Châtel. She is a woman of property, but she has been seduced by a married man, and could not now aspire to a grand alliance. Saccard marries Renée, and his new-found wealth allows him to indulge in speculation. In the Paris of Baron Haussmann, where property must be demolished and owners compensated, there is a promising career for men with foresight and with obliging friends at the Hôtel de Ville.

After the death of his first wife, Saccard had sent his daughter, Clotilde, to his younger brother in Plassans. His son, Maxime, grows up in Paris: spoilt, elegant and vicious. Bored with a life of endless pleasure, he finds himself the companion of Renée. She, too, is bored beyond belief by her existence. Like Baudelaire in *Les Fleurs du mal*, they both long for new experience; and, inevitably, they find it in a relationship approaching incest. In the Café Riche, where their affair begins, in the conservatory of Saccard's *hôtel*, they make love with despair, and without affection. They savour their relationship because it is forbidden, because it brings novelty to their unchanging life. The relationship is complicated by Maxime's ambiguous, almost effeminate character, and by Renée's masterful nature. It is, above all, when they make love in the conservatory that, in Zola's words, 'Renée was the man.' Maxime lies on the black bearskin; Renée, symbolically, looks down on 'this yielding prey which she possessed completely'. She crouches over him like a white sphinx with phosphorescent eyes: a sister of the black marble sphinx beside her. The vision suggests a painting by Gustave Moreau rather than a Naturalist description; it also indicates Zola's own ambiguous attitude to the dominant woman.

Nana will be driven by abundant zest and gaiety. *La Curée* is pervaded by Baudelairean despair. Nana will have no memory of a tranquil past, no regrets for a moral way of life. Renée recalls her childhood in an austere *hôtel* on the Île Saint-Louis. 'I am an honest woman,' she tells Maxime at the Café Riche; and she is not cynical but nostalgic. She recognises where she belongs; and her tragedy is that she had known it from the first. When her life with Saccard has ended, when Maxime has predictably married for money, Renée returns to the *hôtel* beside the Seine. In the old, dusty nursery, 'in a corner, in the midst of this dumb despair, this neglect for which the silence wept, she found one of her old dolls; all the bran had poured out of a hole, and the porcelain head continued to smile with its enamel lips, on top of this limp body, which seemed to have been exhausted by a doll's follies'.[4]

Zola's novels are largely *romans à clef*, and Renée has elements of certain courtesans of the Second Empire. Saccard and Maxime, it is said, owe something to the Houssayes, father and son. Certainly Arsène Houssaye made a fortune out of Haussmann's transformation of Paris; his *hôtel* in the avenue de Friedland may well have suggested details for Saccard's *hôtel*. But Arsène Houssaye was, physically, no Saccard; he was uncommonly handsome. Henry, his son, was no simple *petit crevé*, like Maxime. He was to be an historian and an Academician.

Whatever the originals of the characters, however synthetic they may become, the social climate, the setting of an epoch, are true to life. They are based not only on Zola's notes for *La Curée*. His contributions to *Le Sémaphore*, in Marseilles, from 1871 to 1877, were to give him a wealth of *choses vues* for his novels. The documentation for *La Curée* is at times too evident. Zola took three pages of notes on exotic plants, which may perhaps explain why there are too many plants in Saccard's conservatory. But Zola transcends his documents. In this Second Empire hothouse, the atmosphere of *Les Fleurs du mal*, the sense of impending and inevitable sin, lie heavy on the air. Baudelaire had suggested the correspondences between perfumes, colours and sounds. Zola goes further: his characters often reveal their natures by their smell. Aromas and emanations influence their behaviour, determine their states of soul.

The novel is superbly erotic. Renée's seduction in the Café Riche, the scenes in the conservatory are described with intense, controlled sensuality. Whatever the scientific precepts on which he based his novels, the Naturalist belief in objectivity, Zola already understands pathetic fallacy and symbolism. The view from the café window of the fading lights of Paris, the waiting prostitute in the street, make their comment on the seduction to come; and, as Renée yields to Maxime, the floor shudders beneath her. It is in fact that the omnibus has turned the corner of the boulevard, but the shudder has its significance. The opening description of the drive home from the Bois may owe something to a passage from *Le Figaro*; but, whatever his sources, Zola transforms them into an atmospheric *mise en scène*. At the end of the novel the carriage drive is repeated, but it is not now an October evening, it is a summer day, and Renée is not with Maxime, she is alone. The first drive had suggested the advent of mystery and pleasure; the second drive implies the busy and indifferent world which Renée is about to forsake.

Perhaps the critics were deterred by the thought of the Public Prosecutor; perhaps, as a critic, Zola had already made his enemies. Whatever the reason, *La Curée* was virtually unnoticed by the Press. For a moment, the very future of the Rougon-Macquart novels was in question, for Zola's publisher was going bankrupt. However, when Lacroix found himself obliged to break the contract, Théophile Gautier spoke to Georges Charpentier, who had just taken over his father's publishing house. 'Either I am very much mistaken,' Gautier said, 'or that young man is endowed with a touch of genius.'[5]

Maurice Dreyfous, who was then Charpentier's associate, recalled that Zola was uncouth, and clearly bought his clothes from a multiple store, 'his usual Dusautoy [or tailor] being La Belle Jardinière. He remained faithful to it all his life.'[6] His appearance suggested financial straits; indeed, in the rue de La Condamine, Alexandrine was obliged to accomplish miracles of economy.

Poor, uncouth, aggressive, Zola offered Charpentier two books a year, with exclusive rights for ten years, in exchange for 500 francs a month for six years. 'Agreed!' said Charpentier. 'I like you. I believe in you. That's settled!' It was a bold and generous decision; but Charpentier was to be, from the first, the ideal publisher. He reprinted the works which had been

compromised by the failure of Lacroix; he negotiated for those
to come, and he signed a contract which left the novelist free
from financial cares. Zola was not, in fact, to provide two books
a year, but Charpentier's gesture was to assure the future of his
house.[7]

9

In about 1870, Zola had first encountered Alphonse Daudet.
His wit and sensual good looks gave him 'something of the
French gamin and something of the Oriental woman'.[1]

A nobler, more significant figure had already entered Zola's
life. In 1869 he had met Flaubert. That August, Flaubert had
installed himself in an apartment at 4, rue Murillo. After the
War and the Commune, he returned there, from time to time,
to make himself amends for the provincial solitude of Croisset,
and to delight his Parisian friends.

His lodging consisted of three small rooms on the fifth floor
[Zola recalled]; it looked over the parc Monceau, a superb view
which had decided him. He had the rooms hung with a cretonne
with a large floral pattern; but this was his only luxury and, as at
Croisset, the trinkets were lacking, there was hardly anything except
an Arab saddle, brought back from Africa, and a Buddha made of
gilded cardboard, bought from a second-hand shop in Rouen. It
was there that I entered into his intimacy. He was then very alone,
very discouraged. The failure of L'Éducation sentimentale had been
a terrible blow to him. And then, although he had no political
conviction, the fall of the Empire seemed to him the end of the
world ... On Sundays I found hardly anyone there except Edmond
de Goncourt; and he, too, was afflicted, by the death of his
brother.[2]

Jules de Goncourt had suffered from venereal disease, and it had
affected his mind. On the eve of the Franco-Prussian War he
had died insane. He was thirty-nine.

Another of Flaubert's visitors was Maupassant, then in his
early twenties. When Zola arrived on Sundays, at about two
o'clock, he nearly always found him reading his literary essays

to his mentor.[3] Maupassant would disappear when his elders
came – Daudet and Turgenev among them. 'They were delightful afternoons, with a great underlying sadness.' Zola particularly remembered a Shrove Sunday when he listened, until
darkness fell, to Flaubert and Goncourt regretting the past.[4]

On 14 April 1874 Flaubert and Zola, Goncourt, Daudet and
Turgenev dined together at the Café Riche.[5] This was the first
of the celebrated Dinners of the Five.

There were as many foods as there were temperaments [Daudet
recorded], as many recipes as provinces. Flaubert had to have
Normandy butter and *canards rouennais à l'estouffade*; Edmond de
Goncourt, refined and exotic, demanded preserved ginger; Zola,
sea-urchins and shellfish; Turgenev revelled in his caviar . . .
We used to sit down at 7 o'clock, we had not finished at 2 in the
morning. Flaubert and Zola dined in their shirtsleeves, Turgenev
spread himself out on the divan. We used to send the waiters away,
a very useful precaution, since Flaubert's *gueuloir* could be heard from
top to bottom of the building; and we used to talk about literature.[6]

The gourmet who delighted in shellfish had long seen Les
Halles Centrales as a promising setting for a novel. Les Halles
gave him a theme, a symbol and an antithesis. Opposite Victor
Hugo's mediaeval cathedral he decided to set up the temple of
terrestrial nourishment, the symbol of the nineteenth-century
city. *Le Ventre de Paris* was the first of Zola's novels to have its
setting as its central personage, almost as its plot. He intended
it to complete *La Curée*: 'It is the *curée*, or quarry, of the middle
classes, the rut for solid food and for good, uninterrupted diges-
tion.'[7]

When he was preparing to write his novel, he turned to
Maxime du Camp. A man of letters and a friend of Flaubert,
Du Camp was working on a six-volume survey: *Paris. Ses
organes, sa fonction et sa vie dans la seconde moitié du XIXe siècle.*
The second volume, published in 1870, included a chapter on
Les Halles. Zola also made numerous enquiries on the spot. He
and Alexandrine once spent a night wandering round the stalls,
and revived themselves with the famous soup which the workers
bought for two sous. Alexandrine long recalled its excellence.
Zola approached a head doorkeeper, who took him for a walk
on the roofs of the different wings of the building; he also

escorted him round the cellars. For the next month Zola smelt the pungent smell of accumulated poultry.[8]

Le Ventre de Paris was published on 19 April 1873.

Aristide Saccard had been possessed by the urge to make his millions. Lise Macquart, his cousin, now Mme Quenu, is driven by the urge to be comfortable. The wife of a butcher in Les Halles, she supports the Empire because it represents her tranquillity; and when her husband's half-brother, Florent, comes back from Cayenne, where he had been sent for opposing the *coup d'état* of 2 December, when she finds that he is still a rebel, she sacrifices him to her well-being. She allows him to be re-arrested, and no doubt sent back to the penal settlement. Under her placid, buxom appearance, she keeps the viciousness of a Macquart.

Le Ventre de Paris records a world which cares only for material prosperity. The characters are null and void, but the novel is not so much about people as about Baltard's market, one of the wonders of Second Empire Paris. Here, for the first time, Zola presents an institution with its complex life, its commonplace and picturesque detail. *Le Ventre de Paris* is an Impressionist novel. Zola sees the vegetables, the fish, the meats displayed in the charcuterie, with the eyes of Cézanne. The visible world exists for him; he had noted it in the same way as his artist friends made sketches for their pictures. His notes reveal how faithfully he followed the principles of Naturalism. His novel shows how he transmuted and transcended the recorded facts. The conservatory in *La Curée* had revealed his awareness of scents and aromas, of their influence on behaviour; the market in *Le Ventre de Paris* is pervaded by evocative smells. Zola is not only moving from the realistic to the symbolic, he is again suggesting *correspondances*, the significant relations between the senses. Even now, in the third of the Rougon-Macquart novels, the Macquarts have become comparatively insignificant, the question of heredity is largely forgotten. Zola is already escaping the confines of Naturalism, and giving rein to the poet who remains within him.

The Rougon-Macquart novels were to vary, almost alternately, between the large-scale and the intimate. After *Le Ventre de*

Paris, Zola undertook a novel in which he would study the characters in depth.

La Conquête de Plassans had a double theme. It was intended to represent the provinces under the Empire. It was also 'a *physiological* drama', a study of the relationship which brought husband and wife together and later set them in confrontation.[9] The original idea for the book came from a short story which Zola had written early in his career. This described the case of a man who was constantly told that he was insane; convinced of his own insanity, he finally went mad. François Mouret – the unlikely brother of Silvère – was based on the father of Cézanne: 'sneering, republican, bourgeois, cold, meticulous, miserly'. In his study of Marthe Mouret, the lucid madwoman, Zola used the observations of the neurologist Trélat.

La Conquête de Plassans records the destruction of a household by a priest bent on power. Marthe Rougon, the daughter of Pierre and Félicité, has married François Mouret, a cousin on the Macquart side of the family. They live a dull, undemanding life in Plassans, with their sons Octave and Serge, and their simple-minded daughter, Désirée – a reminder of unhealthy ancestry. Mouret lets a room in the house to a needy priest. The priest arrives, mysterious and louche (Zola's notes record that he had been expelled from Besançon for a physical attack on his superior). Faujas is silent and secret, and has clearly come for some unchristian purpose. Eugène Rougon has in fact sent him to Plassans to ensure that the city remains loyal to the régime. Faujas needs the Mourets' house as a base for his activities. Gradually he assumes direction of the household. The sons leave home, the daughter is sent to live with a nurse. Marthe turns to religion, develops religious mania, and dies. Mouret goes insane, escapes from his asylum, strangles Faujas and sets fire to the house. Both men are burnt to death. There is no victor in this account of frailty and wickedness.

La Conquête de Plassans is a sombre caricature of provincial life. It is also the first of Zola's anti-Catholic novels. In 1874, the year of its publication, Marshal MacMahon was elected President of the Republic. He brought the era of 'the moral order'. Once again the critics chose to ignore Zola's work.

10

In the original plan for his series, Zola had mentioned a novel inspired by the religious fervour of the time. 'The amorous priest has never been studied as a human being. There's a fine subject for a drama there, especially if we set the priest under hereditary influences.'[1]

This concept seems to cover both *La Conquête de Plassans* and *La Faute de l'Abbé Mouret*, and Zola had meant to combine the two themes in a single novel. At one point he had thought of making Faujas the lover of Marthe Mouret. He soon perceived, however, that the subject of the priest in love was itself enough for a book. In *La Faute de l'Abbé Mouret* he effaced the clerical surroundings and set his characters deep in the country: predictably in the neighbourhood of Aix. The village of Les Artaud, where Serge Mouret was the officiating priest, was actually Le Tholonet, some six and a half miles west of the city. As for Le Paradou, Gabriel Faure believed that it was based on the Gallice estate, on the other side of Aix, on the Roquefavour road. In fact, it seems to have had a more complex origin. In his boyhood, on the banks of the Durance, north of Aix, Zola had once come across a small, deserted château. It stood in an abandoned park, where the trees and flowers had grown wild. He had recalled this magical discovery in *La Tribune* in 1869. Then he had read *Les Misérables*, and he had found another secret garden: the garden where Jean Valjean had sought his refuge. By a kind of Proustian process, the real and the fictitious had merged. 'People have claimed,' added Zola, 'that when I described Le Paradou I was describing Monet's paradisiac park, where some wonderful paintings were born. . . . The two resembled each other in the wild abundance of the leaves, the ungovernable flowers. My eyes and my heart brought them together.'[2]

Zola had intended to write a psychological study of celibacy; he finally conceived a pantheistic poem inspired by Genesis. The details of trees and flowers used in the description of Le Paradou were taken from reference works, but they were verified at horticultural exhibitions. Some of them had been

noted at the Jardin des Plantes, they had already been used for
La Curée, and in time they were to serve when Zola planned
his garden at Médan. A note about Le Paradou shows how
carefully he made his characters' emotions coincide with the
different hours of day and the changes of landscape: a procedure
which, again, contradicted the tenets of Naturalism. Zola extended animism to things as well as landscapes. Some critics consider this to be a residue of Romanticism, but it also anticipates
Surrealism.

Zola wrote *La Faute de l'Abbé Mouret* during the summer of
1874 at 21, rue Saint-Georges (since called rue des Appenins)
in Les Batignolles. He had recently moved to this larger house,
and the move marked his final entrance into comfortable
bourgeois life. Every morning he attended early mass at the
little church of Sainte-Marie. He also went to mass at Notre-
Dame. He talked to an unfrocked priest before he wrote about
seminary life. He pursued the studies of a candidate for ordin-
ation. Needing a religious atmosphere, he even bought church
ornaments and clerical vestments. Paul Alexis was to remember
'the two or three readings he gave me from the novel he was
working on. He gave them at dusk, in the stifling little garden,
surrounded by high walls, behind the house.'[3] In this semblance
of a garden, Zola dreamed of Provence. *La Faute de l'Abbé
Mouret* was to be his celebration of the much-loved and familiar
landscape. Alexandrine later told Gabriel Faure that he had
even thought of buying a *tubet* there: a little hut in the heart of
the countryside. But literary work demanded that he lived near
Paris.[4]

La Faute de l'Abbé Mouret was serialised in *Le Messager de
l'Europe* in St Petersburg from January to March 1875. Turgenev
had introduced Zola to the review; he was afraid that his
compatriots might find the novel scabrous, but it enjoyed considerable success. It appeared in France on 27 March, and went
through four editions that year.

Marthe Mouret had been destroyed by a priest. In *La Faute de
l'Abbé Mouret*, her son is destroyed by religion. At the age of
twenty-five he is living with his simple–minded sister and an
elderly housekeeper at Les Artaud. He is devoted to his priesthood, ignorant of the world. His pitifully confined existence is

interrupted when he falls ill with typhoid fever. In his delirium, he loses his memory. His uncle, Pascal Rougon, a doctor, sends him to convalesce on a nearby estate. Pascal, absorbed in his study of the family heredity, is too deep in his books to recognise the living danger. Albine, a wild young girl, tends Serge at Le Paradou. Oblivious of his past, and living alone with Albine in this vast, private paradise garden, he falls in love with her, and she with him. Their love has its spring and summer, and in August it is consummated. 'It is nature which plays the part of Satan in the Bible,' Zola had explained in his *ébauche*. 'It is nature which tempts Serge and Blanche [Albine], and lays them under the tree of evil on a splendid morning.' The parallel with Genesis continues to the end. Frère Archangias, a watching priest – the jealous God – expels Serge from Le Paradou. He returns to his atrophied existence in the Church. 'Serge [is] Catholic to the end,' writes Zola. 'Blanche [Albine] is naturalism, and she moves freely in the direction of instinct and passion.' Albine dies, grief-stricken, with the flowers of Le Paradou around her.

The first and third parts of the novel are harshly realistic; the middle third, as Professor Hemmings says, seems to derive from a different literary tradition. This central episode is a close, deliberate refashioning of the legend of Adam and Eve, and of their fall. It is an anthem to universal love and to the satisfaction of the senses. Nature in Le Paradou is wild, abundant and mysterious. The trees, the flowers, the birds, the very insects urge Albine and Serge to delight in life. Zola writes of human love with the despairing fervour of the chaste. Whatever his scientific precepts, the central passage of this book again reveals the Romantic within him. The youth from Aix has not forgotten his love of the Provençal countryside; and the ideal Ninon to whom he had addressed his short stories has now become an ardent, living creature. The atmosphere of Le Paradou is heady with the scent of woman, the aroma of flowers. The difference between Le Paradou and the world of the Church is emphatically that between life and death. *La Faute de l'Abbé Mouret* is a condemnation of the living death which Catholicism seeks to impose. Zola's terror of annihilation is as clear as his love of life. The antithesis between the two extreme modes of existence, or rather between life and death

itself, is Hugolian in its intensity. It echoes Zola's personal
dilemma. He, too, is torn between his rational pessimism and
the optimism which comes from his heart.

If my opinion is worth anything [Maupassant wrote to Zola], let
me say that I found [the book] very fine. It has extraordinary power.
I am immensely enthusiastic; few books have made such a deep
impression on me . . .
A sort of strong, persistent smell rises from every page . . . Your
book made me completely drunk, and it greatly excited me, too.[5]

When Taine acknowledged his copy of the novel, he took the
occasion to comment on Zola's career.

First of all [he wrote], my heartfelt and most sincere compliments
on your visible progress . . .
Since you have done me the honour of sending me your book,
no doubt you want me to perform my function as a critic. Here,
then, are my objections.
1) You are on Mazeppa's horse. Sometimes it is dangerous and
dizzying; you become, so to speak, drunk with pictures and, even
more, with physical sensations (especially those of smell). You
must always keep control of yourself.
2) Five volumes on madmen or semi-madmen are a lot. In his
thirty dramas, Shakespeare created only one King Lear. A family
in which the original flaw re-appears, in different forms, from generation to generation, is not typical of humanity . . . Take healthy
people from now on, especially since health is more beautiful than
sickness.
3) Apart from Dr Pascal and Renée's father, nearly all the characters are wood-lice and spiders . . . Your sympathies don't seem wide
enough to me; there are happiness, well-being, goodness and even
nobility in mankind . . .
I have no more room, all I can do now is to grasp your hand
and congratulate you, admire you. I also ask you for a little pity
for poor humankind, to which we belong.[6]

La Faute de l'Abbé Mouret has only a tenuous connection with
the Rougon-Macquart. Pissarro found the novel 'a little too
naturalistic';[7] but Zola, like Hugo – perhaps even more than
Hugo – is a pagan, and his paganism is already strangely in
contrast (one might almost say in conflict) with his scientific
principles. La Faute de l'Abbé Mouret already suggests the powerful instincts which he repressed.

It was in the spring of *La Faute de l'Abbé Mouret*, the spring of 1875, that Zola became involved in an extraordinary miscarriage of justice. Until now it has remained virtually unknown, and Zola's comments on it have not been published; but it seems a remarkable prefiguration of the Affair of twenty-three years later.

On 23 April 1875 Zola's friend from Aix, Paul Alexis, was woken early in the morning by two plain-clothes agents, and ordered to appear before the local commissioner of police. On the way to the police station, so Alexis was to remember, his escort gave him permission to call on Zola. 'We interrupted him in the middle of a sentence in *La Faute de l'Abbé Mouret*. He was very disturbed when he heard what had happened . . . "My poor friend, . . . I shall drop everything, snatch a quick *déjeuner*, and jump into a cab . . . You will be free before this evening. I shall begin with *Le Rappel*, where I shall see Lockroy." '[1] Zola's concern for his *déjeuner* is certainly authentic but he was not writing *La Faute de l'Abbé Mouret*, which had been published the previous month. It also seems unlikely that Alexis could have called on him while under arrest. Alexis was a Provençal, and one suspects that his story was embroidered.

His correspondence shows, however, that he enlisted Zola's support; and it was from a cell at the police station that he wrote to him later in the day: 'Apparently I was a *lieutenant*!!! in the 184th, in the Commune, and since 1873 I have been condemned by default to be deported to a fortress.' Four days later, he was transferred to the Cherche-Midi prison. On 28 April he begged Zola: 'Do something for me, and quickly.' On 1 May: '*On the 5th, Friday the 5th*, I am appearing before the court-martial. (My father must not be told beforehand.)'[2]

It was, in fact, a case of mistaken identity. His dossier, marked 'Alexis journaliste', had been confused with another, marked 'Alexis journalier' (a *journalier* was a day-labourer).[3] On 3 May, Zola wrote indignantly to their mutual friend from Aix,

Marius Roux:

I haven't told you the story of P., because I wanted first to get things straight in this stupefying history.

Everything is now explained. These gentlemen made a mistake. It was a question of another P. And *our* poor P. has been in prison for twelve days. Charming, isn't it?

The worst thing is that the military authorities are furious at making a mistake. And so they are looking for a peccadillo to reproach the poor boy with. They have now found that he touched 17 francs which belonged to the Commune. So they are putting him on trial at once. It's no longer a question of deportation to some or other fortress, but of a fine or a few days in prison. More and more delightful, isn't it?

Look at this poor creature: they fling him into the police station, then into the Cherche-Midi; they don't question him for a week, in spite of my supplications; they walk him through the street in handcuffs; they terrify him with endless stories; and then they ask him to account for the 17 francs he touched during the Commune! They should apologise, and they accuse him of lacking 'moral sense . . .'

Anyway, I hope he'll be acquitted. I'm doing everything possible and impossible to ensure it. He's going to be tried on Wednesday [*sic*], the day after tomorrow. Not a word to the family. The government commissioner advised me not to warn the father; no doubt he wanted to frighten P., without pushing things any further. I ask you not to say a word to anyone. I'm keeping a watch on the papers, to see that nobody discusses it there.

Some of the details have been fantastic. I'll tell you about it all when you come back. On Wednesday evening, if there is a verdict, I will drop a note in at your door.[4]

He kept his word. On 5 May he scribbled: 'P. is acquitted. Go on keeping the secret. He means to tell his family himself.'[5]

Alexis was released that evening. He was to recall the episode in *L'Aurore*, in the early days of the Dreyfus Affair.

In 1875 Zola had his own continuing personal problems. In January, dining with Goncourt, Daudet and Turgenev, he had talked about his domestic life, 'where there is no distraction in the evening, except a few games of dominoes with his wife, or a visit from his compatriots [from Aix]'.[6] On 4 April, at Flaubert's, no doubt made garrulous by wine, he told the company 'that, while he was a student [*sic*], he had more than once spent a week in bed with a woman, or at least lived in a shirt with her. . . . Now, he says, he has become very good, and he only has intercourse with his wife every ten days . . .'⁷ The first statement was no doubt embroidered; Zola – like Alexis – had a Provençal taste for exaggeration. The last confidence was unpardonable, but it sounds convincing. Any passion for Alexandrine had long since been spent. Sexually the marriage was a failure. Only, it seems, in his novels, and in free talk among men, could Zola rid himself of his frustration. Sometimes he insisted on his strict morality; sometimes he indulged in outrageous claims. 'No, no, I insist, I have no moral sense. I have slept with the wives of my best friends. I certainly have no moral sense in love.'⁸ Such aggressive – and inventive – talk only proved his oppressive need.

The fact that his marriage was childless was a profound and perpetual sorrow to him and to Alexandrine. She was now thirty-six, and she was still young enough for motherhood. She was maternal by nature. 'Why did he not want children by me, when I could still give them to him?' So she was to ask after his death.⁹ Perhaps she had been unable to have them. As she grew older, as time passed, this barrenness became increasingly painful to both of them. Like many other people whose human relationships are failing, they showed an inordinate love of animals. Zola himself recognised it as 'the ridiculous affection of an ageing couple without children'. But they followed the childhood of Charpentier's son – Zola's godson, Paul – with poignant interest, and Zola confessed to the boy's father: 'His picture is on our mantelpiece, as if he were a child of our own.'¹⁰

Zola poured his emotional energy, his intense frustration, into his books. In the twenty Rougon-Macquart novels the act of creation, the act of birth were to become an obsession. Again and again, in his articles and in his correspondence, he was to insist that the purpose of existence was fecundity. Legitimate or not, the true marriage was the fruitful relationship. The Abbé Mouret had made love only once in his life, but he had given Albine a child; Étienne Lantier, in *Germinal*, was to make love only once to Catherine, but he was to be haunted by the thought that he might have made her pregnant. Dr Pascal was to die in peace, convinced that he had given Clotilde a son. Few writers in French literature have shown such longing for posterity.

Alexandrine had no literary outlet for her emotions. Her frequent ill-health probably owed much to her own profound frustration. During the summer of 1875 she was so unwell that Zola kept her in bed for two months. On 2 August, for the sake of her health, they went to Calvados, and settled at 53, rue des Dunes, Aubin-sur-Mer. Three days later, Zola reported to Marius Roux: 'The accommodation is more than modest, the doors don't shut properly and the furniture is primitive. But the view is magnificent – the sea, the eternal sea! . . . There's nothing grander, especially at night.'[11] On 7 August he invited Alexis to come and stay.[12] He needed cheerful company. Writing to Goncourt, he asked: 'Do you know what's happening to Flaubert? I heard that he had many troubles, too.'[13]

Flaubert was indeed depressed, especially by his financial state. He had had to leave the rue Murillo. On 26 September, Turgenev told Zola: 'Poor Flaubert's morale is quite pitifully low. As you say, all his friends must gather round him, this winter, *if he comes* to Paris; it is not at all certain yet. It is abominably brutal of fate to come like this and fasten on the man who of all men is the least capable of living by his work.'[14] Fortunately Flaubert's niece suggested that he moved to her apartment at 240, rue du Faubourg Saint-Honoré; and here, once again, on his visits to Paris, Flaubert's friends were to come to visit him.

Zola himself still had 'abominable moods of melancholy';[15] but the writer in him remained alert. He was making notes on the sea, 'for a great descriptive episode of some twenty pages which I dream of slipping into one of my novels.'[16] Even on holiday he continued to think of the Rougon-Macquart. One novel was just finished, the next was already dormant in his mind. 'No doubt it will sleep until Paris,' he told Alexis on 17 September. 'I have the broad outline, I need Paris before I can delve into the details.'[17]

On 4 October he returned to Paris. Next day he set to work on *L'Assommoir*.

PART FOUR

THE COMING OF FAME
1875-1887

12

Zola had long thought of writing it. In his original plan for his series he had mentioned 'the novel which will have the working-class world as its setting'.

Show the world of the people [he wrote, now, in his *ébauche*] . . . Show how, in Paris, the drunkenness, the breaking of family bonds, the violence, the acceptance of all the shame and misery come from the very conditions of the worker's existence . . . This fearful picture will contain its own moral . . .

I can only save myself from the platitude of this intrigue by the grandeur and truth of my popular pictures . . . The subject is poor; I shall therefore have to try to make it a miracle of exactitude.[1]

He had at first thought of calling his book *La simple vie de Gervaise Macquart*. When he began to study the language of the common people, he had turned to the *Dictionnaire de la langue verte*, by Alfred Delvau. Perhaps he himself had discovered it; possibly Marius Roux, his willing assistant, had brought it to his notice. In 1869 Roux had published *Évariste Planchu. Mœurs vraies du Quartier Latin*. He had added a postscript to the work suggesting that characters in fiction should speak *la langue verte* where appropriate; he had given a glossary of terms, and quoted repeatedly from Delvau. Oddly enough, he had given 'a Macquart ça!' as the Parisian term for a worthless horse, an animal 'good for nothing except Macquart, the knacker'.[2]

Whoever had suggested the *Dictionnaire de la langue verte*, Zola had studied it, and he had observed the word *assommoir*. Delvau gave it as the name of a wine-shop in Belleville, then by extension as the name for every sleazy bar where the working class drank adulterated drinks. Zola also read about the *assommoirs* in a book by Denis Poulot: *Le sublime ou le travailleur comme il est en 1870, et ce qu'il peut être*. This was a study of working-class milieux at the end of the Second Empire.

There were, it is said, more personal sources of information. Zola himself was *très peuple*. As a child, he had stayed with a relation in one of the large tenements inhabited by the Parisian poor. Alexandrine's family, so tradition goes, had provided him with useful details. Maurice Dreyfous had also obtained permission for him to visit the abattoirs, but Zola had refused the offer; he said he would suffer too much to see animals hurt. However, before he went on holiday in this summer of 1875, he had visited a forge and a laundry.[3]

Early in October, on his return from Saint-Aubin, he began to search Paris for a district in which to set *L'Assommoir*. He spent hours in the boulevard de La Chapelle and the rue de la Goutte-d'Or, taking notes on the shops and houses, the movement in the streets. He and Alexandrine used to sit on benches to catch the working-class conversation. He needed much more than the four hours a day which he was later to give to his writing.

On the 10th I began not only my novel but a large-scale study of Flaubert for Russia [so he told Alexis on 20 October]. And, since the 10th, I have worked nine hours a day, so hard that I am washed out in the evening . . .

I am very pleased with my study of Flaubert, which will go off to-morrow, and [I am] even more pleased with the first chapters of my novel.[4]

He was not always happy with his work. As for re-reading his books, so he was to tell a biographer, 'it was a thing he never did, glad to forget them as soon as they had been disposed of . . . Every morning on sitting down to his table he felt as if the whole of his task were still before him; [he felt] that so far he had done nothing.'[5] Zola was nervous, but he remained determined. Or perhaps it was true, as he surmised, that, in him, determination was replaced by a fixed idea, which would make him ill if he did not follow it.[6] He was renowned for his diligence. As an English writer approvingly observed, 'he was not a literary Bohemian, . . . but an industrious and punctual artist'.[7]

Talking to the Italian critic, Edmondo de Amicis, Zola confessed: 'I do not write [a novel] entirely, I let it write itself . . . I seat myself quietly, methodically, with time-table in hand, like a mason . . . I write almost without correction, . . . and barely is it written when I put the page aside, and never read it again until it is printed. I can calculate the day when I shall finish it . . . I write with the placidity of an old compiler.'[8]

Late in 1875, or early the following year, he explained his way of life to a Russian journalist, Boborykin:

> I live quite apart, in a distant *quartier*, in the very depths of Les Batignolles. I live in a little house with my wife, my mother, two dogs and a cat ... I go out as little as possible. The only writers I visit are Flaubert, Goncourt and Alphonse Daudet. I have withdrawn from everything, deliberately, so as to work as peacefully as possible. I work in the most bourgeois way ... It's like a woman embroidering in wool, stitch by stitch ...
>
> If I didn't write my books, I should like to have a little place in some village or other ...
>
> In art, I really have only one passion, and that is life. I love modern life, all my epoch, with devotion.[9]

Zola loved life; yet he lived apart, distrustful and withdrawn, like a sensitive man who had suffered much, an outsider with a grudge against society, a provincial who felt ill at ease with *l'esprit parisien*. Gabriel Vicaire said that he had the innocent astonishments of those who had rarely ventured far afield, and for whom every molehill was a discovery.[10]

On 25 January 1876, while Zola was still working on *L'Assommoir*, *Le Siècle* began to serialise *Son Excellence Eugène Rougon*. Zola intended it to be a painting of ignorance, baseness and venality in politics. In many respects *La Fortune des Rougon*, *La Curée*, *Le Ventre de Paris* had also been political novels; but *Son Excellence Eugène Rougon* was the first of his books to take political power as its theme, professional politicians as its characters, and parliament and the ante-rooms of ministers as its setting.

In his months as parliamentary reporter on *La Cloche*, Zola had studied political manners. He now read Taxile Delord and Ernest Hamel's works on the Second Empire. He examined the back numbers of *Le Moniteur universel*. A book called *Souvenirs d'un valet de chambre* gave him details of Imperial ceremonial, and recalled the domestic life of the Imperial Household. Flaubert, who had stayed at Compiègne, offered him his observations.

Zola's abundant notes include some sharp political portraits, among them those of Napoleon III, Morny, Persigny, Émile Ollivier and Eugène Rouher. Alexis bluntly insisted that

Eugène Rougon was not Eugène Rouher. Yet Rougon does not simply have some of the Minister's habits. When Zola wrote Rougon's reply to the republican opposition, he used the actual speeches which Rouher had delivered in 1867. However, it would be unwise to be too simplistic. Rougon was a composite character. Henri Mitterand observed that he also owed some features to General Espinasse, Guizot, Persigny, Baroche, Billault and Jules Favre.

Son Excellence Eugène Rougon is not so much a novel as a record of certain stages in a political career. It begins and ends in the Chambre des Députés. The first of these pictures shows the fall, and the second shows the triumph, of Eugène Rougon. Another hundred pages or so, and the pattern of rise and fall and return to power, of intrigue and isolation and further intrigue, would be repeated. Rougon's career reflects not only his own lack of principle, but the instability of the régime.

Eugène Rougon – like Zola – is a parvenu, he is an opportunist who finds himself in his natural setting in Second Empire Paris. He has his moment of passion: his attempt to seduce Clorinde, the adventuress, reveals a brutal sensual streak in him. Yet his desire for her is almost his only discernible weakness; and even this desire may be an aspect of his need to dominate society. Zola emphasises the link between libido and the longing for power. Eugène Rougon is driven by the need to prove his superiority. He has no morals, and no principles except the determination to succeed. He knows how to manipulate his followers; he understands how to encourage his partisans. They, in turn, are driven by the same self-interest. Rougon, the immoralist, is surrounded by men and women who are worth little more than himself; he is simply an immoralist writ large.

Eugène Rougon is matched only by the demi-mondaine, Clorinde. Just as he may owe something to the Emperor's Minister, Eugène Rouher, so she bears an evident likeness to the Emperor's mistress, the Comtesse de Castiglione. Clorinde, the Italian courtesan of mysterious origin, the disturbing, dynamic woman on the fringe of Society, the fashionable woman with a taste for politics, is a characteristic Second Empire figure. She does not forgive Eugène Rougon for once rejecting her: she finally outplays him by proclaiming her liaison with the Emperor, and by ensuring that her husband is given

Rougon's office; and yet, in the final pages of the book, Rougon is again in the ascendant, and she is once again forced to admire him. Clorinde is a Second Empire symbol, almost to the same degree as Nana. She is worthy of a Rougon adversary.

These central characters are drawn considerably larger than life; round them revolves a world of lesser opportunists, cultivating friendships and exploiting their advantages, ready to extol or to defame. *Son Excellence Eugène Rougon* has the amplitude of a fresco. At the end of the novel, the infant Prince Imperial, driving through Paris in his handsome carriage, is spattered with the mud of the streets. It is a felicitous symbol of the contamination of the régime.

Son Excellence Eugène Rougon is a cumbersome novel. It lacks the passion of *La Curée*, the verve that will impel the reader through *Nana* and *Pot-Bouille*, the grandeur that will inspire *Germinal*. It is often close to caricature. There remain some memorable passages: above all, the account of the baptism of the Prince Imperial. Here, already, Zola shows his extraordinary ability to describe the grandiose in detail, to handle multitudes and individuals, to present large-scale impressions and intimate scenes. No doubt this skill owes much to his training as a journalist, but here he turns journalism into literature. He suggests the provincial excitement and impatience of the Charbonnels, as they wait for the procession, he catches the metropolitan airs of the drunken Gilquin. Yet he also sees the procession itself, the scene in Notre-Dame, with the eyes of Constantin Guys.

One point remains to be emphasised. Whatever his debts to contemporary politicians, Rougon himself was more than an historical figure. Paul Alexis recognised him as Zola. Eugène Rougon was, to him, Zola as a Minister, that is to say Zola's secret dream of what he would have been, had he applied his ambitions to politics.[11] 'No, no, not a woman!' Rougon tells Clorinde. 'It takes up too much time.' Zola, like Rougon, was largely driven by the sexual appetites that he repressed. 'I am a new man, I have only my fists.' It is Rougon, or, again, Zola who is speaking. Delestang may express the dreams of a socialist future which Zola himself will profess at the end of his career; Rougon expresses the dreams of the young novelist. Rougon wanders through Paris, and finds it 'made to measure for him,

with enough air for him to breathe'. He delights in his return to
office because it satisfies his self-esteem, his endless appetite
for authority. 'Je suis une force,' he assures Clorinde. Zola had
used the phrase of himself. This novel is, unconsciously, a study
of its author.

Soon after it appeared, the first cartoon of Zola was published
in *L'Éclipse*. It was the work of André Gill.[12] The novel also
earned Zola a prudish notice from Henry James, who was then
the Paris correspondent of the New York *Tribune*. Its success,
he reported, 'is owing partly to its cleverness, partly to the
fact that it is a presentation, through a transparent veil, of
actual persons, and chiefly, I suspect, to its brutal indecency
. . . [Émile Zola] utters his crudities with an air of bravado
which makes them doubly intolerable.'[13]

On 13 April, a few weeks after *Son Excellence Eugène Rougon*
had appeared, *Le Bien Public* began to serialise *L'Assommoir*.
Zola had lost none of his power to outrage his readers. Such
was the commotion caused by the first chapters that on 6 June
the serial had to be broken off. Catulle Mendès offered to
finish it in his review, *La République des Lettres*.[14] The literary
world was still disturbed. Zola, declared Jules Troubat, former
secretary of Sainte-Beuve, had determined to seek popularity,
just as others set out to seek a star; but Zola sought his star in
a sewer. 'I have put my nose into *L'Assommoir*,' Turgenev confessed to Flaubert. 'I am not enchanted with it. This is strictly
between ourselves.'[15] The right-wing critics saw *L'Assommoir* as
an inevitable product of the republican régime; the left-wing
critics also condemned it, and accused the author of insulting
the common people.

The book was published on 26 February 1877. It made Zola
a fortune. Goncourt's jealousy was plain. 'In Zola's enormous,
gigantic, unprecedented success, I seem to see a sign of the
general hatred of style.'[16]

Zola's earlier books had concerned provincial life in a previous
generation, the vices of a Parisian society which – so people
liked to think – had ended with the fall of the Second Empire.
Critics and public could comfortably dissociate themselves
from the pernicious conduct which he portrayed. *L'Assommoir*

still presented an aspect of Second Empire life but, fundamentally, it presented the degeneration of human beings, the destruction of the social order through the influence of drink. Zola presented the brutish drinking of the working class, the stunning alcoholism which could still be found in the depths of Parisian society. It was a continuing problem, and – in the days of absinthe – it was not confined to the plebeian world.

Gervaise Macquart has hardly reached puberty before she is seduced by Auguste Lantier; he gives her two sons, Claude and Étienne. They come to Paris, where he deserts her. She struggles to make a living as a laundress, and she marries Coupeau, a zinc-worker. They have a daughter, Nana, and for a while they live in pitiful contentment. Gervaise sets up a laundry, and she prospers, till the day when Coupeau falls off a roof at his work; as an invalid, he takes to drink. He loses the urge to earn his living, and lives on his wife. Lantier returns, and also finds it convenient to live on her. Once again he becomes her lover; for Gervaise, like Madeleine Férat, is haunted by the first man she had known. Claude, her elder son, had been sent to college in Plassans. An old man there had recognised his artistic gifts and had offered to take charge of him. Gervaise supports two men and two children. She herself turns to drink – it is one of the weaknesses of the Macquarts; her customers desert her, her laundry fails, and she descends to prostitution. Coupeau dies of delirium tremens. Gervaise returns to an unspeakable *hôtel* in the rue de la Goutte-d'Or. She dies in a cupboard underneath the stairs.

Gervaise is among the most immediately felt of Zola's characters. George Moore declared that 'in the line of souls Gervaise is his greatest achievement'.[17] Born in another stratum of society, given a solid husband, she might have led a tolerable life. She is hard-working and well-meaning, and she asks only for love and security. Yet Gervaise is a victim. She suffers from social injustice, from the accident of her humble birth, and from her hereditary weakness. It is a sign of her reality that we do not simply care about her, we speculate on her life outside this book.

It is, then, very largely her reality which inspires *L'Assommoir*; and we are concerned with the Parisian poor because we are concerned with Gervaise. Here is a world of laundresses,

prostitutes and tavern-keepers, a Paris pullulating with the
under-privileged and the oppressed, with the forgotten multitudes who move between their sordid shops and their seedy
lodgings, drinking to escape their existence. Zola had recognised
from the first that his subject demanded authenticity. *L'Assommoir* has an authenticity which is intensified to the point of symbolism. *L'Assommoir* is a novel and a social document. Like
the paintings of Daumier, it has its poetry.

The world of *L'Assommoir* was a world which Parisians were
anxious to forget. Zola saw it through the eyes of its desperate
inhabitants, he described it in their words, with unprecedented
truthfulness and passion. His plebeian style is remarkably un-
forced. It identifies the reader with the characters. We do not
simply observe this world, we are living in it. We accept its
standards, while we deplore them. We understand its aspirations, while we find them pitiful. 'There are certain pictures
which one should not paint,' Victor Hugo explained to his
biographer, Alfred Barbou. 'Don't tell me it's all true, don't
tell me that it happens like this. I know, I went down and
explored all that misery, but I won't have people making a
spectacle of it. You have *no right to strip poverty and misfortune
naked*.'[18] Zola had believed that he had both a right and a
duty.

The first copy of *L'Assommoir* had been sent to Croisset. It bore
the dedication:

> To my great friend
> Gustave Flaubert
> in hatred of taste
> ÉMILE ZOLA.[19]

Flaubert, writing to a friend, observed that 'there are splendid
passages, and the narrative has great allure'. He added that
he found the novel 'too long in the same tone; but Zola is a
strapping fellow, and you'll see how successful he will be.'[20]

Contemporary writers were quick to recognise Zola's triumph.
'This is a very great work,' wrote Mallarmé, 'and it is worthy of
an epoch when truth becomes the popular form of beauty ...
You have given something new to literature.'[21]

It is your best novel [wrote Paul Bourget]. The fury of the attacks
is enough to prove it. You are absolutely on a ground of your own

. . . You have invented a manner. It is disturbing like all discoveries, upsetting so many fixed ideas that one has to dare to admire you as you have dared in order to write . . .

Give us some more books of this power and you will be the Balzac of the *fin de siècle*.[22]

13

Paris was still discussing *L'Assommoir* when Zola set to work on his next novel. *Une Page d'Amour* was to be a simple middle-class tragedy with three characters: lover, mother and child. Zola wanted Paris to play the part of the classical chorus.

In April 1877 he went up to Passy to study the panorama of the city. He often climbed up the scaffolding of the future Palais du Trocadéro, to catch a glimpse of Paris at different times of day and in different seasons. Zola's artistic intentions recall those of Monet, when he tried to realise the various interpretations of a single theme; they also recall those of Guillemet, who painted his broad vistas at different hours. It has been observed that Zola borrowed the actual visions of artists. Thérèse Raquin, naked on her bed, had been a direct memory of Manet's *Olympia*. When the heroine of *Une Page d'Amour* climbed on to a swing in the sunshine, Zola was recalling *La Balançoire* by Renoir.[1] Henri Mitterand ascribes Zola's choice of motifs very largely to specific paintings. It was, says Mitterand, friends like Cézanne and Manet, Pissarro, Renoir and Fantin-Latour who had taught him to look at modern life.[2] Zola admitted this himself. Not long before he died, he confessed: 'I did not only support the Impressionists. I translated them . . . In all my books . . . I was in touch with artists, and borrowing from them. The artists helped me to paint in a new way in literature.'[3]

The aspect of Impressionism which influenced him most was the use of light. His real Impressionist pictures were the novels which he wrote when Impressionism was at its height; and here he recorded the effect of colour, light and texture on the senses. He did not yet consider these effects in depth, but later (in *Germinal*, for example) he began to treat light in symbolic fashion. From about 1880 his belief in Impressionism was fading; he attached more importance to realistic painting. Perhaps this change of attitude owed something to the fact that he now wore his pince-nez all the time, and distinguished detail and composition more clearly.[4]

At the end of May 1877, with all his notes for *Une Page d'Amour*, and his plan already in his head, Zola left Paris for L'Estaque. Today L'Estaque is swallowed up in the suburbs of Marseilles. It was then a little fishing town, huddled at the foot of stark rocks and barren hills. 'The country is superb,' he told Léon Hennique on 29 June. 'Perhaps you would find it arid and desolate; but I was brought up on these bare rocks and in these barren plains, which means that I am moved to tears when I see it. The very smell of the place summons up the whole of my youth.'[5] There was a considerable difference between the Provence of Daudet and that of Zola.[6] Daudet tended to be superficial. Zola took a serious view of things. If, now, he was writing *Une Page d'Amour*, he was well aware that it was only a gentle interlude. 'I have finished four chapters of it [this to Goncourt on 23 July], and I am very pleased with them . . . I am deliberately writing for schoolgirls, I am making myself flat and grey. And then, with *Nana*, I shall go back to the ferocious.'[7]

He cloistered himself in solitude, and he worked on; he sometimes went for three days without leaving his room. By 3 August he had finished the first of the five parts of his novel.[8] 'I work all the morning and read all the afternoon,' he explained to Roux. 'Day follows day, and they are all alike . . . I haven't seen a drop of rain for two months . . . Joking apart, this eternal fine weather is my only criticism of Provence. It puts you off the sun.'[9]

In Paris he had dreamed of Le Paradou and of Provence; now, in Provence, he lost himself in his Parisian novel. He wrote it with apprehension, and with no hope of commercial success. On 5 September he told Roux: 'I'm working at my novel, but less vigorously than I should like. However, I am still determined to stay here until 3 November.'[10] A few days later he felt obliged to tell Hennique: 'I want every note in my series; that is why . . . I shall never regret having done *Une Page d'Amour* . . .

I forgot to tell you that I finally chose this last title. People will think they are drinking a glass of syrup, and that is what decided me.'[11] Zola was accustomed to audacity; he did not want anyone to think him timid.

He stayed at L'Estaque for five long months; he returned to Paris with relief. *Une Page d'Amour* was published in April 1878. Compared with his earlier novels, it is curiously restricted. The action takes place very largely in an apartment in Passy – and in the mind and heart of Hélène Grandjean, a Rubenesque young widow with a daughter on the verge of puberty.

Hélène and Jeanne live a life of seclusion. Jeanne adores her mother, and she is violently jealous and possessive. Emotional to the point of neurosis, she also suffers from chloro-anæmia (Zola had studied the condition in the works of different specialists); she is lethargic, moody, and subject to convulsions. As the book opens, she is passing through a crisis. Her mother goes in search of a doctor. The doctor whom she finds is young, married and handsome; gradually they are drawn together. Jeanne becomes aware of her mother's divided affection, and she hates the man who is trying to cure her; when, at last, Hélène becomes Henri's mistress, the child dies. Hélène marries an old admirer. Two years after the death of Jeanne, they visit her tomb; and Hélène reflects on the curious unreality of her past. Henri has vanished from her life, Jeanne has departed. Paris alone remains.

The action of *Une Page d'Amour* is so restricted that, in Zola's hands, it becomes banal. Hélène merely strikes maternal attitudes or poses as a woman in love. Jeanne does little but demonstrate her ill-health and her possessiveness. Henri Deberle is a nullity. In no other Rougon-Macquart novel does Zola so contrive his situations, so patently force events to meet his needs. He seems more concerned to solve technical problems than he does to represent reality. Hélène is a Mouret by birth, and she has the neurotic nature of her family. Jeanne inherits the instability which had led Tante Dide, *la grande ancêtre*, to an asylum. The theory of heredity is carefully stressed, but Zola lacks the tact and perception to write this study of personality.

Une Page d'Amour is a depressing picture of adultery and a strangely unromantic book. The romance is found, most lastingly, in the five Impressionist panoramas of Paris. Just as the garden of Le Paradou had matched the stages in the love of Serge and Albine, so Paris reflects the stages in the life of Hélène; and, finally, its untroubled sky predicts her untroubled future. Zola had come a long way from the precepts of Taine and the preface to *Thérèse Raquin*.

Une Page d'Amour was greeted with a deference which may now seem surprising. 'It doesn't spoil the collection, don't worry,' Flaubert assured him, 'and I don't understand your doubts about its worth.'[12] Mallarmé confessed:

> I admire your latest work as much as all the others, and perhaps a little more. It seems to me that you have succeeded for the first time, not in creating something magnificent, which you have habitually done, but in creating exactly what you consider to be the typical modern work of literature. A poem, for such it is, unceasingly; and a novel for those who would like to see it just as a fair painting of contemporary life.[13]

'It may not be the most colourful of your novels,' Maupassant told Zola, 'but it is, in my opinion, the most perfect in style, and among the most human and the most true.'[14]

14

In 1877 Zola had left the rue Saint-Georges, in Les Batignolles, for 23, rue de Boulogne. After his return from L'Estaque, in the autumn of that year, he had decided to buy a country house. It is said that he had thought of going to Brittany or Provence, but that the Exhibition of 1878 had led him, instead, to look for a house near Paris. The explanation seems implausible; however, it was at Médan that 'a narrow little house hidden in a nest of verdure, and separated from the rest of the hamlet by a magnificent alley of trees, produced upon him what Stendhal has called *le coup de foudre*'.[1] It was a curious choice, for the main railway line from Paris to Le Havre ran beside the house; but Zola did not seem to be concerned. He saw, however, that the Seine flowed past the garden; and Jean-Claude Le Blond insists that the Seine led Zola to acquire the property: the Seine which had witnessed his wretched youth, the Impres-

sionists' Seine which visited Monet at Argenteuil, lapped
Maupassant's canoe at Sartrouville, and finally reached
Flaubert at Croisset.[2]

Médan, so Edmund Gosse was to write, 'is a very quiet
hamlet, . . . absolutely unillustrious, save that, according to
tradition, Charles the Bold was baptised in the font of its
parish church.'[3] Céard added that Médan was an ancient
seigneurie which had been owned by Parisians since the ninth
century. In the fifteenth century, the château had been restored
by Henry Perdrier, a bourgeois from Paris. In the sixteenth
century, Jean Brinon, another Parisian, and a friend of Ronsard,
had entertained poets there.[4] Now, on 14 July 1878, Zola reported to Marius Roux: 'We are in a green paradise here. I
have gone back to my work, but I am still a little shaken by all
the upheaval of moving in. In a few days all will be well.'[5] On
9 August he announced to Flaubert: 'I've bought a house, a
rabbit hutch between Poissy and Triel, in a charming spot on the
banks of the Seine. Nine thousand francs, I'm telling you the
price so that you don't feel too respectful. Literature has paid
for this modest rural retreat. It has the advantage of being a
long way from any station and of not counting a single bourgeois
in the neighbourhood.'[6]

From this moment, Zola never stopped enlarging and trans-
forming Médan. Alexandrine supervised the workmen, and
ensured that his plans were carried out. He did not want an
architect. Like his father, he wanted to build. He preferred to
imagine his own buildings, just as he imagined his own literary
constructions (had he not said that he wrote like a mason?).
He had bought the little house from the profits of *L'Assommoir*.
As fast as his novels accumulated and his wealth increased, the
buildings and the garden also grew. A wing was added, the
neighbouring fields were turned into a wooded park. The island
in the Seine was transformed with its châlet, shrubs and lawns,
and the transformations were to date from *Nana*. The hot-houses,
stables and hen-houses were to be Zola's reward for *Pot-Bouille*.
A second wing, with a large drawing-room, was to represent
La Joie de Vivre. Ernest Vizetelly later recorded:

The whole place was lighted by electricity, . . . after a series of
experiments with acetyline gas which led to several explosions . . .
  [Zola] liked to show one his grounds and his flowers – the bright

red rose being his favourite, though he also had a taste for peonies and dahlias. At times he would lead one to the farmyard, and feed the houdans, guinea-fowls, ducks, geese and turkeys . . .[7]

According to her husband's wishes, Alexandrine planted the first stake of every path, the first tree of every clump; she laid the foundation stone of every building. There was a certain solemnity about these occasions. She and Zola would seal up a commemorative scroll in an iron box, and the box would be bricked up in the wall. 'On 27 September 1880,' Alexandrine was to record, 'I laid the first stone of this house, on our island, which we called Le Paradou'; and Zola added modestly: 'I was present at the laying of the first stone by my dear wife.'[8]

In time Médan was to become a considerable estate. Near the main building rose 'the friends' pavilion', where, in a more conventional setting (the bedroom curtains were floral chintz), Zola's guests could live as they chose, without changing their daily habits. In later years his publisher came to stay so frequently that 'the friends' pavilion' came to be called *le pavillon Charpentier*.

One of the most remarkable features of Médan was Zola's farm. The stables were built of marble. The mangers were overlooked by a sort of gallery in carved oak, from which he could watch his animals eating. 'They say,' he observed, 'that there are people who don't love animals . . . Who can say that he does not love them, since he needs them so as not to feel alone, terrified and desperate?'[9] On 26 September 1881, Léon Hennique duly reported from Ribemont: 'Your white rabbits, with red eyes, black ears, tail, nose and paws, will leave here today at four o'clock, and will therefore be at Triel tomorrow morning, Tuesday. There are a male and a female . . . So mind you keep an eye on their escapades, in order that the race may be preserved.'[10]

From the moment he acquired the house, Zola used to spend six or eight months of the year at Médan. In Paris he did little but document himself for his books. It was in the country that he wrote them. The servants used to arrive in advance to open the house for the season. The gardener, Octave Lenôtre, and his wife, lived in a lodge by the kitchen garden, and they looked after Médan in Zola's absence.

His way of life in the country was bourgeois in its regularity.

He rises at eight in the morning [wrote Sherard], and dresses in very rustic attire, his favourite apparel being a suit of brown corduroy velvet, with heavy shooting boots. Directly after rising he takes a walk with his dogs ... The house is reached again by a quarter to nine, when the first breakfast [*sic*] is served ... Zola, however, takes no liquids, and, believing in working on a well-nourished frame, invariably takes a couple of eggs on the plate – that is to say, fried eggs – for breakfast. He is very particular that these eggs should be cooked just to the point at which he likes them.[11]

At nine o'clock, precisely, he went up to his workroom: a huge room, over fifteen feet high, twenty-seven feet broad and thirty feet long. Over the mantelpiece, traced in letters of gold, was the exhortation: 'Nulla dies sine linea.' In the middle of the room was a large table, covered with writing materials, all arranged in methodical order. Here Zola wrote, uninterrupted, until one o'clock, when *déjeuner* was served. At two, he took his siesta. At three the postman arrived.[12] At four o'clock Zola rowed on the Seine – or, in later years, took a bicycle ride. Dinner was served at half-past seven; tea was served after dinner, and might be followed by a game of billiards. At ten o'clock, precisely, he retired to his room to read. He rarely went to sleep before two in the morning.[13]

Some visitors, it must be said, observed Médan in a less kindly light. One day towards the end of the 1880s, with Valentin Simond, editor of *L'Écho de Paris*, Edmond Lepelletier went to dine there. 'A marvellous dinner,' reported Goncourt. 'Domestic in white tie. Mme Zola low-cut, bare-bosomed. Seven glasses, with the wines specified ... In this comedy of elegance, Zola playing the genial host, but Mme Zola apeing the Princess ... In fact, such an act at this rustic dinner that the two guests came out and burst into laughter.'[14]

Goncourt was almost always malicious, and possibly inventive. The ostentation at Médan was poignant. Alexandrine, the disappointed woman, was consoling herself with what she considered social prestige. Zola still needed to make amends for his impoverished past. 'He always seemed a very quiet, unassuming man,' Julian Osgood Field was to write, 'quite unlike what one would picture him to be, but exactly what he

originally was, a clerk behind a counter.'[15] Zola was all too
conscious of his origins, all too anxious to become respectable.
He did not understand that, in his search for dignity, he might
sometimes seem ridiculous. '*Mon ami* [this to Céard], would
you have somewhere about you, among your papers, the arms
of Dourdan (Seine-et-Oise) and those of Médan? I mean the
shields, with the indication of the heraldic colours. I need these
documents for my new billiard-room.'[16] The grandson of the
house-painter of Dourdan (Seine-et-Oise) was eager to proclaim
an ancestry. Albert Laborde recorded that outside the billiard-
room there stood a suit of armour. The 'knight' wore a helmet
and held a pike in his mailed fist.[17]

Céard saw it all with sympathy. Zola, he explained, sought
only the pleasure of the moment. Perhaps, in the disparate things
around him, he found rest for a mind which was tired by con-
ceiving such organised books.[18] Marie Belloc Lowndes agreed
with the suggestion. Zola's only form of relaxation seemed to
her to be a visit to the Hôtel des Ventes.[19]

In about 1876, even before he bought his country house, a
group of Naturalist writers had formed around him. It was to
be known as the École de Médan.

Paul Alexis, a novelist and dramatist, had attended the
Collège Bourbon a few years before Zola; he had met him
again in Paris at the end of the Second Empire. Alexis had come
to know Léon Hennique on *La République des Lettres*, and he
introduced him to Zola. In April 1876, Henry Céard, a clerk
at the Ministry of the Interior, had called on Zola in the rue
Saint-Georges. Céard had been born in Paris in 1851. After
the Franco-Prussian War, he had entered the École de médecine.
In 1873 he had abandoned his medical studies, and gone into
public administration. Céard – himself a novelist – helped Zola
in the research for his novels, and in settling small domestic
matters. In time he was to help him in the most critical moments
in his private life. During his first meeting with Zola, Céard
mentioned Joris-Karl Huysmans: a colleague at his office who
was also a man of letters. Zola read *Marthe*, and recognised the
novelist's promise.

On 16 April 1877, at Trapp's, at the corner of the passage
du Havre and the rue Saint-Lazare, Maupassant had organised

a dinner which brought the École de Médan together, and inspired them to assert their existence. *La République des Lettres* had published an imaginary menu. It ended with Parfait Naturaliste, Vin de Coupeau and Liqueur de l'Assommoir.[20]

On Sundays, the group used to spend the day with Zola in the country.

Oh, how happy Médan used to be in those days [Alexandrine was to recall]! Maupassant enlivened the house with his joyous energy. I can still hear his carbine shots echoing endlessly in the garden . . . As he was then a great canoeist, he was entrusted with buying us our first boat, a very ordinary boat, a family boat, which was given the rather unsuitable name of *Nana* . . .

Céard delighted us with his delicate wit . . .

Huysmans endeared himself to us with his erudite conversation . . .

Hennique used to bring us parrots, which one of his brothers sent him from Senegal . . .[21]

Even Léon Daudet, the cynical son of Alphonse, was mellowed by the atmosphere of Médan.

Here is Médan on a hot June day, powdered with gold. Huysmans is there, mocking and gaunt, with the visage of a tamable vulture, his familiar irony . . . Hennique, Céard, Paul Alexis, Frantz Jourdain join in in turn, and sometimes all together, in the conversation between the master of the house, Goncourt and Alphonse Daudet. My father, as usual, animates everything, projects his good humour . . . Zola is much more amiable, in better form at home than he is anywhere else. He has a feeling and a taste for hospitality. He suggests an outing in a boat. They follow him; and to see these writers at the height of their fame, or on the road to fame, so light-hearted, open and natural, bent over their oars, talking and singing, no-one would imagine that the future would soon hollow out such chasms between them.[22]

In this setting, in the massive chair inscribed 'If God wills, I will,' in the summer of 1878, Zola settled down to work at *Nana*.

15

Legend says that when Manet finished reading *L'Assommoir*, he wondered what had happened to the daughter of Coupeau and Gervaise. He saw her as a *fille de théâtre*, and as such he painted a portrait of her. His guess could only have been inspired – or suggested by conversation with Zola; for Manet painted his picture in the winter of 1876–7, and *Nana* did not begin to appear in *Le Voltaire* until October 1879. However, it is probable that Manet's painting inspired an episode in Zola's novel.

Buried at L'Estaque in the summer of 1877, Zola had told Mme Charpentier: 'I'm dreaming of an extraordinary *Nana* . . . We shall be murdered on the spot, Charpentier and I.'[1] His achievement was indeed to be extraordinary. But for the few uncomfortable occasions when he had been to Arsène Houssaye's, he had not set foot in a fashionable *hôtel*; nor had he visited a courtesan. He therefore had recourse to a *bon viveur* whom he had met at Flaubert's. They went to *déjeuner* at the Café Anglais; and there, in a private room, the very scene of his exploits, his host recalled the courtesans of the Second Empire. It was Blanche d'Antigny who held Zola's attention. She anticipated his vision of Nana. In his imagination, Blanche and Nana were henceforward the same creature. Nana was to have the build and complexion of Blanche, and her theatrical and amorous careers were to be based on those of the *grande cocotte*. Julian Osgood Field, an American man-about-town, confirmed: 'Blanche d'Antigny was, of course, the original of Nana – everyone knew that; and, in fact, Zola told me so himself.'[2]

In the late 1870s, as a dramatist and critic, Zola was concerned with the theatre. It was no doubt this interest which led him to make much of Nana's theatrical career, and some *zolistes* have been tempted to recognise in *Nana* a repetition of the themes which he had developed in his journalism. Certainly he turned to a noted figure of the Second Empire theatre. Ludovic Halévy, Offenbach's librettist, gave him anecdotes about Blanche; and, on 19 June 1878, Halévy recorded: 'Did a plan of the theatre, the wings and corridors of the Variétés for Zola. The heroine of his next novel, *Nana*, will sing in operetta at the Variétés. Zola knows very little in this field, and he asked me to take him to the theatre one evening – which I did in April – and to send him a small plan with notes about the place, which I did this morning.'[3]

Zola had also to visit the *hôtel* of a cocotte. Hennique introduced him to that of Mme Valtesse de Bigne, in the boulevard Malesherbes. Mme Valtesse showed him her salons, her dining-room, conservatory and stables, and allowed him into her bedroom, where he was free to study her bed. On this he was to conjure up the naked figure of Nana. 'Do you know what Zola's done?' cried Mme Valtesse. 'He's put a soldiers' moll in my bed!' She was outraged when the book appeared.[4]

Thank you a thousand times for your notes [Zola wrote to Céard on 26 July 1878]. They are excellent, and I shall use them all ...

I've got the plan of *Nana*, and I am very happy with it. I spent three days finding the names, and some of them seem to me to be successful .... I already have some sixty characters. I can't start writing for another fortnight, I still have so many details to settle.[5]

Perhaps he turned again to Du Camp's survey of Paris. In the chapter on prostitution, Du Camp laid much of the blame for 1870 on the corrupting influence of the courtesans: 'When France sought within herself for the men she needed, she saw a void and she found nobody. In this work of social decomposition and decay, the courtesans were instruments of the first importance.'[6] Du Camp not only offered Zola pages of details, he anticipated the theme of the novel.

The preparatory dossier for *Nana* includes 344 pages of notes; among them were Zola's comments on the identities of the characters. Fontan owed something to Coquelin *cadet*, Lucy Stewart to Cora Pearl. Zola seems to have remembered the Prince of Wales's visit to Hortense Schneider's dressing-room. He also made lists of technical terms relating to the theatre, and he recorded observations on the make-up of an actress, which Halévy had enabled him to watch. On 9 August he announced to Flaubert: 'I have that slight trembling of the pen which has always announced the happy birth of a good book. I expect to begin to write about the 20th of this month.'[7]

In the same letter, Zola turned to a less satisfactory subject. 'You know,' he told Flaubert, 'that your friend [Agénor] Bardoux [the Minister of Public Instruction], has just played an unworthy trick on me. After proclaiming for five months to all and sundry that he was going to decorate me, he replaced me on his list at the last moment by Ferdinand Fabre; so there I am, a perpetual candidate for the decoration, although I personally asked for nothing, and cared about it as much as a donkey cares about a rose.'[8]

For someone who professed indifference, Zola was remarkably angry; but he himself was to ensure that authority frowned upon him. On 1 September, in *Le Messager de l'Europe*, he published an outspoken study of contemporary French novelists. On 22 December it was reprinted in the literary supplement of *Le Figaro*. It seems that Zola was, after all, to have had his decoration in the new year; he disappeared again from the list. Maupassant, who worked in Bardoux's office, wrote to Flaubert: 'Zola is not decorated because of the article he published in *Le Figaro*!!! ... How does a critical article destroy Zola's talent?'[9] Goncourt, dining at Brébant's, chanced to meet Bardoux, and asked him why he did not decorate Zola. Bardoux replied that he had met formal opposition from the Council of Ministers.[10]

Meanwhile, in the summer of 1878, Zola immersed himself in his work. Boborykin, the Russian journalist, called on him again in June, and found him 'conscious of his powers; he is sure of himself,' wrote Boborykin, 'without being arrogant; he calculates his interests, but at the same time he is devoted to the idea of art.'[11]

Zola's self-confidence hardly seemed to be impaired by his failure to be decorated. He wrote *Nana* with more gusto, more contentment than any other novel in his career. 'I've finished the first chapter of *Nana*, and I'm enchanted with it!' he told Flaubert on 19 September.[12] A week later: 'I am working hard ... I sometimes long never to go back to Paris, I am so peaceful here in my desert. I have never seen more clearly.'[13]

On 14 October, still at Médan, he announced to Goncourt: 'I don't expect to go back to Paris before the end of December . . . *Nana* is getting on slowly, but I'm very pleased with her.'[14]

It was, it seems, on Zola's return to the rue de Boulogne that a young Swiss author, Édouard Rod, decided to study what had become the Zola Question. The result was to be his monograph, *A propos de 'L'Assommoir.'*

This vigorous painter of the muddiest layers of our society, this man who is quick to attack and quick to retaliate, is [decided Rod] a good bourgeois, who lives a peaceful life and hardly ever leaves home . . . In Paris he lives in an apartment in the rue de Boulogne. It is there that you must see him, if you want to know his tastes; they are those of a collector, or rather of a lover of everything old . . .

The bedroom is especially curious. There is stained glass in the windows, and . . . there is a Louis XIII bed, tall and massive, adorned with chasuble trimmings in Genoa velvet . . .

In this room you breathe in a real fragrance of the past; it disposes you to dreams, it makes caprice run riot, it bears the imagination a long way away from the Rougon-Macquart.[15]

It warmed the Romantic heart of Flaubert. 'I have always dreamed of sleeping in a bed like that,' he said. 'It is the bed of Saint-Julien l'Hospitalier.'[16]

The bedroom was not the only astonishing room in the apartment. As Rod continued:

It communicates with a salon, which brings us back to modern times, thanks to the walls which are covered with very modern paintings: a view of Aix signed by Guillemet; works by Manet, Monet, Berthe Morisot, Pissarro, Cézanne – the terrible Impressionist. To the right of the door, hanging over a red velvet sofa, you notice the life-size portrait of M. Zola, painted by Manet ten years ago. The author of the Rougon-Macquart has changed a good deal since those days: he has grown stouter, and his hair is thinner than it was, but he has kept his kindly look, his benevolent smile . . .

The curtains in this room are made of appliqué lace from chasubles, the fireplace is decorated with Italian lace of great beauty . . . In front of the table is a big Portuguese armchair, in solid rosewood, upholstered in red velvet [red was Zola's favourite colour] . . .

The man who, in the heart of Paris, has created himself such a peaceful setting, collected so many mementoes of the past, escapes the accusations of ignorance and bad taste – to say nothing worse – which have been levied at him. He lives in peace, surrounded by these things, each of which has a history. After the struggles of his youth, tranquillity is dear to him.[17]

Zola was soon to be involved in controversy once more. On 18 January 1879 *L'Assommoir*, in five acts and ten tableaux, taken from his novel by William Busnach and Benjamin Gastineau, was to be staged at the Théâtre de l'Ambigu. 'Everyone says it will be a battle,' Céard wrote on 21 December. '. . . It is you, and only you, they are aiming at. I should be very surprised if people didn't try to take revenge on the play for the success of the novel.'[18] Two days later, Céard added: 'Maupassant has recently been appointed private secretary to Bardoux. He has just come to see me and confirmed my observations. There's a real commotion. Yesterday Coquelin *aîné* was dining at Mme Pasca's, and he thundered against you.'[19]

Three weeks before the first performance of *L'Assommoir*, all the seats left free by the management had been taken. Theatre agencies negotiated ruthlessly for the few tickets at their disposal. The management of the Ambigu announced that the box-office would be closed on 18 January. None the less, two or three hundred people waited outside the theatre. Inside, the auditorium was packed. Sarah Bernhardt, in a stage box, applauded with such vehemence, so the legend went, that she broke her chair. In the stalls were such Nanas of the stage as Léonide Leblanc and Hortense Schneider. The critics were present in force. There were several theatre directors, eager to know how to plan their repertoires.

'Much ado, too much ado, about this first performance,' Halévy recorded. '. . . They just performed a big melodrama, indifferently put together; it was like all other melodramas.'[20] 'I am pleased about the financial success for Zola,' Flaubert announced to Maupassant. 'But that does not consolidate Naturalism (we are still waiting to have it defined), and that does not establish our friend as a dramatist. It is now for him to write a play according to his system.'[21]

However, from the first performance, *L'Assommoir* was a

triumph; and if Charles Floquet, the politician, attacked 'the unhealthy, filthy work of Zola,' such vehemence only served to increase its interest. Parody and caricature increased it even more. At the Cercle des Hydropathes, Galipaux recited 'a comico-realist poem', *En rev'nant de L'Assommoir*; at the Théâtre des Bouffes-du-Nord, Maurice Ordonneau showed a three-act vaudeville, *L'Assommoir pour rire*. On 3 May the Cirque Franconi advertised *L'Assommoir*, 'a parody-pantomime in five tableaux'. The Folies-Bergère announced a number called *Les Assommés*.[22] It was little wonder that the play itself ran for some three hundred performances.

The theatre has long had a special significance for French writers. It has been a means of adding a dimension to their work, but, above all, it has been a platform for their theories. To write for the theatre has been a status symbol and a coveted means of communication. The theatre, Zola said, was a luxury which he could only allow himself when he was very old. In fact, he had aspired from the first to see his work on stage. Until a literary movement had conquered the theatre, it had not really acquired *le droit de cité*. Zola needed his *bataille d'Hernani*.

Already, in the 1860s, he had written a three-act drama, *Madeleine*. When he had failed to place it, he had expanded it into his novel *Madeleine Férat*. In staging his *Thérèse Raquin* he had hoped, once again, to bring Naturalism to the theatre. Some critics consider that the play was Zola's most effective dramatic work. Others find it a melodrama as dated as any by a Romantic playwright; and, staged at the Théâtre de la Renaissance on 11 July 1873, it ran for only nine performances. In *Les Héritiers Rabourdin*, Zola set aside the demands of Naturalism, and wrote a pastiche of a seventeenth-century farce. It has engaging vitality, the sort of bitter comedy which was to inspire his novel *Pot-Bouille*. It deserved more success than it enjoyed. In fact it was staged at an inferior theatre, the Théâtre Cluny, on 3 November 1874. It had seventeen performances, and its poor reception embittered him. Introducing the printed version, he observed that 'novelists are the literary princes of the age; they do honour to our degraded stages when they condescend to set foot on them'. *Le Bouton de Rose* was a comedy about fidelity. He wrote it to divert both himself and the audience. It was launched at the Théâtre du Palais-Royal on 6 May 1878. Flaubert found it 'pitiful'; it lasted for seven performances. A few days after it had failed, Zola declared: 'I have a great deal of stubbornness and patience. People have actually finished by reading my novels, they will end by listening to my plays.'[23]

His ambition was no doubt fired by the enthusiasm of Sarah Bernhardt. She saw herself as Renée, in a play based on *La Curée*. 'This modern Phèdre is my ideal,' she had told him in 1877. 'I am very unfortunate to have so much power over everyone since you, Émile Zola, refuse to listen to me.'[24] On 5 December 1877, Turgenev assured Flaubert that Zola 'was definitely going to write a play for Sarah Bernhardt'.[25] He finally made a five-act drama out of *La Curée*. 'Without Mme Sarah Bernhardt,' he explained himself, in the preface to *Renée*, 'I might never have written the play.' It was one of the few occasions on which he hesitated. He felt that – whatever the implications of *Phèdre* – the theme of virtual incest would be unacceptable to the Théâtre-Français. He solved the problem by writing a play in which Renée's marriage had been nominal. Another problem arose, for early in 1880 Sarah Bernhardt broke with the Comédie-Française, and embarked on a tour of America. She did not appear in a play by Zola. *Renée* was finally performed in 1887, and condemned by Goncourt in his *Journal*. As Zola said, a drama was not left in a drawer for years without growing old.

More than one Rougon-Macquart novel was, however, to inspire a stage production. *Germinal* was to be given at the Théâtre du Châtelet in 1888; *Le Rêve* was to be produced in Brussels in 1891. Among Zola's papers is a letter from Leoncavallo, asking permission for Franchetti 'to turn your *Faute de l'Abbé Mouret* into a musical poem'.[26] Massenet suggested to Zola that he might base a score on *La Faute de l'Abbé Mouret*. The same idea occurred to Alfred Bruneau, who was then almost unknown. Zola considered himself to be pledged to Massenet. However, after Zola's death, Antoine, then director of the Odéon, thought of staging a play in dialogue based on the same novel. Bruneau undertook the musical setting and the theatrical adaptation. The play was first performed in 1907.

During the last decade of Zola's life, when he turned from

Naturalism to visionary and symbolic novels, there was a cor-
responding change in his theatrical interests. Under the influence of Bruneau, he became drawn to operatic form. His
libretto for *Messidor* echoes his familiar theme: it sings the praise
of love, the parallel fecundity of the earth and of humankind.
Plot and characters are embarrassingly poor for the man who
had written *La Terre*. Vizetelly wrote that *Messidor* had a cool
reception. 'The book was pronounced absolutely trivial, and
the music of the ballet, a principal feature of this so-called
lyric drama, was considered to be lamentably deficient in
rhythm and movement.' None the less, there was another work
in collaboration with Bruneau. *L'Ouragan* was a violent drama
about desire, love and revenge; it was performed unsuccess-
fully at the Opéra-Comique in 1901.[27] In *Violaine la chevelue*,
Zola returned to his literary beginnings, his *Contes à Ninon*. He
might perhaps have been better advised to write his work as
a fairy-tale. Understandably, it was not performed on stage.
Much the most felicitous of his *poèmes lyriques* was *Lazare*. In
this one-act piece which, once again, Bruneau set to music,
Jesus raises Lazarus from the dead, but Lazarus asks only to
return to his long and peaceful sleep. One wonders if, as in
La Joie de Vivre, Zola had identified Lazarus with himself. This
comédie lyrique has an urgency which suggests that it coincided
with some personal grief.

For all his persistence, Zola did not establish himself in the
theatre. It demanded a skill and flair which he did not possess.
A play did not allow him the luxury of description, it rarely
concerned large movements or collective emotions. It could not
be constructed from documents, as he constructed a Rougon-
Macquart novel, and this was the method of writing which he
best understood.

Yet, though he was no dramatist, his friendship with André
Antoine was significant in the history of the theatre. Zola saw
the Théâtre-Libre, which Antoine had founded in 1887, as the
home of modern progressive drama. In 1889 he gave the
theatre his *Madeleine*. Antoine also staged his *Jacques Damour*,
adapted by Léon Hennique, and *Tout pour l'honneur*, adapted by
Henry Céard. Zola rejected the thought of collaboration in
the novel; genius, he said mildly, must stand alone. He had no
genius in the theatre, and he was obliged to recognise that on

stage he could not walk unaided. However, though his own work for the theatre was undistinguished, he had helped some dramatists who were to be admired by posterity.

Cher maître [Strindberg wrote to him in an undated letter],

I do not want to importune you with a regular correspondence, but I cannot refrain from telling you that your famous *Thérèse Raquin* has just been performed at the Theatre Royal in Stockholm . . .

It was an event for us Naturalists, and all the more remarkable since the literary and political reaction has treated our young school roughly for some years . . .

I myself have regained my courage since the performance of *Ghosts* in Paris. At the risk of appearing a nuisance. I am emboldened once again to trouble you to read a play. For the past year, M. Antoine has kept this and another play (not to mention *The Father*), and he has not made a decision.

If you deigned to consider the pressing circumstances of an author relegated to the end of the world, an author who has so often succumbed in an unequal struggle, dragging on an existence which is painful for his family, you would not reproach me for my persistence.[28]

Zola not only encouraged Strindberg; he already shared with Antoine the distinction of introducing Ibsen to the French theatre. He himself had urged Antoine to stage *Ghosts*, and he had even found him a translator; soon after Zola's intervention, Antoine had cast the play.[29]

16

'I saw Zola yesterday evening, and he said you weren't coming to Paris this winter.' So Maupassant had written to Flaubert on 13 January 1879. '. . . Zola is desolate that you aren't coming; he said that people don't meet each other unless you are there, and he's going to spend a solitary winter.'[1] Zola was increasingly concerned with Flaubert and with his well-being. Flaubert was now confined to Croisset with a broken leg.

No doubt you have been reassured about his accident [wrote Gustave Toudouze, the novelist, on 30 January]. Just in case you have not, let me send you a few lines from a letter from M. Laporte:

'There was a very bad sprain, and a fracture of the base of the fibula. The inflammation has already disappeared, but he has been ordered to take a complete rest for some time. There is no need for anxiety.'

Forgive me for writing to you unsolicited, like this, but I thought that everyone who loves Flaubert would like to be reassured about him twice rather than once.[2]

Flaubert's troubles were not only physical. He was still in financial straits. His friends had hoped to find him a sinecure as a librarian; but rumours of their activities had leaked into the Press, and they had brought him only vexation. 'Flaubert is better in the mind and quite as bad as far as his purse is concerned,' Céard had told Zola late in 1878. 'The attempts to make him accept a librarianship will be fruitless. Maupassant quoted me phrases from one of his letters, heartrending phrases which refuse in the loftiest manner.'[3] However, Baudry was appointed to the Bibliothèque Mazarine; he created an additional post for Flaubert, and Flaubert finally accepted it.[4]

Flaubert was the only contemporary whom Zola always recognised as his superior in literature. 'I beg you once again, don't be sad; on the contrary, be proud. You are the best of us all.'[5] Flaubert was nineteen years his senior; he was the paternal figure which had long been lacking from Zola's life. Antoine Albalat said that Zola could not speak of Flaubert without emotion.[6] Alexandrine said that her husband felt 'immense friendship' for him. Maurice Dreyfous was moved by the visible affection which Flaubert and Zola felt for one another. Flaubert behaved like a loving elder brother; Zola showed him filial devotion.[7]

Flaubert was not uncritical. Zola, he lamented, was not concerned 'with what, to me, is the aim of Art, that is to say with Beauty'. Zola's error, so he told Mme Roger des Genettes, was 'to have a system, to want to establish a school ... He lacks two things: (1) He is not a poet, and (2) he has no reading, or rather he is ignorant.' Yet, for all his criticism, Flaubert considered Zola 'a real artist'. He gave him an understanding which was untinged with jealousy or bitterness.[8]

Now, in the early months of 1879, Flaubert remained at Croisset; and 'Zola asked me to say that he was waiting for you impatiently,' wrote Maupassant, 'so as to give the dinner he

promised for the 50th edition of *L'Assommoir*. He hopes that
you will be here at the beginning of May, because he wants to
leave immediately afterwards. He has put off his departure for
this.'[9]

While theatregoers applauded *L'Assommoir*, and readers revelled
in it, Zola continued to work on his new novel. 'There are
ridiculous rumours going round here about *Nana*,' Céard
reported from Paris on 30 May. 'In a Franco-Russian *salon*
where I set foot again the other evening, a gentlemen affirmed
in all seriousness that Nana was Valtesse. He also quoted the
names of three or four other very expensive women on the
Parisian market, who were, he said, to figure in your next
novel. I did not even try to disillusion him, what was the
use?'[10] Visitors to Parisian *salons* were perhaps more inspired
than Céard knew.

The story of *Nana* demanded a day at the races. Zola seems to
have used the account of the Grand Prix which he had published in *Le Messager de l'Europe*. He also wanted a fresh impression, and on 8 August he and Alexandrine set out for Longchamp. Armed with binoculars, Zola studied the various
aspects of the course. Marpon, the publisher, who was with
him, offered to make him win twelve hundred francs. Zola
refused. Marpon betted for him, and won. The Grand Prix was
won by Nubienne. Zola went back to Médan with pages of
notes. Pleasantly interrupted by a visit from Cézanne – who
painted Alexandrine in the garden – he began Chapter XI of
his novel.[11] 'With your fishing-rod in one hand,' wrote Alexis
on 9 August, 'and the pen for writing *Nana* in the other, you
must have forgotten Paris completely.'[12]

As usual, when Zola had written some two-thirds of his book,
he was to start publication in serial form. On 15 September he
warned Jules Laffitte, director of *Le Voltaire*: 'Don't begin your
publicity too soon, . . . or else you would exhaust your readers'
patience.' Whatever Zola's counsels, Laffitte did not spare
publicity. Red posters burgeoned all over Paris, displayed
themselves on the windows of the trams and on the bridges of
the *bateaux-mouches*. They perambulated along the boulevards
on the backs of sandwichmen. *Nana*, as Auriant observed, 'said
psitt! to readers on every pavement in the capital'.[13] On 15

October, Céard reported: 'There's enormous curiosity about *Nana* . . . It's becoming an obsession and a nightmare.'[14]

Next day the novel began to appear in *Le Voltaire*. The public avidly followed an author who hesitated at nothing. 'The chaste writer,' Zola himself insisted, 'is recognised at once by the exacerbated virility of his touch . . . Chastity has been the spur of powerful men of genius.'[15] As Claude Lantier was to paint in *L'Œuvre*, so Zola wrote 'with a passion for nakedness desired and never possessed, a powerlessness to satisfy himself, to create as much of this flesh as he dreamed of embracing with his two despairing arms'.[16]

The publication of *Nana* continued in Paris, the writing of *Nana* continued at Médan.

When there's a marriage in high society, do they give a ball, and, if so, which evening [this to Mme Charpentier on 22 November]? The evening of the contract or the evening of the church ceremony? I should prefer the evening of the church ceremony . . .

I'm being so pushed that I no longer dare to risk a detail. I've just been arguing with my wife about all the questions I put to you, and I'm taking you as an arbiter. Give me as many details as you can, I shan't tell a soul that you have collaborated in *Nana*.[17]

On 14 December he announced to Flaubert: 'I'm finishing *Nana* . . . You can't imagine the trouble that my novel has given me – and is still giving me.'[18]

He was now preparing to describe the death of Nana. Céard, obliging as ever, had offered to get into the Grand Hôtel du Louvre, where she was to die. 'Here you forgotten what I suggested for the notes on the Grand Hotel [Céard enquired on 14 December]? First of all I shall go and see what a cursory inspection can reveal. If this examination doesn't seem enough, nothing is easier than to spend a night there.'[19] Among the notes for *Nana* is the plan of room 401, looking over the boulevard des Capucines, with the exact description of the furniture. Céard added the price of the room (12 francs a day), and the comment that from the room you could hear the sounds on the boulevard. The former medical student also had his professional advantages. On 16 December he told Zola: 'I still have a friend or two under the white aprons of the students at the Hôpital Lariboisière. I shall write to one of them. With any luck, there will be a corpse of a smallpox victim in the amphitheatre. The friend will let me know, and I'll go and take all the necessary notes *de visu*.'[20] On 18 December, Zola acknowledged the book on smallpox which Céard had sent him. 'That will obviously be enough. I shall *invent* a mask, which is more original in its horror. Only I must admit that, if you can see a corpse without too much trouble – a curious commission, isn't it? – I should be glad.'[21] On 7 January 1880 he told Céard not to trouble about the face of the corpse. He was so pleased with what he had written that he would not change it.[22]

That day he finished *Nana*. Exhaustion and hypochondria overcame him. They were prolonged. On the last day of the month, Turgenev gave a farewell dinner before his departure for Russia. Zola arrived leaning on a stick. 'He had a rheumatic pain in his thigh which seemed just like sciatica . . . Then [he] listed the morbid phenomena which made him afraid that he would never be able to finish the eleven volumes which he still had to do.'[23]

On 5 February the last instalment of *Nana* appeared in *Le Voltaire*. On 15 February the book was published. Charpentier had printed 55,000 copies – an enormous printing for the period. He saw that day that he should have printed more.

Nana seems like a novel written with consummate ease, it has such life and spirit. Some critics have wanted to see it as pornography, but it is in fact a savage condemnation of the Second Empire courtesan. Nana was – in Zola's eyes – the golden fly on the dungheap; she signified a nation methodically corrupted. *Au Bonheur des Dames* was to be the poem of modern activity; *La Terre* was to be the poem of the earth. Zola intended *Nana* to be the poem of male desires.

Nana, the courtesan, launched at the Théâtre des Variétés, is the incarnation of sexuality. Nana is Woman, she is the Whore, and all the world is instantly enthralled. Nana pursues her career, off stage, with warmth and calculation. She destroys the honest and the virtuous, and she exploits the wealthy. She falls from success to poverty, walks the streets, goes back to the theatre, and finally returns to an old lover: Comte Muffat, a member of the Imperial Household. She ruins him financially, wrecks his marriage and career, and irremediably corrupts his nature. She is unable to be faithful, either for love or wealth. Perhaps, in her contempt for men, she finds more pleasure with her own sex. Zola gives her Lesbian tendencies.

Nana is corrupt and corrupting. She dies of smallpox, but one suspects that this was a euphemism for venereal disease. It is strange that Zola was not more outspoken. Nana dies, symbolically, on the eve of the Franco-Prussian War, with the crowds outside her window chanting: 'À Berlin! À Berlin!' She is identified with the vices of the Second Empire, and, as it ends, she ends. The obscene decomposition of her corpse is Zola's comment on her career.

It is a measure of his power that he conveys both Nana's viciousness and her attraction. Nana lacks the virtues of women: even maternal instinct is denied her. In her affection for the youthful Georges, her devotion to the brutal Fontan, she allows herself, briefly, to be guided by her heart. Otherwise she is driven only by her sexual needs, by her desire for wealth and status, and by her contempt for society. Into her profession she puts the amorality which she has inherited. Yet her Macquart ancestry, which Zola is at pains to emphasise, becomes almost irrelevant. What Zola paints, with all the power of repressed sexuality, with all the guilt and fascination which the theme arouses in him, is the all-pervading, overwhelming power of sexual attraction.

Nana is a force of nature, a ferment of destruction, but she hardly understands her powers. She keeps a certain curious innocence. When a malevolent journalist describes her as the corrupter of society, she hesitates to recognise herself. Yet she becomes increasingly concerned with material rewards, largely as a compensation for her wretched youth, as a sign that she is equal to the society she scorns, the society which uses but condemns her. When she smashes all the presents sent by her admirers, when she tramples on Comte Muffat's uniform, she is showing her contempt for men and for the social order. She is not hateful, but she becomes unbalanced with power. Like her mother, Gervaise, she is drawn in the round. She is one of Zola's most convincing creations. She also remains a symbol. As Flaubert wrote, admiringly: 'Nana veers towards the myth, without ceasing to be real. This creation is Babylonian.'[24]

Nana gives a rich impression of a world and a way of life. It is brilliant with colour, and it is remarkably organised. Aurélien Scholl maintained that it was a Parisian novel to provincials, and a provincial novel to Parisians. The witticism was wide of the mark. *Nana* remains among Zola's most spectacular achievements.

It created consternation. In Copenhagen it was banned as an outrage to public morals, and the translator was prosecuted. In Dresden, the proprietors of reading-rooms were fined for lending the volume to subscribers. In France itself, Zola was castigated by literary critics. But, as he observed: 'The whole thing is to move the masses. Only indifference kills.'[25]

There was no indifference. On the day of publication, Huysmans wrote to him: 'I have emerged from *Nana*, amazed ... Glory be, it's all superb!'[26] 'A gigantic book, *mon ami*,' wrote the author of *Madame Bovary*.[27]

17

Soon after the appearance of *Nana*, the public was presented with *Les Soirées de Médan*. Maupassant and Hennique, Céard, Alexis and Huysmans had found themselves dining with Zola, and recalling the war of 1870. Some of them had been volunteers or conscripts; Zola doubtless made his comments as a political journalist, an aspirant in the corridors of power. The conversation had become increasingly animated, and Zola had thought of turning it to account. He had suggested that they produced a book of short stories in which the events of *l'année terrible* would be studied and narrated in the Naturalist style. Twenty-one years later, he talked to André Antoine about the day when everyone had brought his piece for *Les Soirées de Médan*. After Maupassant had read his 'Boule-de-Suif', they had all had the feeling of a masterpiece.[1]

'Boule-de-Suif' revealed Zola's contribution, 'L'Attaque du Moulin', as a superficial melodrama. The short story was not a genre suited to his style. Zola needed the scope of a novel. Strangely enough, the most effective of his short stories are those which he wrote without reference to Naturalism. Among them is 'La Légende du petit manteau-bleu de l'amour': a lyrical tale rather in the style of his *Contes à Ninon*. In his *Nouveaux Contes à Ninon*, in 1874, he had also published his memories of his Provençal youth. In his introduction he had addressed himself, once more, to his ideal love. 'I need all my vigour. Later, oh later! I shall come and find you again.' Zola thirsted for the truth, but even now he could not suppress his dreams.

The year 1880, which saw the appearance of *Nana* and *Les Soirées de Médan*, also saw the publication of *Le Roman expérimental*: a collection of critical articles, most of which had appeared in *Le Messager de l'Europe*. Brunetière dismissed the collection as a mixture of paradoxes and banalities. The judgment was harsh, but the articles add little to our knowledge of Zola's creed: his resolute belief in work, his insistence that the novelist must be impersonal. The Naturalist writer, Zola repeats, is a scholar, an analyst and an anatomist. He is moral and austere. He teaches the bitter knowledge of life.

In 1881, in *Les Romanciers naturalistes*, Zola returned to the theme. Balzac, he explained, 'had created the naturalist novel, the exact study of society . . . It was the most striking affirmation of modern evolution.'[2] In *Documents littéraires*, that year, Zola insisted, once again, on the paramount need to be modern.[3] He also took the occasion to make another apology for Naturalism. 'It rests on the intellectual and social movement. And, as it has progressed parallel to the sciences, as it has gradually gained all the forms of the written word, . . . I foresee that it is the beginning of an immense evolution which will continue for centuries.'[4]

Some already doubted this. Flaubert, writing to Turgenev in 1876, deplored the effect of Naturalism on Zola. 'The *System* is leading him astray. He has Principles which shrink his mind . . . He thinks he has discovered "Naturalism"! As for poetry and style, which are the two eternal elements, he never mentions them!'[5] And again: 'After the Realists, we have the Naturalists and the Impressionists. What progress! A bunch of jokers, who want . . . to convince us that they have discovered the Mediterranean!'[6] Maupassant also asserted his incredulity and his independence. Whatever his respect for Zola and for the École de Médan, he had confessed as early as 1877: 'I don't believe in Naturalism and Realism any more than I do in

Romanticism. To my mind, these words mean absolutely nothing . . . Zola is now a magnificent, brilliant and necessary personality. But his manner is one of the manifestations of art, and not a *summary*.'[7]

Maupassant had touched the truth. Zola might have christened his school the 'zolistes'; the term was to be used by one of those whom Jules Huret interviewed for his *Enquête sur l'évolution littéraire*. Many of those whom he questioned in 1891 were to limit Naturalism to Zola. Lemaître said categorically: 'Naturalism is Zola, and Zola alone.' Gabriel Vicaire had suspected this in about 1880: 'Could it be that Naturalism is simply the glorification of M. Zola?'[8] Naturalism was a European movement, originating in France but spreading over the Continent and to America; yet everywhere it was Zola's name and Zola's theories that counted.[9]

The literary society in which Zola moved was chronicled by some lively observers. In 1880, in the *Century Magazine* of New York, Daudet had described the Sunday meetings at Flaubert's. Mme Daudet, in her turn, recalled the Charpentiers' Friday evenings. 'In their salon, for a decade, there assembled all the famous names in politics, literature and the arts . . . It was at our friends the Charpentiers', . . . in their small salons on the quai du Louvre, that my husband introduced Edmond de Goncourt to me.'[10] Goncourt remained the most sensitive and difficult of men. Michel Robida, great-nephew of Mme Charpentier, recorded how, when Goncourt came, the publisher used to hide Zola's books so as not to offend him. He added that, when Goncourt had refused to speak to Zola, the Charpentiers had organised a dinner of reconciliation.[11] Goncourt and Zola were not born to be in sympathy. Goncourt the aristocrat despised Zola the parvenu; Goncourt the unpopular resented Zola the best-selling author. J.-H. Rosny, describing Goncourt's Grenier, wondered 'if Zola was aware of the sullen face of the host at his approach, and the tension of the forearm which accompanied the extra-limp handshake. The master of the Grenier detested Zola. Apart from a few obligatory words of praise, he never failed to be malicious about him. It was a subject on which he became almost eloquent.'[12]

Only close and proven friends were admitted to Zola's

Thursday evenings.[13] In March 1884, however, Mme Daudet recorded her impressions of the rue de Boulogne. Much might be read between the lines.

The Zolas' apartment pleases me [explained Julie Daudet] because of the kindness and eagerness of the hosts, and because one can guess something of the difficult beginnings, of the pleasures tasted, little by little, in buying works of art and decorating the home.

The man . . . is affectionate, good, discreet . . . He seems to have a tender love for his wife – and she deserves it. I remember her in former days, in the little lodgings in Les Batignolles, knowing the many burdens and fatigues of housekeeping. She keeps house wonderfully, . . . and she makes her own dresses. She shows all the signs of a woman who has long been used to doing things for herself.

At Médan, as in Paris, these people are – quite obviously – happy in each other.[14]

The comments were condescending, and they were not wholly true. It was clear to the most casual observer that the Daudets were absorbed in one another. Early in their married life, Alphonse had been struck by a crippling form of rheumatism. Julie cared for him devotedly, and helped to make him the writer he became. Her reserve and charm concealed much intelligence and determination. Zola considered Daudet's marriage 'a final and supreme piece of good fortune'. He himself was fond of Alexandrine, and to the world at large he might seem to be a loving husband. Yet for some time the relationship appears to have been under strain. On 14 February 1881, he had published 'Le Divorce et la Littérature'. The article in Le Figaro sounds like a comment on his own unhappy alliance, which had then lasted nearly eleven years.

When one is married, I think the best thing is to put up with one's lot, and to be married as well as possible. That depends absolutely on the man and woman. They must learn to tolerate each other, since the continual cohabitation of two people is most often disagreeable . . .

There is no conjugal hell which one cannot bear when on both sides there is a little good sense and a great deal of pity.

18

On Easter Sunday, 28 March 1880, Zola and Goncourt, Daudet and Charpentier went to spend twenty-four hours with Flaubert at Croisset.

Zola [recorded the diarist] is as happy as an auctioneer's clerk who is going to make an inventory . . .

'Here we are! Look, after the bridge!' It is Zola announcing his property at Médan. I catch a fleeting glimpse of a building in a feudal style. It seems to be planted in a field of cabbages.

Maupassant comes to meet us in a carriage at Rouen station . . .

The dinner is very good; one particular cream sauce on a turbot is a marvel. We drink many wines of all sorts, and spend the whole evening telling broad stories.[1]

The visitors left Croisset delighted with their escapade, and touched by Flaubert's hospitality. They agreed to meet in Paris early in May. On Saturday, 8 May, a telegram arrived at Médan. It said simply: 'Flaubert dead.'

It was Maupassant, remembered Zola, 'who sent me those two words by telegraph, without explanation. It was a knock-out blow, straight to the head.'[2] The explanation came from Heredia.

My dear Zola [he wrote that evening],

Flaubert, our great Flaubert, died of a stroke this morning at Croisset. As she was leaving for Rouen, his niece asked me to tell you this fearful news. She promised to let me know the day and time of the funeral. I'll send you a telegram immediately . . .[3]

'I am crazy with grief,' Zola wrote to Céard. '. . . Nothing is worth the trouble of living.'[4]

Until Tuesday, 11 May, the day of the funeral, the presence of Flaubert remained with him.

He haunted me, especially at night; suddenly he arrived at the end of all my thoughts, with the cold horror of never again . . . On the Tuesday morning I left for Rouen, I had to go and catch a train at the nearby station, and cross the countryside in the early sunlight . . . I felt tears rising to my eyes . . . He would never see the sun again.

At Mantes, I caught the express. Daudet was on the train . . . There were carriages waiting at the station, and we set out once more on the journey which, six weeks earlier, we had made so happily. But we were not to go as far as Croisset. We had hardly left the Canteleu road when our driver stopped and drew up against a hedge; it was the funeral coming to meet us, still masked by a clump of trees, at the turn of the road. We got out of the carriage, and bared our heads. In my grief, the terrible blow was inflicted on me there. Our good and great Flaubert seemed to come to us, lying in his coffin. I still saw him, at Croisset, coming out of his house, and kissing us on both cheeks, with big resounding kisses. And now it was another meeting, the last. He came forward, again, as if to welcome us. When I saw the hearse with its hangings, its horses moving slowly, its gentle and funereal swaying, emerge from behind the trees on the empty road and come straight towards us, I felt a great coldness and I began to tremble . . .

Daudet and I were standing at the side of the road, speechless and very pale. We had no need to speak, our thought was the same, when the wheels of the hearse brushed against us: it was *le vieux* who was passing.[5]

The service was held at Canteleu, in an old church on the hilltop, among the trees. Flaubert was buried at the Cimetière Monumental, on the far side of Rouen. His coffin was too big for the grave. The undertakers struggled with it, forced it in head downwards, made desperate attempts to straighten it. The mourners begged them to wait until the funeral was over. The ceremony was overwhelming, and it was grotesque.

When Zola tried to read Céard his account of that day, he wept silently, and he wept beyond control.[6]

Flaubert's death was followed by another death which touched him profoundly. His mother was now sixty-one, and she suffered from a heart condition. She was staying with one of her brothers in Verdun when she had a stroke. The local doctor assured her that she could travel to Médan. Alexandrine went to meet her in Paris, and she was shocked by the sight of her swollen legs.[7] The doctor in Paris tried to dissuade Mme Zola from going further, and warned her that the journey might be fatal. She insisted on going to Médan. As soon as she arrived, she retired to bed. She struggled against heart failure and dropsy, became delirious, and recalled the past. Zola wandered in the fields, or shut himself in his study. He was anxious only to escape her. Alexandrine cared for her devotedly; and her care was all the more remarkable since Mme Zola conceived a horror of her, and accused her of wanting to poison her.

She died on 17 October. The staircase was so narrow that her coffin had to be lowered from her bedroom window. Zola was rarely to set eyes on the window again without wondering who would be the next to die.

He and Alexandrine escorted her coffin to Aix, so that she could be buried beside her husband. The funeral took place on 20 October. The death of his mother was an event which Zola recalled with horror, long years afterwards.[8] His grief was genuine, it was profound, and it was permanent. It was tinged with his native superstition. Henceforward he would not embark on any enterprise on a 17th, the anniversary of his mother's death. He also had the double nature of the creative artist. He saw the event as material for his work. He was later to describe it with precision.

19

After *Nana*, Zola had meant to write a novel on a different note, the one he was in time to publish as *La Joie de Vivre*. He was to put some personal reminiscences into it, including an account of his mother's death. But his grief was still too acute, and he decided instead to embark on *Pot-Bouille*. The original idea for the novel had occurred in an article in *Le Figaro*, published in March 1881: 'L'Adultère dans la Bourgeoisie'.

As usual he turned to his friends for help in his research. On 6 June 1881 he asked Huysmans for some notes on an architect's status.[1] Huysmans obligingly sent him details. On 20 June, still from Médan, Zola thanked him, and added: 'If I'm going to spend August and September by the sea, I shall try to get through a lot of work . . . I find the summer melancholy, this is the dark season for me.'[2]

It was indeed a dark season. George Moore, who called with Alexis one May morning, found Zola 'sorrowful in that dreadful room of his, fixed up with stained glass and morbid antiquities'.[3] Zola was not the only person to be melancholy at Médan. The Daudets, the Charpentiers and Goncourt came for the day in June, and 'as dusk falls,' reported the diarist, 'there rises from the treeless garden, from the childless house, a sadness which catches Daudet and me'.[4] Alexandrine, too, was sad. Zola described her condition as a nervous disorder; certainly it brought severe depression. At Médan, for all its comfort, she must have felt imprisoned: driven in, unbearably, on herself.

Late in July, she and Zola found themselves at Grand-Camp, near Saint-Vaast, in Calvados: an overwhelmingly dismal part of the coast. Zola escaped, as usual, into his work. 'We are very comfortable here,' he told Roux on 31 July, 'and my wife is better already. Our house is in the sea [*sic*], there are masses of fish. I have settled down to do two months' work in peace.'[5] Alexandrine's improvement was only temporary. On 7 August he reported to Céard: 'The nervous disorder ... has grown more acute in the last few days. It is a very unpleasant crisis. I've decided that, if her condition doesn't improve, she must have a very strict treatment as soon as we return to Paris.'[6] Her condition did not improve; on 21 August he recorded that she was 'middling, better one day, worse the next.'[7] They were due to leave Grand-Camp on 15 September. On 1 October, from Médan, Zola finally announced: 'My wife is somewhat better, and we are preparing to spend a winter of peace and work.'[8]

He constructed his novel as a clockmaker assembled the movement of a clock. It was a question of many wheels, which must be made to work with meticulous care. He wrote on, mechanically. In mid-December he told Roux that he was 'up to the neck' in his book, and that he did not expect to finish it before 15 February. 'And then we shall go and spend six weeks in Paris. If you don't see me, it's because I only make flying visits to Paris. Besides, I have a flock of masons and navvies here, because I've bought the neighbouring field and I'm getting organised.'[9]

In *Pot-Bouille* (published on 12 April 1882), Octave Mouret arrives in Paris from Plassans. He takes a room in an imposing *hôtel* in the rue de Choiseul. The proprietor, M. Vabre, is a retired notary; he lives on the premises with his son-in-law, a counsellor at the Court of Appeal. His two sons have their separate apartments, and one of them has recently taken over the silk mercer's shop on the ground floor. Among the other tenants are a diocesan architect, Campardon, with his wife and daughter; and the Josserands, with a simple-minded son and two daughters of marriageable age. There are also an author (Zola himself), a clerk and his wife, and a number of servants. Despite its outward respectability, the *hôtel* is buzzing with unorthodox activities. Campardon's wife is ailing from some unspecified illness, and he instals his mistress in their apartment. The clerk's wife, Marie, is an easy conquest for Octave Mouret; and the Josserand household is constantly resounding with Mme Josserand's matrimonial plans. She finally marries her daughter, Berthe, to Auguste, the landlord's son. The marriage is unhappy, and Berthe in turn becomes Octave's mistress. The *hôtel* echoes with cries of surprise, desire and despair, with the opening and closing of doors, with footsteps approaching and retreating. Behind their social pretensions and their claims to virtue, the characters are almost all deplorable. The bourgeois are intent on their love-affairs and their financial interests. Their wives console themselves for their husbands' adultery and seek nothing but their social advancement. The servants corrupt the children, sleep with any willing man, and keep silent, when expedient, for money. Masters and servants, husbands and wives have little but contempt for one another; they are guided by self-interest. Octave Mouret is perhaps the most despicable character of all.

When, in time, he becomes the hero of *Au Bonheur des Dames*, Zola will emphasise Octave's virtues; in *Pot-Bouille* it is hard to discern them. Octave is a Second Empire Julien Sorel. He exploits all women and despises them. He is self-seeking. He behaves according to a plan. Like Zola himself – though he shows a brutality foreign to his creator – Octave means to dominate, to compensate himself for his past. Like Eugène Rougon, he is an outsider who intends to arrive. The aggressive parvenu is a type which recurs so often in the novels that it must surely represent their author.

Pot-Bouille is an indignant picture of middle-class corruption and cant. It is written with unceasing verve. Mme Josserand, dominant and vulgar, fills the book with her machinations and her outrageous conversation. Vital, appalling and outsize, she is one of Zola's most memorable creations. Octave Mouret, the scion of the Rougon-Macquarts, is dwarfed by such a figure. But, when the book ends, the young man from Plassans has learned the usefulness of sexual relations, the need for hypocrisy and ruthlessness. His future is assured.

The bourgeoisie had applauded *L'Assommoir*. They refused to tolerate *Pot-Bouille*. It was permissible to describe the plebeian world; but Zola had dared to reveal defects on which it was essential to be silent. 'Zola only really knows the working-class woman,' Mme Daudet was to decide. 'His Renée of the Empire, Nana, his perverted middle-class women in *Pot-Bouille*, are apocryphal figures, put together from information and documents.'[10] Juliette Adam was perhaps thinking of *Pot-Bouille* when she wrote of Zola: 'This man, with his talent, is a danger to the morals of France.'[11]

Zola found an unexpected ally. Writing in *La Revue des Deux Mondes*, Ferdinand Brunetière suggested that, if Zola had not committed the crime of *lèse-bourgeoisie*, the public would have recognised a masterpiece.[12]

20

The idea of the sequel had long existed in Zola's mind. Years earlier, when he listed the Rougon-Macquart novels, he had noted: '*The novel about merchants*, linendrapers. Octave Mouret'. 'In *Au Bonheur des Dames*,' he explained, now, in his *ébauche*, 'I want to write the poem of modern activity.'[1]

Zola was the first to divine the poetic interest of the modern stores. Among those who helped him in his research was Frantz Jourdain, who was later to earn fame as the architect of La Samaritaine. Jourdain recalled how Zola had summoned him to Médan, and asked him for a plan, 'just as if the store were to be erected. He was informed about the choice of materials, the fitting-up of the interior, the decorations, the technical terms and total estimate . . . He criticised some of the arrangements, made objections, and discussed particular proportions; . . . in short, he examined the project like the proprietor and builder.'[2]

Jourdain was not the only source of information. M. Beauchamp, of the Magasins du Louvre, and M. Carbonnaux, of the Bon Marché, told Zola about the habits of the staff and the amorous adventures of the directors. Alexandrine introduced her husband to a saleswoman, Mlle Dulit, who gave him the physical likeness of his heroine, Denise.[3]

On 29 April 1882, Zola wrote to Céard from Médan: 'We are installed here, once again. On Wednesday I settled down to write my novel.'[4]

He wrote it apprehensively. He felt that he would never write another novel as moving as *L'Assommoir*, as commercially successful as *Nana*. He was restless and dissatisfied. In April he had longed to leave Paris. Now, in July, Goncourt found him frustrated at Médan. Goncourt touched the truth again. 'A couple can do without children in an apartment in Paris, but not in a country house. Nature calls for children.'[5]

That no doubt remained the unacknowledged reason for Zola's unremitting regrets. It explained his perpetual need to escape; it explained, perhaps, why he found no satisfaction in success, why he was always lost in work, preoccupied by health, beset by his fear of death. He longed, with increasing desperation, to be assured of his posterity. Céard, who also went to see him, found him suffering, once again, from nervous exhaustion. 'I had to go to bed after you left,' Zola told him on 19 October, 'and since then I have gone from bad to worse. Yesterday I tried to work, which brought on another attack of nausea and shivering . . . But it's nothing dangerous, these are nervous troubles which come over me from time to time, and they take every form.'[6] On 22 December, writing to Théodore Duret, Zola added: 'I am here for another month, deep in the end of my novel. I haven't budged since June, and I must admit that I'm very weary.'[7]

He finished *Au Bonheur des Dames* on 25 January 1883. It was published on 17 March.

Octave Mouret had eventually made sure of his fortune by his marriage to Mme Hédouin, part owner of Au Bonheur des

Dames. The death of an uncle had left her sole proprietor of the growing enterprise. Even while the store was being extended, she had died, through an accident on the site, and Octave had become the unchallenged ruler of his empire.

He shows no sorrow at her death, and he finds it easy to console himself. In his pursuit of power he is indifferent to real relationships, indifferent to the suffering he causes. The small shopkeepers in the district find their premises threatened, their livelihood destroyed, by his progress. The store becomes an inescapable part of their lives, a reminder of their inevitable ruin. Baudu, who sells cloth across the road, is hurt when his niece arrives from Valognes and goes to work at Au Bonheur des Dames.

However, from the moment she sets eyes on this commercial palace, Denise is hypnotised. She bears with the malice of the staff, the pitiful pay, the rudeness of the customers; she is wrongfully dismissed, but she returns to the vast emporium. She, alone, refuses the advances of Mouret; and her repeated refusals count, ultimately, more than his commercial triumph. On the day he first makes a million francs, he is finally convinced of the futility of wealth and power. He offers her marriage; and she accepts him, not because he is rich, but because she loves him.

Au Bonheur des Dames reveals Zola's understanding of a whole commercial enterprise, its effect on society, its everyday routine. He presents the hierarchy in the store itself, their rivalries, ambitions and private lives; he presents the compulsive buyer, even the shoplifter. He is in the accounts department, in the director's office, devising new publicity, arranging sales and window displays. The documentation is exhaustive but rarely obtrusive; we see the institution from within. The characters themselves are drawn in remarkable relief, and even the minor figures have vitality.

Few characters in the Rougon-Macquart cycle are entirely good human beings, but Denise is one – and she alone is properly rewarded. No doubt this is because she is Zola's own ideal of womanhood. Denise is the woman of the Greuze engraving: a country girl who is untouched by money, revolted by the thought of promiscuity, and moved to action only by her heart. While Denise seems to represent Zola's perfect woman, Octave Mouret reflects his creator. In Mouret's recognition of the uselessness of wealth, in his fundamental loneliness, we see the problems Zola encountered. Mouret's despair at what he feels to be rejection echoes Zola's own despair at his failure to find love. Mouret was an unreal figure when he first appeared in *Pot-Bouille*; he becomes authentic in *Au Bonheur des Dames* because he is approaching a self-portrait. In Mouret's final conquest of Denise, Zola allows himself to fulfil his dream.

Au Bonheur des Dames was greeted by a sympathetic Press. It seemed to conform to conventional morality. Five weeks after it was published, Zola set to work on its successor.

In April 1880 he had explained to Fernand Xau that he wanted to write an intimate novel, in a simple style, as a sort of reaction against his earlier work. At about the same time he had drafted an *ébauche* for a novel which would develop the idea of goodness and suffering. The heroine was to be Pauline Quenu, daughter of the *charcutier* in *Le Ventre de Paris*. She was to symbolise vitrue just as Nana had symbolised vice. The original plan for *La Joie de Vivre* had been replaced by a second, third and fourth; but the bereavements of 1880 had prevented Zola from writing the novel. Now, three years later, when he had recovered enough to embark on it, he had begun again at the beginning. He wrote another three *ébauches*. He passed from the worldly pessimism which had been in vogue in 1880 to the ardent belief in life which had been imposed on him by his own deep despair. His conviction fired the book. He wrote it with extraordinary speed, and he finished it in seven months. It was published on 8 March 1884.

After the death of her parents, Pauline Quenu comes to live with their cousins, the Chanteaus, in the coastal village of Bonneville, near Arromanches. The setting – based on Grand Camp, in Calvados, where the Zolas had stayed in 1881 – is dismal in its wildness and isolation; and the Chanteaus are likewise depressing. Chanteau himself is stricken with gout; his wife, who is socially his superior, has long ago abandoned her hopes for him, and she has transferred them to their son. Lazare is gifted but lacking in ambition and self-discipline, and he is already neurotic. The family, in financial straits, is looked after by Véronique, an embittered and outspoken maid.

Pauline, engaging and ten years old, brings gaiety and sanity to the household; but she is exploited from the first. She looks after the irascible Chanteau so devotedly that Mme Chanteau postpones her plans for sending the child away to school. In time, Mme Chanteau sees her as the obvious wife for her son. However, while Pauline becomes enamoured of Lazare, he is attracted by a young girl who comes to stay with the family. Pauline is brokenhearted; but not only is her peace of mind disturbed, her financial security is destroyed. Mme Chanteau persuades herself that Pauline's inheritance is her own, and the family live on the girl's future. Mme Chanteau's guilt turns to hatred and mistrust. She dies of heart disease, accusing Pauline of dosing her with poison. Pauline sacrifices herself, and urges Lazare to marry Louise; but the marriage proves to be unhappy, and she and Lazare recognise that they should have married one another. Pauline helps to deliver Louise's baby. Véronique, the maid, hangs herself. Pauline's destiny is clear: henceforward she will live on with old Chanteau, and with the married couple and their child. She will be the perpetual sacrifice.

Pauline Quenu is a Macquart who is wholly good; she also expresses one of Zola's most profound emotions. In her, with irony and anger, he presents the unfulfilled woman, the maternal woman cheated of a child. Zola's accounts of menstruation and childbirth go beyond the demands of Naturalism; they reflect his own obsessive longing for posterity. *La Joie de Vivre* is in other ways an extremely personal book. The death of Mme Chanteau reflects the death of Mme François Zola, and Mme Chanteau's demented accusations of Pauline are those which Mme Zola had made of Alexandrine. Lazare's obsessive fear of death, his neurotic habits, were those of the novelist himself. Lazare is one of the half-dozen characters scattered through Zola's novels who reflect a facet of the author; he is the incarnation of the weaknesses Zola himself had needed to conquer. In *La Joie de Vivre* Zola attempts to discard a burden by projecting it into fiction.

La Joie de Vivre is a bitter title; but it underlines the truth that despite the pain, monotony and injustice of life, most

people cleave to it. When Véronique commits suicide, Chanteau cries indignantly: 'Must be a fool to kill yourself!' This
cry of Chanteau's is the key to the work. 'I have loved life,'
Zola was to say, 'however black I have painted it.'[8] *La Joie de
Vivre* is Zola's most profoundly depressing work. It is also a
condemnation of pessimism.

21

In his study of *Germinal*, Richard Zakarian suggests that 'the
date of the formal genesis may be approximately set at January
16, 1884'.[1] The statement is pompous. It is, however, certain
that for some time Zola had thought of writing a socialist novel.
'This plan became more definite,' he explained to Van Santen
Kolff, 'when I understood the vast socialist movement which
is working through old Europe in such formidable fashion.
The setting of a strike imposed itself on me quite naturally as
the only dramatic one, the only one which would give the facts
the necessary emphasis. *Germinal* is, then, the complement to
L'Assommoir, the two faces of the working man.'[2]

Zola used the *Gazette des Tribunaux* for the details of the
strikes at La Ricamarie, Rive-de-Gier and Aubin in the
Aveyron in 1869. He was also to make an occasional reference
to the strike at Fourchambault in 1870. The strike at Montsou,
in *Germinal*, was to be a sort of synthesis of industrial conflicts in
France.

Zola had hesitated over the setting for his book. The coalfields of the Loire and the North had both attracted him.
However, during a stay in Brittany, he had met Alfred Giard,
the radical Deputy for Valenciennes. It was Giard who decided
for him.

Events played into Zola's hands. On 21 February 1884 a
strike broke out in the northern coalfields of Anzin; it was to
last until 17 April. Giard had to visit his constituents, and he
took Zola with him, ostensibly as his secretary. Through this
subterfuge Zola attended several miners' meetings. Giard
returned to Paris; but, accompanied by Alexandrine, Zola
stayed in Valenciennes, and from there he travelled through

the country, talking to miners and mining officials. M. de Forcade, the manager of the Anzin mine, had given him permission to visit the company's establishments 'below ground and on the surface'. Guided by an engineer, he went down more than two thousand feet into the Fosse Renard. Overweight though he was, he crawled along the narrow galleries, and he made notes on the experience.

By 8 March he was back in Paris. On 16 March he announced to Édouard Rod: 'I have all my documents for my socialist novel, and I am going to shut myself up in the fields from the end of the week.'[3]

'There are two things in a work such as I understand it, there are the documents and the creation.'[4] So Zola was to say. He invented more than he observed. Truth, for Zola, was amassed in his documentation; and the documents enabled his imagination to take flight. 'I have the hypertrophy of the actual fact,' he explained to Céard, 'the leap into the stars from the trampoline of exact observation. Truth rises with its wingbeats to the symbol.'[5] Zola anticipated the cinematic use of the symbol; like the film director, he used the technique of directed vision. He prolonged reality into symbolism. He chose to set *Germinal* in a mine because his characters had to suffer in the dim labyrinth of the unconscious. Zola's fear of tunnels had haunted him when he had typhoid, it had haunted the Abbé Mouret in his delirium. Tunnels were to have a sinister significance in *La Bête Humaine*. The tunnel deprives man of light and air and of hope itself; it is full of mystery, and it is hostile. The mine brings disease, explosion, flooding, suffocation; ever deeper and more dark, it is the modern version of Dante's Hell.

Zola remained superstitious. He began to write the novel on his forty-fourth birthday: 2 April 1884. It was, he explained, to be about the struggle between capital and labour. 'I want it to predict the future, and to ask the question which will be the most important question of the twentieth century.'[6] In *Germinal* the hero, Étienne Lantier, was to be given his socialist education.

'It is one of those books that you do for yourself, out of conscience,' Zola wrote to Céard. 'We shan't go to Mont-Dore until the end of July; which reminds me, write and tell me which of the three first-class hotels we should choose . . . Which is the one which is nearest the thermal establishment?'[7] It was, in fact, on 5 August that he and Alexandrine left Paris. He invited Céard to dine with them at the Gare de Lyon.[8]

He was always made uneasy by a change in his routine, and he was soon disorientated in the Puy de Dôme. He was also bored. 'Don't you see curious things in the hotel where you're staying?' Céard asked him, hopefully. '. . . I still think one can get something simple and new out of Mont-Dore.'[9] But if the Hôtel Chabaury *aîné* gave the Zolas comfort, it seems to have had no literary use.

They returned to Médan, and once again Zola settled down to *Germinal*. On 1 December he confessed that he had doubts about the book, and that he still had six weeks' work ahead.[10] On 18 January he told Céard:

No, *Germinal* is not finished . . . This devil of a novel has given me a great deal of trouble. But I am very satisfied, especially with the second half, and that is the essential . . .

We shall hardly come back to Paris except from the 12th to the 14th. I want to get rid of my last proofs here . . . Besides, Paris tempts me very little, and I really think I should not set foot there but for the few friends whom I may still have there. My only thirst is for work.[11]

On 23 January he finished his novel. Two days later he confessed to his publisher: 'Oh, how I need a little idleness!'[12]

Germinal was published in March. It appeared, symbolically, with the spring.

Étienne Lantier is the son of Gervaise Macquart by her first lover. He has inherited his parents' alcoholism, and the Macquart tendency to violence. Like his mother, however, he is hardworking; he also wants to establish social justice. He is already driven by revolutionary zeal when he arrives at a mine near Montsou in search of work. He is hired, and so horrified by conditions at the pit face that almost at once he is tempted to leave; but, perhaps for love of Catherine, a young ore-carter, perhaps because he senses revolt, he decides to stay.

He is soon given his chance to lead rebellion. The company who own the mine contrive a new financial arrangement which is grossly unjust to the miners. Étienne urges the miners to strike. The strike drags on, the miners are driven to despair and violence by their hunger, but they refuse to return to the pit. Finally they are starved into capitulation. Souvarine, a Russian revolutionary, goes to the pit-head at night and saws a panel out of the wooden shaft. Those who choose to return to work, to abandon the cause, are going, all unknowing, to their deaths. The pit is flooded; there is a series of explosions. The ground subsides, the workings of the mine are engulfed, and a canal bursts its banks and submerges them. Trapped in an underground gallery, Étienne murders Catherine's lover. Then, as they wait for the waters to cover them, he makes love to her for the first time. Just as the spectre of Camille had haunted Thérèse Raquin and her husband, so the floating body of Catherine's former lover returns, repeatedly, on the rising waters, to come between Catherine and Étienne. Catherine dies just before Étienne is rescued – prematurely white – from this subterranean hell.

When he is strong enough, he sets off for Paris. As he strides away from the coalfields, he hears the miners shifting the coal, with blows from their picks, deep in the ground below him. But the black and red inferno is now in the past. The sun is rising, the trees are turning green, the fields are shimmering with the growing crops. It is Germinal, the springtime of the Revolutionary calendar; and the avenging army, underground, are sowing seeds which will burst the earth asunder.

Henriette Psichari was later to note a few of Zola's factual errors and improbabilities. He had disregarded the law which decreed that no working man could be hired without presenting his 'book'. Étienne had been hired without credentials. Zola had been impressed by the current wave of anarchy and terrorism when he was writing in 1884; but in 1865 – when the action of the novel occurred – there had been no trace of anarchy in France, or even in Russia. Then, again, Zola was carried away by his medical research. Bonnemort had had the incurable illnesses of miners: black bronchitis, hydropsy, paralysis. Zola had not paused to ask if one person could have them all.[13] Such errors are blatant; but *Germinal* presents a different order of truth. At times it is what Victor Hugo called *la réalité historique devinée*; at others it is truth raised to the power of symbolism. *Germinal* records violence and poverty, a whole primitive community, with a disturbing power and directness. It makes *Les Misérables* seem like seminary reading.

In *Germinal*, Zola proclaims his concern for the working man; but the collectivism of Lantier – like that of the novelist – springs from poetry and not from science. His aspirations are not those of a Marxist, they are those of a mystic humanitarian. Yet if Lantier is the prophet of the socialist future, he is also – like many heroes in the Rougon-Macquart novels – the outsider who imposes his will. He is, yet again, the Zola who is seeking compensation for his past; he is the youthful Zola of Aix-en-Provence and the early years in Paris. He is also the embryo of the Zola who, in later years, will preach the doctrines of Fourier and write Les Quatre Évangiles.

Étienne Lantier is a new pilgrim making his progress. *Germinal* is among the finest Naturalist novels, but one may also see it as an allegory of man on the road to tolerance, enlightenment and justice. This sense of allegory is heightened by the poetry of the work: the sense of an invisible, implacable authority for whom the miners daily risk their lives; an awareness of the mine itself, a giant maw devouring humankind. There is an ominous vastness about the mine which recalls the Romantic engravings of John Martin, and Doré's illustrations for the *Inferno*.

The symbolism of *Germinal* is intensified by Zola's use of colour. Black and red have a complex significance; by their continual repetition they accumulate associations. There is the black of night as Étienne arrives at the mine, there is the blackness of the mine itself, the blackness of the bodies of the miners. Old Bonnemort, who has spent most of his life at the pit face, spits black, for his lungs are full of dust. Black is punctuated by red: the recurrent red of fire and blood. Black and red represent the curse that lies upon the mine. Weight is another malediction; in *Germinal* we are constantly told of the heaviness of things. We are made aware, too, of imprisonment, of the suffocation and crushing of men, and of the temptation of oblivion. Sleeping, dreaming, madness, drunkenness are escapes from reality. The sexual act is itself, in Zola, a passionate escape out of oneself and out of the world.

Zola aimed to create a sense of life. 'Have I given breath to my characters, have I engendered a world? . . . If so, my task is

done, and it matters little where I found the clay.'[14] He created
a world in *Germinal*. It was, in general, a sombre world. Yet
green is the colour of hope, and there was also a world of green
which Étienne finally attained.

Germinal made a profound impression on Zola's contemporaries.
Jules Lemaître defined it as 'a pessimistic epic of human
animality'.[15] 'I am quite prepared to accept your definition,'
wrote Zola, 'on condition, however, that I explain this word
animality . . . You put man in the head, I put him in all his
organs. You isolate man from nature, I do not see him without
the earth, from which he comes and to which he will return.'[16]
Monet read the serial version of *Germinal*, and found it
'admirable, . . . magnificent'.[17] Huysmans agreed that *Germinal*
was 'damned fine. If ever the theory of milieux has produced
magnificent results it is certainly in this book, where the mine
is gigantic and grips you like a nightmare.'[18] Maupassant was
in Sicily with his friend Amic. His health had not yet reached
the point of irremediable decline, but he now found it hard to
use his eyes; he had *Germinal* read to him by his companion.

Let me tell you at once [he wrote to Zola] that I find this book the
most powerful and the most astonishing of all your works . . .
In reading you one feels the soul, the breath of these people, and
all their tumultuous animality. You have obtained an effect as
astonishing as it is superb; and the setting of your novel remains
before one's eyes and in one's mind, as if one had seen these things
. . .
When I come back to Paris, in about a month, I shall come and
greet you at Médan. I am constantly thinking about you, and I very
much wish I could talk to you more often.[19]

22

'Oh, how I need a little idleness!' Zola had exclaimed. He
could not bear idleness for long. On 7 March 1885 *Le Matin*
had announced what he planned to do after *Germinal*. 'First of
all,' he said, 'I shall probably do a short work, with very few
characters, which is set in an artists' milieu . . . Then I shall

begin the novel which I am so anxious to write: the novel about peasants.'[1]

The short work which he had in mind was *L'Œuvre*. He had begun to write it on 12 May. It has a central place in the Rougon-Macquart cycle. It was not only a study of a Macquart as artist. Two of the characters were to represent Zola himself. 'Pierre Sandoz,' he wrote in his notes. 'My portrait modified.'[2] He put himself into *L'Œuvre* as Sandoz, but he did so only in order to give his ideas about art. Sandoz was Zola the author of the Rougon-Macquart novels: a man who was driven, unsatisfied, by his obsession for work. Sandoz was Zola the pessimist; he was also Zola the bourgeois, calculating the usefulness of marriage. Sandoz was a devoted son and a practical, selfish husband: intent on being loved and being comfortable, showing no deep love for his wife. Sandoz was kind to his friends but, like Zola, he lived in isolation; and his Thursday evenings, like those of Zola, reflected the breaking of old friendships, revealed the absence of familiar faces. When Zola came to write *L'Œuvre*, the friendships with Goncourt and Daudet were strained. Huysmans seemed to have broken with the writers of Médan on the publication of *À Rebours*, and Maupassant was clearly independent. The École de Médan was disintegrating.

The origins of Claude Lantier have often been discussed. More than one critic has compared Lantier and Cézanne. In his manuscript notes, Zola admits: 'Claude . . . is a Manet, a Cézanne, more of a Cézanne.' Claude Lantier was in fact to have the physical appearance of Cézanne. Robert Niess observes that, while Zola was working on *L'Œuvre*, Cézanne spent a few weeks near Médan, and during that time he visited Zola. Yet the paintings described in the novel, and the artistic themes advanced there, do not resemble his own. Lantier's artistic efforts may, at most, symbolise the struggles of the young Cézanne, and Niess maintains that Zola did not mean them as a prophecy of his failure. Zola's conception seems to him to owe much more to Balzac in *Le Chef-d'œuvre inconnu* than it does to his own memories. It is hard to determine the truth.

It is, however, clear that Lantier was a composite figure. Manet, like Lantier, had dreamed of decorating the new Hôtel de Ville. His *Déjeuner sur l'herbe* had created a scandal at the Salon des Refusés, just as Lantier's *Plein-air* was to do. Manet, Cézanne and Monet – like Claude Lantier – had each had a mistress and a son before they married. Monet had tried to kill himself in 1868; Claude Lantier committed suicide. André Gill, the cartoonist, was, like Lantier, overwhelmed by a sense of failure. He died in the asylum at Charenton, and his death was reported in *Le Figaro* on 2 May 1885, ten days before Zola began to write his novel.[3]

L'Œuvre contains some likenesses of Zola's contemporaries, and some ill-digested comments on art theory, but the importance of the novel seems to be autobiographical. At different levels, Sandoz and Lantier represent their creator. Much the most important element in Lantier is the element of Zola himself. 'With Claude Lantier,' he explained, in his notes, 'I want to paint the struggle of the artist against nature, the effort of creation in the work of art ... In short, I shall describe my own life of production, this constant and most painful engendering.'[4] Lantier is nearer to Zola than he was to Cézanne. In Lantier (as in Lazare in *La Joie de Vivre*) Zola laid a ghost: the ghost of what he himself might have been had he not remained in control of his career. Claude Lantier, like Zola, is torn by his desire to dominate, and by self-doubt. Lantier, like Zola, is neurotic, passionate, and – when art reclaims him – determined to sublimate human love. Perhaps for Zola, as for him, marriage had come too late; the wife had diminished the mistress.

L'Œuvre is almost certainly a record of Zola's own detachment from Alexandrine. For many months, Christine and Claude had lain in bed, side by side, like strangers, 'after a slow rupture of their physical relationship: a deliberate abstinence, a chastity of theory which he must attain to give all his virility to painting – [a chastity] which she had accepted, in proud and silent grief'. At the end of the novel, Christine reminds her husband: 'It's eight months and seven days, I've counted them! It's eight months and seven days since we had anything together.' Her lament has the ring of reality; and so has the explanation: 'Often, at first, when he had a good deal of work next day, and she held him tight when she went to bed, he would say no, it would tire him too much ... And, little by little, the break had come like that, a week to wait for a picture to be finished, then a month so as not to disturb the preliminary work for another, then dates put back again, occasions neglected, the slow breaking of a habit, the final forgetting.' Claude's detachment from Christine is mentioned three times in the dossier. They are married after some seven years together, and he agrees to the marriage only out of compassion. Quite early in Zola's marriage, if we are to trust Goncourt's comments, Zola was moving away from his wife.[5]

His marriage was made more melancholy by Alexandrine's continuing ill-health. Her nervous disorder was still not cured; and Goncourt referred, maliciously, to her 'fishwife's nerves'. She did not give her husband emotional stability. Their neuroses fed on one another. Goncourt, dining with Zola on 19 March 1885, had reported: 'His wife is suffering from an arthritic knee; she is going to bed for a month to-morrow.' On 8 May: 'Mme Zola did not dine at Charpentier's to-day. She had cried all night, she was so frightened by her affected knee, and the poor woman found her eyes too red to venture into society this evening.'[6] Alexandrine's nervous state was pitiful. Some might interpret it as an unconscious demand for attention, an unspoken need for Zola's love. But he could not give her what she needed.

In this summer of 1885, they found themselves again at Mont-Dore; and from here, on 23 August, Zola wrote to Céard, whose mother had just died: 'The only thing is work. Create some enormous task for yourself, give yourself an aim; that is the only possible way to forget life.'[7] He himself often needed to forget. Alexandrine had a weak chest, and she was always afraid of pneumonia or bronchitis. She was now suffering from bronchial trouble, and the raw climate did not improve it. She remained confined to a hotel bedroom, afraid she might get congestion of the lungs. When at last she took the waters, the treatment made her worse. For a moment, Zola thought of writing a novel about watering-places, and the exploitation of invalids. Only a few notes remain, but perhaps some of his ideas later found their way into *Lourdes*.[8]

On 2 September he told Céard, with evident relief: 'We are leaving Mont-Dore at eight to-morrow morning! And without regret, I assure you, for this year our season here has been

particularly oppressive. My wife is very tired, and she has been
stunned by the severity of the treatment.'[9] Her ill-health
continued for at least two months.[10]

The winter came and went and, as usual, he lost himself in
work. Methodically, every day, he approached the end of
L'Œuvre. On 23 February 1886 he wrote the last words of the
novel in which, as he told Céard, 'my memories and my heart
have overflowed'.[11]

Claude Lantier – son of Gervaise – is living and painting in an
attic on the quai de Bourbon. One night, he comes home in
heavy rain to find a young girl sheltering in the doorway. He
takes her in. Next morning he discovers her naked and asleep,
and recognises her as the perfect model for his picture. He
sketches her, but he sees her purely as an artist, and he makes
no physical advances. She leaves. He does not seek her out, but
from time to time she arrives to talk, to bring a bunch of roses,
to watch him working; when his picture is exhibited and
derided by the public, Claude returns to his attic to find her
waiting.

Their love-affair begins. They escape to the country. Their
son is born, and art is forgotten. Then Claude meets a Paris
friend, by chance; and, gradually, art reclaims him. The
family return to Paris. Once more he is lost in painting. His
son dies; Claude draws his dead child (as Monet had once
painted his dead wife), and he exhibits his picture. This
picture, again, is treated with derision. Claude's vision remains
beyond his reach. He is artistically impotent. His marriage –
for he has at last married his mistress – is a travesty of a relationship. Christine becomes embittered and jealous because
he thinks of nothing but his dream. Finally she persuades him
to make love to her; soon afterwards he hangs himself in front
of his unfinished painting. Woman, the idol on the canvas, has
destroyed them both. Art has defeated them. The instability
and the violence of the Macquarts have at last found their
expression.

L'Œuvre records the gulf between dream and achievement,
the transience and venality of love, the material advantages
of mediocrity and conformity. *L'Œuvre* describes the disappointment of artistic hopes, and disillusionment in love and

E

friendship. Claude Lantier dominates Paris at last, but he does so from his grave on the heights of Montmartre. That is the meaning of the book, and perhaps it is Zola's comment on himself.

L'Œuvre was published on 6 April 1886. Some time later, André Antoine attended the inauguration of a monument at Père-Lachaise. After the ceremony, he noticed, Zola 'stayed for a long while in contemplation before the immensity of Paris spread out at his feet.'[12]

Jules Lemaître was deeply impressed by *L'Œuvre*. 'You will find, on almost every page, a terrible sadness, a hyperbolic violence of vision which overwhelms and hurts. No-one has ever seen the whole outward aspect of the human drama more tragically. There is some Michaelangelo in M. Zola.'[13] Banville thanked Zola warmly for *L'Œuvre*. 'I am glad to possess and re-read this fine book in which, so eloquently, you describe the most touching and the most terrible of all martyrdoms.'[14] On 4 April, Cézanne in turn thanked Zola for 'this good token of remembrance'.[15] Then he read *L'Œuvre*, and saw in it Zola's condemnation of his painting. The friendship of some thirty years was broken.[16]

L'Œuvre was harshly judged by all the artists whom Zola knew. In March 1886, Pissarro noted: '[Huysmans] is completely of my opinion. It seems that he had a showdown with Zola . . . Since *L'Œuvre* was published, Guillemet's enthusiasm has melted like butter in the sun.'[17] On 5 April, with sadness rather than anger, Monet acknowledged his copy of the novel. 'It has always given me great pleasure to read your books,' he wrote to Zola, 'and this one particularly interests me because it [deals with] questions of art . . . I have just read it, and I must confess that I am still troubled and disturbed.'[18] Monet thought he saw Manet in Claude Lantier, and he was distressed by such disloyalty to a dead friend. Zola's long friendship with Manet, wrote George Moore, 'only enabled him to imagine that hollow abortion Claude Lantier; and we gather how much he understood of his friend's genius from the statement which I once heard him make: "Claude Lantier is infinitely greater than Manet." '[19]

Moore was malicious and unreliable; but Zola's appreciation

of Manet must still be questioned. In April 1900 Adolphe Retté, the Symbolist poet, told Zola how he admired the portrait which Manet had painted of him.

He answered: 'Yes, that portrait isn't bad, yet Manet wasn't a very great painter. He had an incomplete talent.'

That opinion, so expressed, rather surprised me [admitted Retté]. because I recalled many pages in which Zola had warmly praised the art of the promoter of Impressionism. I could not refrain from saying so.

'Ah!' he replied, 'I was young, I was looking everywhere for weapons to defend the doctrine on which I based my books. Manet took care to choose contemporary subjects, and his attempt at realism seemed to me worth supporting. But, to tell the truth, his painting has always rather disconcerted me.' . . .

Perhaps [continued Retté] these *actual* words of Zola's may displease some people. But what can I do? . . .

'Besides,' Zola went on, 'I cannot grow enthusiastic about painting . . . It's like music, when I listen to it I soon become distracted and think of something else . . . In fact I have never felt, I never feel, really passionate except about literature.'[20]

Zola had little understanding of painting, added Michel Robida, and he showed it by writing *L'Œuvre*.[21]

Zola's appreciation of art was discussed with more sympathy, and with more scholarship, by Jean and Hélène Adhémar. He had, they emphasised, an artist's vision. He had known and admired the Impressionists since the beginning of the movement. He had underestimated Cézanne, but his underestimation had been exaggerated by the malicious inventions of some of Cézanne's biographers. One must also repeat that Zola was frequently inspired by the work of the Impressionists, and that they in turn exhibited pictures which had been suggested by his novels. Distinguished artists – including Renoir – illustrated the popular edition of his works. Zola was not a professional critic of art, he offended the world of art in *L'Œuvre*, but he remains a figure in the history of Impressionism.[22]

On the day he finished *L'Œuvre*, he himself told Céard: 'I am already bitten by the novel on the peasants. It is working at me, I am going to settle down at once to the hunt for notes and the plan.'[23]

23

It was probably when Zola undertook *La Faute de l'Abbé Mouret* that he had first studied the peasants, and surmised their potential importance in his work. However, the most important factor in the genesis of *La Terre* was probably his purchase of Médan. He had bought the property in 1878, and early in 1880 there had come a public announcement that he intended to write a novel on the peasant world.

When Zola settled in the little commune, all the inhabitants earned their living by farming, or by rearing cattle. Apart from the owners of the château, he was almost the only bourgeois, the only Parisian in Médan. To the local peasants 'Zola was the "Monsieur", to whom everybody applied in moments of need or emergency. In earlier years,' recorded Vizetelly, 'they called on him with their many doleful tales of bad crops, accidents, illnesses, or wrongs incurred at the hands of malicious neighbours.'[1]

According to the census of 1881, Médan consisted of 62 houses and 65 households. There were 198 inhabitants, and many of them seem to have been related, to judge by the recurrence of certain names. Some of the names which Zola gave his characters in the notes for his novel were those of inhabitants of Médan. On 16 January 1881 he had become a member of the municipal council. The record of his attendances at meetings suggests that communal interests were not his main concern. He himself confessed as much. In 1887 he explained: 'I let myself be appointed a municipal councillor, which has allowed me to extend my investigations. Indeed, I have used every means available. I have made my servants talk – and the peasants proved more confiding with them than with a bourgeois.'[2] Henri Cavillier and his wife Zélie were the Zolas' valet and cook. They helped in the research for *La Terre*.

If the Rognes of Zola's novel owed something to Médan, it was, however, set elsewhere in France. His mother's family came from the Beauce, and he chose to go there for his documentation. Perhaps he was guided by filial piety, but he did not mean to write a subjective novel.

I have been here since yesterday [this to Céard from Châteaudun on 6 May 1886], and I have got the corner of the earth I need. It is a little valley four leagues from here, in the canton of Cloyes . . .

The day after tomorrow I have a meeting with a farmer, three leagues away, in the heart of the Beauce, to see his farm . . . Today I stayed in Châteaudun to attend a big cattle market.[3]

Alexandrine was with him. They hired a two-horse landau. It was like a mobile study in which he could spread out his maps and plans, and consult his books. His notes were the colourless raw material for his poetic mind. He studied the background of his fresco, and he found the motifs for his narrative. Many of his novels had a recurrent motif. In *La Curée* it had been the congested traffic in the Bois de Boulogne and on the boulevards; in *L'Argent* it was to be the portico and columns of the Bourse. Now, in *La Terre*, it was the monotonous, grandiose landscape of the Beauce, and the growing corn. 'What you call repetitions are found in all my books,' Zola was to tell a correspondent. 'It is in fact a literary device which I used timidly at first, and then perhaps carried to excess. As I see it, this gives more body to the work, strengthens its unity. There is something there like the theme tunes of Wagner.'[4]

In his draft for his novel, he explained: 'I have wanted to do for the peasant, in *La Terre*, what I did for the lower classes of Paris in *L'Assommoir*: write their history, describe their habits, passions, sufferings as they are fated to be by their surroundings and by historical circumstances.'[5]

By mid-June 1886, he was once again at Médan, 'I am still working at *La Terre*, but I haven't yet done half of the book,' he told a correspondent on 9 November. 'I had to take a holiday this summer, as I was very tired.'[6]

The correspondent in question was Jacques Van Santen Kolff, a Dutch man of letters. He was one of the men who worked most effectively to renew Dutch artistic life in the last thirty years of the nineteenth century. He had been born in Rotterdam, and now lived in Berlin. He was chiefly interested in music and painting, but he was an able literary critic. Van Santen Kolff kept Zola informed about the reception of his novels in Holland and Germany; he sent him articles and reviews. He translated several of his works into Dutch. Since 1880 he had been a demanding correspondent.

'I am still only two-thirds of the way through *La Terre*,' Zola told him on 12 March 1887. 'This novel will be the longest I have written, and it's giving me a great deal of trouble. I am pleased with it, as much as I can be, that is to say with my continual fever and my eternal doubts.'[7] He had once confessed that he wept with rage over his manuscripts, and that he never published a book without thinking it inferior to the rest.

La Terre demanded more of Zola than his normal working hours. He was 'slaving away over phrases till two o'clock in the morning,' so he told Céard on 26 May.[8] Two days later, *Gil Blas* began to serialise the novel. 'I wish,' wrote Maupassant, 'that all your friends, everyone who admires you as I do, begged you never to serialise these very grand and large-scale works again. Their composition and powerful effect almost completely vanish when they are cut up in a paper.'[9]

Zola was to ignore this advice. He worked on, and provided the copy from day to day. *La Terre* already roused public protest, but it had almost reached its end when, on 18 August, *Le Figaro* published a violent attack on Zola himself, an angry repudiation of his novel. 'The master has sunk to the depths of filth . . . [We must protest] with all the power of our hard-working youth, with all the loyalty of our artistic conscience . . . We must protest in the name of healthy, virile ambition, in the name of our cult, our deep love and supreme respect for *Art*!'[10] The Manifesto of the Five was signed by Paul Bonnetain, J.-H. Rosny, Lucien Descaves, Paul Margueritte and Gustave Guiches. Four of the Five were later to repent what they came to see as a youthful error. But they wanted now to affirm their independence and, no doubt, to attract attention.

Maurice Le Blond said later that the Manifesto had been planned while Goncourt had been staying with Daudet at Champrosay. He wondered if both of them had known of Bonnetain's idea, and favoured it. Daudet himself had denied this vehemently when he thanked Zola for an inscribed copy of *La Terre*.

It touches me, this inscription, because it proves to me that you have forgotten what people have tried to put between us, the calumny which for a moment you [seem] to have believed: that I inspired, prompted, or even remotely knew about the article ... I know that Goncourt has explained himself, but I should like to tell you now that if I had known of this plan for a public protest, I should have begged the authors ... not to publish it, for their own sakes and especially for mine. It seemed to me that nothing in our relationship entitled you to believe me capable of such a mean trick.[11]

But, my dear Daudet [Zola answered], I never ever thought that you had known about the extraordinary Manifesto of the Five! ... What is astounding is that you turned me from a victim into a culprit, and that instead of sending me a handshake, you nearly broke with me. You must admit that this was a bit excessive.

Personally I have never borne you a grudge. I know quite well how the Manifesto was written, and I have to smile. All the same, my dear Daudet, your letter gives me a lively pleasure, since it puts an end to a misunderstanding which had already delighted our enemies.[12]

A few years earlier, the Manifesto might have passed unnoticed. In 1887, however, there was a general movement from science to religion, from Naturalism to idealistic literature. The Symbolists were concerned with mood and soul, with landscapes which were inwardly perceived. On 28 August Anatole France published his condemnation of *La Terre*. It would, he said, have been better if Zola had not been born. On 1 September, in *La Revue des Deux Mondes*, Ferdinand Brunetière discussed 'La Banqueroute du Naturalisme'. On 9 September *La Gazette de France* denounced Zola's novel, 'this monument of dung, of physical and moral dirt, erected to contemporary progress'.[13]

Zola himself had taken a much-needed holiday. On 30 October he told Van Santen Kolff: 'I have just got back to Médan, after an absence of two months ... I spent six delightful weeks at Royan ... I'm sunburnt, I have never been so calm or lighthearted as I was during this idiotic rumpus.'[14]

Le Père Fouan divides his land between his three children; the division rouses primitive greed and hatred. Buteau, one of Fouan's sons, marries a cousin, Lise. Jean Macquart has been

working at a local farm since his return from the Italian
campaign; he marries her sister Françoise. La Grande, Père
Fouan's sister, determines that Françoise and Jean shall have
Buteau's house, and Buteau and Lise are evicted. Françoise
becomes pregnant, and Lise and Buteau see that her child
might one day inherit it. They find her in the fields. Lise holds
her to the ground while Buteau rapes her. Then she throws
her on to a scythe. As she is dying, Françoise contrives to let
Père Fouan know the truth. Buteau is haunted by the thought
that his father knows of the crime, and he stifles him as he is
sleeping. Even before the old man is dead, Buteau and Lise
set fire to the body. Jean Macquart leaves Rognes to rejoin the
army.

There were good characters in *La Terre* as there had been in
L'Assommoir, but Zola did not know how to make them live. It
sometimes seemed as if he could animate only crime and
degradation. Buteau is a bestial figure. Old Fouan is a symbol
of cunning and rapacity before he becomes a kind of peasant
Lear. Most of the women in *La Terre* are hardened by poverty.
Blood relationships are forgotten. Human kindness is ignored.
Copulation is not an expression of love, except for the pitiful
Palmyre, who sleeps with her simple-minded and ostracised
brother. The world of *La Terre* is a world without morality,
and Françoise, the one good Fouan, is cheated of her inheritance, of her child and, at last, of life itself.

La Terre is among the most savage of the Rougon-Macquart
novels; but, like other novels in the cycle, it clearly has a dual
identity. It is a Naturalist work: exact to the point of crudity.
It is also, quite as certainly, a poem of the earth. The recurrent
theme is that of generation, the insistent song of the powers of
the flesh. There is a constant and emphatic parallel between
the birth and death of the seasons and the birth and death
of mankind. The narrative is punctuated by lyrical visions of
the Beauce, of the seasons of the year, the everlasting cycle of
life and death in the countryside. These visions recur, as Zola
intended, like the familiar themes of a symphony. They help
to unify the work, to give this sober, factual book another dimension. Like the paintings of Millet, they emphasise the eternal
quality of peasant life. *La Terre* begins with Jean Macquart,
sowing the seed with a hieratic gesture; it ends with the sowers

once more at their task. Just as the peasant in *La Débâcle* will plough his field during the battle of Sedan, so the work of nature continues, despite all human failings, in *La Terre*. The novel is another affirmation of Zola's faith in life, of his fundamental optimism.

PART FIVE

FULFILMENT
1888–1893

24

Honoré Champion, the publisher, was a friend of Zola's. They had been booksellers' clerks together, and Champion boasted that it was he who had prompted Zola to write *Le Rêve*. He had reproached him, he explained, for making his Rougon-Macquarts the most despicable of human beings, and he had reminded him that even the most decayed of forest trees might produce healthy shoots. 'I think,' he said, mildly, 'that *Le Rêve* was the consequence of the lecture which I gave him.'[1] Michel Robida suggested another source of inspiration. Georgette Charpentier, the publisher's young daughter, had asked if she might read one of Zola's books. It was for her, said Robida, that he wrote *Le Rêve*.[2] There was also, perhaps, a literary reason for the novel. Zola had become aware of the current religious revival, the interest in the occult sciences. He meant to introduce 'something of the beyond, the dream, the unknown, the unknowable,' into his book. The heyday of Naturalism was over. The Manifesto of the Five and the article by Anatole France had done their work.

There remained a more significant explanation for *Le Rêve*. Zola was determined to renew himself. He intended the critics to recognise him as a psychologist. He was also tempted to write a love story between a man of forty and a girl of sixteen. After a struggle with his conscience, the man was to give up the girl to the young man whom she really loved.' That would be good, symbolic, it would show him desperately seeking the unknown, letting youth go by, not loving, in search of a dream (Myself, work, the literature which has eaten up all my life, and the turmoil, the crisis, the need to be loved, all this to be studied psychologically). I shall also put in the [present] moment, the reaction against Naturalism, the eagerness for the beyond, the need for an ideal, the destruction of faith. All that with dreams . . . And life breaking into it with the young girl.'[3]

It is clear that as early as 1887 Zola passed through a personal crisis. Almost a decade ago, in 1878, he had confessed that he felt a persistent longing to sleep with a girl who had not reached puberty: 'not a child, but a girl who was not yet a woman: "Yes, that frightens me . . . I can see the Assizes and all the rest of it." '[4] Goncourt recorded the confession; he was always eager for scandal. Yet there seems to be, here, an element of truth. Alexandrine, who was blind to her husband's needs, deaf to the warnings of Mme Laborde, had now engaged a young maid on whom, wrote Goncourt, crudely, 'the good Zola began to practise his touch'.[5] The girl was dismissed; but Zola remained desperate for love, for the warmth which Alexandrine could not give him.

He had grown grossly overweight, no doubt from sedentary work and from years of consoling good living. He determined, now, to regain his youthful figure. Late in 1887 he began to diet. His determination was, as usual, inflexible. Goncourt met him on 4 March 1888, and reported that he had lost two stone in three months; he had begun to look like his Manet portrait again.[6] In November, Goncourt noted: 'It is no longer the head of the Manet portrait . . . It is the head of a spectral being.'[7]

For eighteen years Zola had borne with Alexandrine's ill-health and nervous problems, with her profound depressions, her inability to give him the physical love, the children for whom he longed. 'Sandrine' was now forty-nine, at an age of particular stress; he himself was forty-eight, aware that youth had gone, and that he had missed his happiness. He suffered such crises of despair that he sometimes wept for hours; he felt crushed by the sadness of existence.

In the spring of 1888 his life was transformed. Twenty-eight years ago, he had come across a Greuze engraving. 'It was a young peasant girl, tall, of uncommon beauty of face . . . I looked for a long while at that engraving, and vowed that I should love the original, if such a portrait – doubtless an artist's dream – can have one.'[8] Now, in the spring of 1888, Alexandrine unwittingly found her, and, despite the earlier experience, despite the repeated warnings of Mme Charpentier and Mme Laborde, she engaged her as a laundress and sempstress at Médan.

Jeanne-Sophie-Adèle Rozerot had been born at Rouvres-sous-Meilly, in Burgundy, on 14 April 1867.[9] She was just twenty-one – twenty-seven years younger than Zola. She was the second daughter of a miller, Philibert Rozerot, and (according to Guillemin) his Swiss wife. Rozerot had been widowed in about 1870, and Jeanne had suffered greatly from her mother's death; all the more so, as her father had re-married, and found himself with a large family to support.

Jeanne was the incarnation of the Greuze engraving. She had dark hair, large, bright and gentle eyes; she was placid and modest, and she did nothing to attract Zola's attention. She was amazed that a man of his distinction should notice her, and she was no doubt touched by his need of her. Perhaps, unconsciously, she wanted an older man to replace the father whose affections had been so divided.

Since the days when he had pleaded for women's education, Zola had changed. He no longer sought 'a devoted equal', a woman who was 'his sister in her thinking'. 'What he most prizes in a young woman,' Dr Toulouse was to write, 'are freshness and health, physical and moral harmony, and also gentleness and charm; he attaches no importance to dress, and he would be rather put off by a woman's intellect.'[10] Jeanne had all that he prized in a woman, and he loved her from the beginning.

Zola's sexuality was inhibited but intense. He had been faithful to Alexandrine, but they had given one another occasional appeasement rather than love. His love for Jeanne was the result of years of disaffection; it was also the fulfilment of his dream. Jeanne was not only the peasant girl of *La Cruche cassée*; she was the Ninon of Provence, she was Denise Baudu, whom Octave Mouret had needed more than worldly success or wealth.

In this summer of 1888, a London paper, the *Daily Telegraph*, published a series of letters on the question: 'Is Marriage a Failure?' Their Paris correspondent, Mr Lonergan, was asked to find out Zola's opinion. He called at Médan, and reported that Zola 'had just finished *Le Rêve* and looked completely *éreinté* or used up . . . The traces of intense application . . . were observable in his features and in his conversation.'[11] The conversation was still rewarding. 'So far as France is concerned,' said Zola, 'I think that marriage is, like the Church, an old and faulty institution. It will have to go on until something better be found to replace it.' Lonergan asked innocently what he thought about free love. Zola answered: 'I think that the *collage* system ... may be every bit as good as matrimony ... There are cases of French couples who have carried on *collage* for years, and have been united as if in the bonds of wedlock.' He added: 'In any case, marriage ... is a failure and a grievance. So, too, is everything in our modern society. We are all going to universal rottenness.'[12] The comments were brash. No doubt they were meant to disguise his emotions; and so they did. Lonergan somehow concluded that Zola was 'the most moral of married men'.[13]

This summer, once again, Zola went on holiday to Royan. The Charpentiers were astonished to see him so idle and so happy. Alexandrine did not even now suspect the truth. At Royan he paid court to Jeanne, whom they had taken with them. Later in the year he installed her at 66, rue Saint-Lazare. It was, it seems, on 11 December that she became his mistress.[14]

The year which brought him happiness also brought him official recognition. On 14 July he was finally decorated. Édouard Lockroy, the new Minister of Public Instruction, pinned on the cross in Mme Charpentier's drawing-room. 'Every man of letters who was decorated,' wrote Coppée, 'was rather ashamed of being so, because you were not. It was an unforgivable oversight, a gross injustice, which M. Lockroy wanted to rectify. The thing has no importance for you, but it has for the profession.'[15]

The effect on Zola – legend says – was instantaneous. The following week he announced to Mme Charpentier: 'There were two paths I could have followed: the official path or the other. I didn't think about the first at all. You led me to it. I must follow it to the end ... I shall be Grand' Croix of the Légion-d'honneur. I shall be a Senator, since the Senate exists. And, since an Académie exists, I shall be an Academician.' Camille Doucet, the permanent secretary of the Académie, was asked if he thought that Zola would be elected. 'I do not doubt it,' he replied, 'for a single moment ... I don't say that he'll pass the first time, but you can take it for granted that he will be elected without serious difficulties.'[16] Doucet's predictions were repeatedly to be disproved.

On 27 July, Émile Blavet, of *Le Figaro*, found himself in a suburban train; as he waited for it to start, a belated traveller hurried in, and collapsed on to the opposite seat. It was Zola himself, 'but a new-style Zola, a Zola who was young again, dashing, with a well-trimmed beard, an impeccably knotted cravat, sprightly, brisk, almost slim, the newly-tied piece of ribbon casting pretty pink reflections on his fined-down face'. Blavet, a born journalist, asked at once if it were true that he was standing for the Académie. Zola – also a journalist – replied that *Le Figaro* should clip the wings of this *canard* once and for all.

He had, he admitted, finally let them 'violate his buttonhole'. 'It was not unimportant for my work, for my self-love as a writer, and for the dissemination of my ideas, that I should enter the great family of the Légion-d'honneur.' He was not at present standing, he said, for the Académie; but he intended to do so: again because it would publicise his work and his ideas. The conversation ended at the station at Poissy (Zola was returning to Médan). It was duly published in *Le Figaro*.[17]

In the meanwhile his acceptance of the Légion-d'honneur amazed and even angered his friends. They saw it as a lack of principle, a contradiction of his published views on the award of honours for the artist. They could not reconcile it with his attacks on the Establishment. They did not see that it meant a change of heart. Maupassant seems to have needed an explanation. 'I accepted after long reflection,' Zola assured him, '. . . and the acceptance goes beyond the cross, it extends to all rewards, even the Académie . . . I think this is good, and besides it would be only the logical result of the first step which I have just taken.'[18] Goncourt, who was jealous of Zola's material success, was vexed by this official recognition.

Why blame me for accepting the cross [Zola asked], when I accepted it in the same conditions as you? I had my hand affectionately forced by Lockroy, just as you had yours forced by Princess Mathilde . . . The cross was a consecration for you; why should it not be one for me?

And, one thing more: be sure that if ever I present myself to the Académie, I shall do so in conditions in which I shall not need to abdicate any of my pride or independence.[19]

There was another, unspoken reason for Goncourt's annoyance. In 1874 he had drawn up a will, which set out his plan for an Académie Goncourt; Zola was to be among its members. Goncourt denied that he had founded this Académie to rival the other, but it was clear that whoever stood for the Académie Goncourt was thereby to exclude himself from the Forty. When Zola finally stood for the Académie-Française, Goncourt crossed his name off the list.[20]

As for Daudet, in consenting to become Goncourt's executor, he had, in a sense, become the patron of the future institution. In 1888 he barred himself from the Académie-Fançaise: he published *L'Immortel*, a satirical novel about the Forty.

It is certainly . . . the most living and, let me add, the fiercest of your works [Zola told him on 12 July]. Once upon a time I reproached you for always keeping a honeycomb for the public. The honeycomb is no longer there. I have had my throat cut for books which were not as hard as yours, and I say that to you as praise.

You have pages of intense life . . . And above all you have abridgements which I greatly admire, since I always need to spread myself. You can rest assured that this work has a note which is all its own, and that it is a note which will endure.[21]

The letter was generous, but it did not end the arguments about Zola's aspirations. These continued into the autumn. On 21 October he wrote reproachfully to Daudet: 'This stupid question of the Académie should not even exist between us, because I am quite sure that you will understand my position, the day when it suits me to stand, just as I should have understood you, if you had thought you owed it to your situation to want a Chair.'[22]

On 15 October, a week before this letter was written, Charpentier had published *Le Rêve*. Writing to Van Santen Kolff, Zola had explained: 'It will be a question of a wild shoot of the Rougon-Macquart transplanted into a mystic milieu, and submitted to a special culture which will modify it. That is the scientific experiment.'[23] *L eRêve* bears small relation to his theories of heredity. It owes less to Taine and to Dr Lucas than it does to Bernardin de Saint-Pierre. 'Let us re-do *Paul et Virginie*,' Zola had written in his *ébauche*. He needed to express the Romanticism which he had tried so long to contain.

Angélique is the daughter of Sidonie Rougon, better known as Mme Touche, the courtier and money-lender in *La Curée*; but there is little of the Rougons in her nature, except perhaps her passion and determination. She is an idealised figure, a modern Juliet who falls in love, again, with the impossible; she is a nineteenth-century Cinderella who would not be recognised as the niece of Aristide Saccard. Angélique proves, if anything, that human beings cannot be explained by race, environment and time. She is hardly modified by her surroundings. Like her uncle, Doctor Pascal, she seems to demonstrate that some escape hereditary taints.

The Huberts are a loving couple who are desperate to have a child. One winter morning they see a young girl huddled on the steps of the cathedral in Beaumont, in the snow. They take her in, and find that she had been a foster-child, and that she had finally escaped from the custody of a drunken tanner and his wife. The Huberts keep her as an apprentice, and she helps them to embroider chasubles for the cathedral; they bring her up humble and devout, and assured of their affection. At moments Angélique reveals her inner violence, her pride and independence; but she is often lost in reverie. She dreams, like a girl in adolescence, of a prince, but she dreams of him with the certainty that he will come. He comes in fact into her life. He is the only son of a prince of the Church, the Bishop of Beaumont. The Bishop had taken orders when his wife had died, and he has only recently felt able to see his child. Angélique and Félicien de Hautecœur fall in love, with passionate innocence. The Bishop forbids the marriage, and Angélique fades away with grief. Only when he gives her the last rites does he relent. She recovers, and she marries Félicien. As they emerge from the cathedral, she kisses him, and dies. 'She dies content, enchanted,' noted Zola. 'She is borne away in the realization of her dream, just as she was entering reality.'

Le Rêve lacks cohesion and conviction. It is a clumsy lyric, a mawkish literary exercise. 'I confess,' wrote Anatole France, 'that M. Zola's purity seems to me most meritorious. It has cost him dear: it has cost him all his talent.'[24]

On 16 November Zola announced to Van Santen Kolff: 'I

am looking for my next novel . . . I shall put some terrible drama
in the setting of the railways.'[25]

25

Van Santen Kolff asked for details; but there was silence. He
seems to have sent a further letter.

My dear colleague [Zola wrote at last, on 6 March 1889],
Haven't I told you before not to worry when you received no
answer from me? I am the laziest man in the world, when I am not
the most industrious. It is quite true that I am going through a crisis,
no doubt the crisis of the 50th year; but I shall endeavour to turn it
to the profit and honour of literature. Forgive me, then, for my long
silence. There are weeks, and months, when there is a tempest in
my being, a tempest of desires and regrets. The best thing then would
be to sleep.[1]

That day, from Paris, he confessed to Huysmans: 'I should
hardly need to make an effort not to touch a pen again.' Mr
Lonergan, aware of this crisis of indifference, referred to Zola's
'next and perhaps last work'.[2]

Zola was more informative, more enthusiastic, in the inter-
view which appeared in *L'Événement* on 8 March.

Yes, I'm working on a novel . . .
The subject? . . . A crime committed on a railway . . .
As for the setting, I've chosen the Ligne de l'Ouest . . .
I applied to the Compagnie de l'Ouest, and I'm glad to record the
courtesy and kindness with which its senior officials put themselves
at my disposal.[3]

He had been given permission to travel from Paris to Mantes
and back on the footplate of an engine. M. Clérault, the engineer
in charge of rolling-stock and traction, had offered to accom-
pany him, and so had M. Pol Lefèvre, deputy head of traffic.
On 15 April, Antoine recorded: 'Zola arrived late, this evening,
at the rehearsal of his *Madeleine*. He collapsed rather heavily on
to the big red divan in the salon, and said that during the day
he had been from Paris to Mantes on the footplate of an engine
. . . He complained that the shaking had broken his legs.'[4]

In Paris he inspected the Gare Saint-Lazare with M. Lefèvre, who explained the train movements to him. Lefèvre also escorted him to the depots at Dieppe and Malaunay.

The plan for *La Bête Humaine* had been set down in principle in 1869. In his list of novels, which dated from 1871, Zola said specifically: 'The judicial novel (railways). Étienne Lantier.' His ideas had now been modified. The main line from Paris to Le Havre ran beside his house at Médan; he had recognised the symphonic rhythm of the endless traffic, he had grown aware of the poetry of machines. Above all, he had discovered how the railways would let him show the result of scientific progress in the hands of violent and primitive people. The railway had come to dominate the novel, and the criminal intrigue had become secondary.

The legal cases which Zola used were the Fenayrou affair of 1882 and the Barrème affair of 1886. M. Barrème, the Prefect of the Eure, had been found murdered on a railway line between Paris and Mantes, in circumstances which remained a mystery. As for his railway accident, Zola used the details of recent disasters: those of Cabbé-Roquebrune, Charenton, Groewendaël, la Hulpe and Monte-Carlo. Maxime du Camp, in his survey of Paris, offered a chapter on the railways, and a section of this was concerned with accidents.

Zola's chief problem lay in the choice of his main character. In his original plan, this was to be Étienne Lantier, but Étienne had since become the hero of *Germinal*. Once again, Zola modified his genealogical tree. He gave Claude and Étienne another brother, Jacques. There had been no question of him in *L'Assommoir*.

Zola set down sixty ideas for the title of the book before he finally chose *La Bête Humaine*.

After *Le Rêve* [he noted in his *ébauche*], I should like to write a quite different novel; to begin with, in the real world; and then without description, without visible art, written more fluently; a simple narrative; and, for its subject, a violent drama to give a nightmare to the whole of Paris, something like *Thérèse Raquin* . . .

The interest of the book would lie . . . in its contemporary human problem. One would have to return to the theory of the right to murder.[5]

The right to murder was a subject much discussed in the
1880s. Dostoievsky treated the question in *Crime and Punishment*.
Paul Bourget's *Le Disciple* was published when Zola was working on *La Bête Humaine*. The second French edition of Cesare
Lombroso's *L'Homme criminel* appeared in 1887. Lombroso believed that 'born criminals' were produced by alcoholic and
criminal parents. Zola could have found no clearer *ex post facto*
approval of his own Rougon-Macquart.

As for the initial murder in his novel, Zola noted: 'The whole
State shaken by the crime, because the Empire is going through
a crisis . . . It is here that the book touches the history of the
Second Empire.' *La Bête Humaine* was to touch the régime in
symbolic fashion. Already, in his *ébauche*, Zola saw the end of
the novel: the stoker and the engine-driver falling, locked in
combat, from the train, and 'the machine going on, at full
speed, perhaps in the night . . . Have the train full of light-
hearted soldiers, careless of danger, who are singing patriotic
songs. The train is then the image of France.'[6] The songs of
the soldiers echoed the shouting of the crowds outside the
Grand Hôtel du Louvre as Nana was dying. The two novels
were to converge on the same point in history.

On 5 May 1889, Zola began to write *La Bête Humaine*. 'I have
set to work with fury [this to Céard on 31 May]. Age hardly
calms me. I hoped that, as I grew older, I should grow a little
wiser. But I can never ever act except in bursts of passion. How
curious it is! For, deep down, I judge myself very coldly, and
I even feel contempt for my enthusiasm.'[7] He worked on,
fiercely. 'I have finished the first chapter,' he told Alexis on
5 June, 'and I am attacking the second. There will be twelve,
there's enough work there for at least eight months. What a
terrible trade, where you are always beginning again, and
always with the same problems and the same agonies!'[8] Next
day, to Van Santen Kolff, he added:

I am very happy with the plan, which is perhaps the most complex that I've done . . . What is original is that the story takes place,
from beginning to end, on the Western railway line, between Paris
and Le Havre . . . You hear a continual rumbling of trains. It is
progress passing, on its way to the twentieth century, and this in the

midst of an abominable drama, mysterious, unknown to everyone.
The human beast under civilisation.[9]

He wrote, now, like a man possessed. It was twenty years
since he had written the first Rougon-Macquart novel; he was
working on the seventeenth, and his zest for the enterprise was
fading. He knew that Naturalism was in decline, he recognised
the old and persistent Romantic impulse within him. Above all,
he no longer needed the Rougon-Macquart novels in which to
express his own ambitions, rid himself of his guilt and misery.
The cycle now belonged to his past, and the past had ended
with the advent of Jeanne. Literature no longer dominated his
life. It was at last eclipsed by life itself.

I am seized by a wild longing to finish my Rougon-Macquart
series as soon as possible [this to Charpentier on 27 August]. I should
like to be rid of it in January 1892 . . .
I'm going through a very healthy period of work, I'm wonderfully
well, and I feel as if I were twenty again . . .
We are going back to Paris on 10 September, to settle at our
leisure in our new apartment [21 *bis*, rue de Bruxelles] . . . We shall
come back to Médan in December . . .
Oh, *mon ami*, if I were only thirty, you'd see what I should do!
I'd astound the world![10]

Zola was youthful, exuberant. Never had he felt so at peace
with himself. For Jeanne was now heavily pregnant. 'Nothing
is founded without the child,' so he was to write. 'It is the living
work, . . . continuing today by tomorrow.'[11] On 20 September
the living work was done. Jeanne gave birth to their daughter
Denise. He gave thanks in a sentence which moves us, even now,
by its passionate intensity of feeling, by the depth of gratitude
it holds. 'By her grace, at last, beneath my lips, a child's warm
hair to kiss.'[12]

On 14 November, while Zola was still writing *La Bête Humaine*,
La Vie populaire began to serialise it.
Roubaud, the son of a carter at Plassans, has married Séverine
Aubry, a gardener's daughter. Séverine is the godchild of her
father's employer, Grandmorin, once President of the Compagnie de l'Ouest; and, thanks to his influence, Roubaud is now
assistant stationmaster at Le Havre. As the book opens, he is

in Paris. A quarrel with a passenger has brought him a reprimand from authority, but his patron has saved him from dismissal. As he celebrates with his wife, he gradually comes to suspect the nature of her relationship with the old man; and he drives her to confess that she had been his mistress. Roubaud compels her to write a note, urging Grandmorin to catch a certain train to Le Havre. During the journey, with her assistance, he cuts the old man's throat, and throws the body out beside the track.

An enquiry is opened. The murder had been witnessed by Jacques Lantier, an engine-driver who had happened to be by the track that night. Lantier is a son of Gervaise, of *L'Assommoir*, and he has inherited his father's violence and his parents' alcoholic tendencies. He rigorously avoids strong drink; he also avoids women, for when he is sexually aroused he has a compulsive urge to kill.

The Roubauds understand that Jacques knows of their guilt, and they determine to buy his silence. They make him virtually one of their household; and, while Roubaud loses himself in gambling, Séverine becomes Jacques' mistress. In time she comes to hate her husband, and she urges her lover to murder him. As Roubaud is about to arrive, unsuspecting, to be killed, Jacques is overcome by desire, and by Séverine's description of the murder of Grandmorin. He cuts her throat, brutally, in the same fashion, and he escapes.

The steam-engine, La Lison, had once been his compensation for chastity, his escape from his perpetual nightmare. Jacques tries to lose himself, again, driving an engine; but he quarrels with his drunken stoker, and in the struggle they both fall from the footplate to their death. The express train, full of troops drinking and singing, speeds on, uncontrolled, into the night.

La Bête Humaine is a study of a Macquart who fights in vain against heredity. Yet it is more than the history of a reluctant murderer, or an analysis of a *crime passionel*. The artist in Zola appeals against the implications of his own scientific theory; the novel is, above all, a compelling horror story, a pretext for presenting a background with magisterial power. *La Bête Humaine* contains factual errors, and anachronisms, but it remains an indelible impression of the world which the railways have brought into being.

This world is presented in detail, and yet on the epic scale which seems to suit Zola best. It has, indeed, as he intended, a quality of nightmare. Like the world of *Germinal*, it is claustrophobic, hermetically sealed. An extraordinary atmosphere of secrecy and suspicion pervades it. Almost all the characters have some adultery, some act of violence, to hide. Many of them live in apprehension, wondering if their guilt has been suspected; others eavesdrop on their neighbours, imagine nonexistent liaisons, spread malicious gossip, and further their own interests by assiduous disparagement of neighbours. Almost every character lives under some emotional strain which will finally break him. The physical violence in the book is primitive and constant; yet even this is less oppressive than the brooding atmosphere.

No doubt this atmosphere was Zola's own deliberate creation; but it extended well beyond the needs of character or plot. Zola's most successful novels generally reflect some more or less conscious aspect of himself. *La Bête Humaine* was the first novel which he had written since his love-affair began; and, while he was writing it, Jeanne gave birth to their daughter. Her apartment was near the Gare Saint-Lazare, near the room where Roubaud conceived the murder of Grandmorin, and Lantier first thought of killing Roubaud: the room where Lantier made love to Séverine. The very setting of the book brought Jeanne to Zola's mind; the theme of adultery and jealousy was ever present to him. Like Lantier and Séverine he had a love-affair which at all costs he was forced to hide.

Zola's critics were bewildered by the contrast between *Le Rêve* and *La Bête Humaine*. On 8 March Aurélien Scholl explained in *Le Matin* that, 'in Zola, the pig was doubled up with a tiger'.[13] However, on the same day, in *Le Figaro*, Jules Lemaître acclaimed the book. Zola, he wrote,

is the poet of the shadowy depths of man, and it is the whole of his work which should bear the title *La Bête Humaine*.

Our mean and transient personalities are only the infinitely small waves of an ocean of forces which are impersonal, eternal, and blind; and beneath these waves there remains an abyss. This is, in fact, what *La Bête Humaine* expresses with melancholy and savage majesty. It is a prehistoric epic in the form of a contemporary story.[14]

Next day, in *Le Temps*, there appeared a still more remarkable review. Since he had attacked *La Terre*, nearly three years earlier, Anatole France had become aware that his comments had been excessive. Rather than admit it frankly, he chose the subterfuge of a conversation about *La Bête Humaine*. One of the speakers insisted that Zola was a poet. 'The Greeks created the Dryad, he has created La Lison; these two creations are equal, and both are immortal. He is the great lyric poet of our time.'[16]

Banville, too, thought of Greek mythology. On 10 March he wrote to Zola: 'I am still burning with the admiration which *La Bête Humaine* has inspired in me. Over this terrifying epic the cruel Eates are hovering like the Gods. It reminds me of what is greatest in the past.'[16] 'I have read your book with passion,' Heredia added, the same day. 'What I admire more than anything, more than the terrible drama, more than the grandiose conception, the audacious style, is the really marvellous composition . . . It is as great as a poem, and it is worked out, perfect like a sonnet.'[17] Mallarmé told Zola: 'For a long time, with all my soul, I have admired this art, your own, which can . . . satisfy the masses and still surprise the man of letters; and never, I think, has the torrent of life flowed as it does in this abyss hollowed out by your drama between Paris and Le Havre.'[18]

On 1 May 1890, fortified by such appreciation, Zola stood for the Académie-Française. He paid the visits which, according to tradition, a candidate must pay to the 'Immortals'. He called, it is said, on the critic and man of letters, Xavier Marmier. 'You have written some superb books, monsieur,' so Marmier explained, 'but . . . you have tarnished admirable pictures with blemishes which are condemned by morality and by good taste. Your success at the Académie will be doubtful for a long time.'[19]

Charles de Freycinet, President of the Council of Ministers, was chosen in preference to Zola. At subsequent elections, Zola was to be defeated by a long series of contenders. Among them was Ferdinand Brunetière, the critic and the enemy of Naturalism. In 1894 both Zola and Verlaine stood for election. Both were rejected, and Heredia was chosen. 'Zola will never enter the Académie,' said the new Academician. '. . . Anyway, I shan't vote for him.'[20]

Talking to Sherard in November 1890, Zola confessed that he wanted recognition in his lifetime. He also wanted recognition for the Naturalist novel. He felt himself to be the heir and successor of a number of rejected men of letters. It was their battle as much as his own that he was fighting.[21] Édouard Pailleron, sometime director of *La Revue des Deux Mondes*, suggested that he had a less noble motive: 'the enormous impetus to the sale of his books.'[22]

Zola's detractors accused him of seeking material gain; in fact he was sometimes strangely unconcerned about his own financial interests. He never had a bank account. He drew what he needed from his publisher. Success brought him comfort, it freed him from the anxieties which had embittered his youth and early manhood. He respected money, but he despised it. Money, he was to write, 'has been among the most powerful factors in civilisation, but it has brought with it every abomination and every iniquity.'[23]

26

No special predilection for money led Zola to write *L'Argent*; but the idea of the novel dated from the time he published the first volume of the Rougon-Macquart. 'Since then,' he explained to Van Santen Kolff, 'I have always kept a compartment for what I called my novel on the Bourse ... I wanted to take up Saccard and Rougon again, to oppose the liberal Empire to the authoritarian Empire, and finally to study the political crisis which preceded the collapse of the régime.'[1]

The subject of the Bourse was essential to his series, but aesthetically it seemed unrewarding. Early in 1890 he embarked on his research. He began by reading *Les Mémoires d'un coulissier*, by Ernest Feydeau, the author of *Fanny*. Feydeau had been a *coulissier*, or stock-jobber, for nearly twenty-five years. His memoirs recalled the world of finance as it had been in about 1860. Zola also sought inspiration from the collapse of L'Union Générale. This had happened over the years 1878–1885; it had been among the financial scandals of the Third Republic. An engineer called Eugène Bontoux had been the central figure of this *cause célèbre*, and he had published a book about it. Zola read it. He also procured the run of *Le Droit*: the paper in which the case was recorded. In Zola's novel, L'Union Générale becomes La Banque Universelle. Saccard exploits the projects of Bontoux.

The documentation of *L'Argent* cost Zola a considerable effort. He approached bankers and financial experts, and he re-read Karl Marx. He learned about the episode of la baronne Sandorff – the scabrous episode of the novel – from Maxime du Camp. The heroine had been Edwige Sapia: the mistress of the Imperial Prosecutor, Chaix d'Est-Ange, and of the financier Jules-Isaac Mirès. An embittered lady's maid had ushered Chaix d'Est-Ange into a drawing-room where her employer found herself half naked with Mirès. Chaix had later taken his revenge by having the financier prosecuted.

Finally Zola wrote his *ébauche*:

I don't want to end this novel by expressing disgust with life, or pessimism. Life as it is, but accepted, in spite of everything for its own sake . . .

As for money, do not attack it, and do not defend it. Do not oppose what we call our century of money to what we call the centuries of honour (those of the past). Show that, for many people, money has become the dignity of life; it gives freedom, it is hygiene, cleanness, health, almost intelligence. Contrast the well-to-do and the poor. Then, the irresistible power of money. There are only love and money.

I shall therefore be obliged to come to the social question, for in fact it is almost completely contained in the question of wealth . . .

Finally, I must remember that the Jewish question is going to lie at the bottom of my subject. I can't touch money without evoking the whole rôle of the Jews, then and now . . .[2]

Zola's attitude to the Jews was still distinctly hostile. Madame Caroline, Saccard's mistress, was to attack anti-Semitism. Yet even now one feels that Zola, like Saccard himself, 'had the ancient racial rancour against the Jews which one finds especially in the South of France'. Saccard admired the achievements of the Jews, but he felt an instinctive aversion to 'this cursed race which no longer has a country of its own, . . . this race which lives like a parasite among the nations'. Saccard's antipathy is expressed with such conviction that the reader suspects that it was shared. Even the Dreyfus Affair was not entirely to change Zola's sympathies. In *Vérité*, Marc Froment (a self-portrait of Zola) was still to feel 'a sort of atavistic repugnance and mistrust' for the Jewish race.[3]

On 10 June 1890, Zola began to write *L'Argent*. On 9 July he told Van Santen Kolff: 'I have just done the first chapter ... Charpentier will put the book on sale in the second fortnight in March.'[4]

It was in fact published on 4 March 1891, some ten days earlier than he had predicted.

L'Argent is not merely a novel about the Bourse, it is a novel about money: the lust for it, the power it confers, the benefits and tragedies it brings. Saccard, the husband of Renée in *La Curée*, is now a widower. Ten years of speculation on the transformation of Paris have left him ruined and burnt out; but he is dreaming of a new career. He learns from a young engineer, Hamelin, of unexploited silver-mines in Palestine, of a probable unexplored vein of iron. Hamelin has studied a new means of extraction; he only needs to raise the capital. Saccard is fired by the prospect, by the thought of railways to be built in Asia Minor, by the political power to be gained. He raises the capital, and founds La Banque Universelle. The rich, the audacious, the hopeful and the poor are in turn fired by his passion. The shares of La Banque Universelle reach extraordinary heights; but Saccard is brought down by the calculating Gundermann (a character modelled on Baron James de Rothschild). The battle in the Bourse is between two temperaments. It demands calculation rather than fervour. Yet the spirit has not died in Saccard, any more than it had died in his brother, Eugène Rougon, after his political fall. It is Rougon, now a Minister, who avoids a prison sentence for him, by allowing him to slip abroad; and, as the book ends, Saccard is already involved in a project in Holland: the reclamation of marshes by a system of canals.

Much as Zola may regret the destruction of the innocent, he patently admires Saccard's spirit and his irrepressible powers of survival. As Georges Chennevière observed: 'Saccard would like to mould the whole of humanity. He is much superior to Octave Mouret: he surpasses him with all his lyricism, he feels the poetry of numbers and of power.'[5] Zola calls him simply 'the prince of the million'. In this obsession with money, the main theme of *L'Argent*, we feel the falseness of Second Empire values, and the imminent end of the régime, the approaching end of a world. It is one of Zola's achievements that he also shows the spell of money. He endows it with a life, a sinister vitality of its own.

'I am finishing your magnificent book *L'Argent*,' Léon Hennique wrote to him on 20 March, 'and I must congratulate you at once . . . I met Maupassant yesterday, and he said that you had a very good chance of entering the Académie this time.'[6]

L'Argent had not in fact increased Zola's chances of election. On 15 January 1891, when the serial version was still appearing, and the manuscript itself was still unfinished, a new Academic vacancy had been discussed. 'Not Zola, whatever happens,' d'Haussonville had said. 'He has just written more filth in *L'Argent*.'[7] Zola campaigned, but Pierre Loti was elected. In 1892, at his official reception, there was 'a triple salvo of applause when he *charged* on Naturalism and spoke of Zola's *monstrous* talent. Zola was attending the session with his wife. He looked like a furious Christ.'[8] Loti had been obliged to read the speech he had prepared; but even he had found himself embarrassed by Zola's presence. After the session he apologised to him, and they shook hands. The public gesture was noble, but the private feelings were not recorded.[9]

Zola was already standing again for election. 'Thank you for your kind literary sympathy which I am told will turn militant in my favour [this to Dumas *fils* on 25 May]. I certainly think the Académie will exercise my patience for a long while; but that still further increases my gratitude to the few friends who are good enough to support me there.'[10] Two months after Loti was received into the Académie, Zola was rejected yet again. On 4 May 1893 Camille Doucet, the permanent secretary, simply wrote to him:

The Académie has just decided that it will proceed to the election of the successor of John Lemoinne on Thursday 8 June.

It is of course understood that, unless you advise me to the contrary, I shall maintain your candidature.[11]

Dumas *fils* suggested that this time they should agree to accept him. 'No,' said Pailleron. 'He has talent, but he has brought crapulence into literature.'[12] Among Zola's papers is a note from François Coppée, who was suffering from tuberculosis. 'Unfortunately I am still very ill, and on my doctor's advice I am going to spend the winter in Algeria. Of course I shall not go until I have dropped a persistent 'Zola' in the Academic ballot-box. I was assured that Dumas was voting for you.' The note is undated, but one might perhaps set it late in 1893.[13] On 24 February 1894, after another predictable rejection, Zola wrote again to Dumas *fils*: 'I thank you all the same, and with all my heart [for your support]. It is my own fault, since the Académie is so impassioned about it. The worst thing is that I shall always stand, because I have no other means of protesting.'[14] In 1895 Jules Claretie wearily recorded: 'Zola is still a candidate.'[15] After Zola's death, Claretie confessed that the votes for him had decreased with every application. 'The last time there was only one. That vote – I can say so now – was mine.'[16] It had been Zola's twenty-second attempt to enter what Anatole France called 'la Sainte Chapelle'.

Zola was to be rejected with unfailing constancy, but he remained undefeated. He also remained absorbed in his enterprise. Two days after *L'Argent* was published, he had told Van Santen Kolff: 'I am beginning to collect the documents for my next novel, *La Débâcle*.'[17]

27

Anatole France had predicted that, sooner or later, Zola would write a military novel, but that the army which he presented would be 'an historic army of which only memory remains . . . M. Zola, held back in the Second Empire, is,' said France, 'a kind of Walter Scott.'[1] The army was indeed to be the army of the Franco-Prussian War; but *La Débâcle* was not to be an historical romance. It was to be, above all, a record of the truth.

The subject, Zola later explained,

was to be War. I had to consider War in its relation to the various classes of society . . . How the war was brought about – that is to say the state of mind of Frenchmen at the time – was a consideration which also supplied me with a number of characters . . . Then, having, with a stroke of the rake, dragged together all that I could find as likely to illustrate my period, both historically and psychologically considered, I wrote out rapidly – the work of one feverish morning – a *maquette*, or rough draft, of all I wanted to do . . . [I then had] to see the place, to study the geography of my book.[2]

According to *Le Petit Ardennais*, Zola arrived at Vouziers on 17 April 1891. He spent the night there, and next day he stayed at Le Chesne. Alexandrine was with him. They followed the route which the Seventh Corps had taken, and travelled by landau from Rheims to Sedan. Zola recorded the landscape, the villages, the inns, the innkeepers and their curious stories.[3] He could not bring himself to ask for a passport to Alsace or Lorraine. Despite the peace terms, they still seemed to be part of France. He contented himself with impressions which were given to him by a friend.[4] However, he returned to Paris with one hundred and ten pages of notes. His journey had been announced by the Press. Veterans of 1870 wrote to offer him their *carnets de route*. Corporal Fernand Hue was one of the few surviving chasseurs of the Margueritte division; he and five or six other old soldiers provided the basic material for the novel.

Zola, complained Maurice Barrès, told the story of *La Débâcle* by setting himself at the level of a private soldier, and of a cowardly soldier at that.[5] Georges Duhamel made a technical criticism. When he first read the novel, he had recently taken his medical examination; he had been astonished to find that all the details of one incident came from a text-book which he had just studied. This was *Précis du Manuel Opératoire* by L. H. Farabeuf, which had appeared in 1885.[6]

Zola spent fifteen months in preparation for *La Débâcle*, but the novel was not his only literary occupation. On 6 April 1891 he had been elected President of the Société des Gens de Lettres. He was also interviewed by the journalist Jules Huret, who was making an enquiry into the decline of Naturalism.

Zola as a child. From a
daguerreotype.

Zola in his days of hardship.
A photograph taken when
he was twenty.

Alexandrine Zola. From the
pastel portrait by Manet, 1879.

Alexandrine in middle age.
From a photograph.

Alexandrine (centre) sets out for a drive at Médan. This
photograph was taken by Zola.

Médan. From a photograph taken by Zola.

Alexandrine with friends at Médan. Another photograph taken
by her husband.

Zola at home in the rue de Bruxelles. Manet's picture of him may be seen on the wall.

Zola the photographer: a picture taken at Médan towards the end of the century.

'I vowed that I should love the original, if such a portrait – doubtless an artist's dream – can have one.' Zola was enamoured of *La Cruche cassée* from his youth. He found the Greuze figure incarnated in Jeanne Rozerot.

Zola and Jeanne. This studio photograph by Petit was taken in the early years of their liaison.

Jeanne Rozerot sewing at Royan. From a photograph taken by Zola in the summer of 1888.

Jeanne, Denise and Jacques. This photograph of his mistress and children was taken by Zola himself.

'He has a serious, anxious, unhappy air which is peculiar to him.' Zola at the end of his life.

'Aha!' the master said to me, smiling, as he shook hands. 'You have come to see if I am dead! Well, you can see that I am alive! My health is excellent, ... [and] I have never been more serene. My books are selling better than ever.'

Zola himself insisted that Naturalism was well, and Paul Alexis underwrote his words. When Huret asked him for his views, for his *Enquête sur l'évolution littéraire*, Alexis sent a telegram: 'Naturalism not dead. Letter follows.'[7]

Yet the great majority of men of letters whom Huret interviewed agreed that Naturalism was dying. It had in fact been dying for some years. When Eugène-Melchior de Voguë published *Le Roman russe* in 1886, he had helped to determine the new direction of French literature. De Voguë maintained that French realism no longer had a soul; he wanted to renew it by putting it in touch with the Russian novel. He emphasised the idealism of the Russian novel, the evangelical spirit which imbued it. The reception of *Le Roman russe* showed how well he had understood the inner need of his contemporaries.

Translations of Russian novels multiplied in France. In 1889, by way of England, where the critic William Archer had introduced them, the mystical works of Ibsen and Bjørnson had become known to French readers. That year, in the preface to *Le Disciple*, Paul Bourget had insisted: 'There is a reality which you cannot doubt, since you possess it, feel it, see it every minute, and that is your soul ...' In his novel, Bourget showed the danger of certain determinist and scientific ideas, when they were put into practice by a biassed mind; he also preached the moral responsibility of the philosopher who put these ideas within reach of the young. The philosopher in his novel, André Sixte, was supposed to be modelled on Taine. Taine himself read *Le Disciple*, and wrote to its author: 'I have only one conclusion, which is that taste has changed, and that my generation is finished.' On 19 April 1890, in *Le Journal des Débats*, Ernest Lavisse published an article 'La Jeunesse'. 'One of the marks of modern youth, I mean of thinking youth, is [he wrote] nostalgia for the divine.' The days of Naturalism were truly over.[8]

On 4 September 1891, Zola told Van Santen Kolff: 'I am leaving on a little journey to the Pyrenees. I shall come back in the first days of October.'[9]

F

The timing of his 'little journey' was significant. He wanted to avoid suspicions, to ensure that Alexandrine remained in ignorance of his double life. Jeanne was expecting their second child late in September. Zola had chosen to be away from Paris at the time, and he had arranged that Céard should keep him informed of events. 'If you have something to tell me, write to me at M.A.B. 70, at Biarritz, poste restante. I shall stay there until the 25th. And I also beg you, when J. has been delivered, and the doctor has given you news, to put a note in the personal column of *Le Figaro*, signed Duval, in which you inform me in code. Put "pheasant" for a boy, "hen-pheasant" for a girl.' On 25 September Jeanne gave birth to his son, Jacques. *Le Figaro* duly announced: 'Fine pheasant, arrived safely.'[10]

It was, apparently, in November, after her return from the 'little journey', that Alexandrine received an anonymous letter. It revealed the existence of Zola's second household.[11]

It was surprising that the secret had been kept so long, for more than one of Zola's friends had known it, and so had some observers who were less disposed in his favour. Two years earlier, on 21 November 1889, Goncourt had recorded: 'Paul Alexis comes today . . . He confirms me in the certainty that Zola has a little ménage. Zola had confessed to him that his wife had great qualities as a housekeeper, but many *chilling* things, which had led him to seek a little *warmth* elsewhere.'[12] Zola himself had often been far from discreet: he had defiantly allowed himself to be seen in Paris with Jeanne. He had also taken care not to alter his routine. Now Alexandrine did not merely learn of his infidelity. She learned of a virtual second marriage: a marriage which was illicit, but secure in the youth of Jeanne and in the existence of a son and daughter. For a woman of fifty-two, childless but maternal, after twenty-one years of married life, the betrayal and the shock were shattering.

On 11 November Zola sent a telegram to Céard: 'My wife is going mad. Can you go to the rue Saint-Lazare and do what is necessary? Forgive me.'[13] Presumably Alexandrine had broken open his desk, and found the letters which Jeanne had written to him. This discovery had brought on a violent crisis. Zola wanted Céard to warn Jeanne, and no doubt he wanted her to guard against a threatened visit from his wife.

Céard found himself, now, in an impossible situation. He was Zola's confidant. He received Jeanne's letters. He was the godfather of Denise. He had also become the unwilling confidant of Alexandrine. 'My dear friend,' she wrote, with emotion, 'in the name of the deep affection I have for you, in the name of those who have been dear to you, come and give me a few minutes at Médan, from Wednesday onwards. You and my poor Amélie [Mme Laborde] now share all my affection between you.'[14] Albert Laborde, Alexandrine's godson, knew nothing about the drama; but he remembered how, one day, she had welcomed him with a warmth which had strangely impressed him. 'I felt myself more than usual in her arms.'[15]

28

When Zola came back from Sedan, he had found himself 'surrounded with huge mountains of hewn stones, mortar and bricks, and all that remained,' as he told Sherard, 'was to build the best structure that I could'.[1]

Zola more than once disclaimed any moral intentions in his writing; but, as he later explained, he had endeavoured in *La Débâcle* 'to speak the plain truth without fear or favour. The reader will be aroused to compassion with the sufferings, bodily and mental, of the heroic and martyred army, just as he will be aroused to downright indignation at the conduct of its chiefs, which fell little short of downright dementia.'[2] Zola also chose this moment to enlarge on his purpose as a novelist. 'My novels have always been written with a higher aim than merely to amuse . . . I have chosen [the novel] as the form in which to present to the world what I wish to say on the social, scientific and psychological problems that occupy the minds of thinking men . . . [*La Débâcle*] is a document on the psychology of France in 1870.'[3] Jean Macquart was to count for less than the Franco-Prussian War. In these later novels, Zola was more concerned with writing a social or philosophical treatise than he was with questions of heredity.

He finished *La Débâcle* on 12 May 1892, and it was published on 24 June.

La Débâcle presents a passage of history in close detail. Zola follows the campaign, the catastrophe of Sedan, the continuing warfare and the Commune, largely through the eyes of two soldiers. Maurice Levasseur is a product of the Second Empire: nervous, effeminate, quick to enthuse and quick to despair. His psychology is to explain, in part, the defeat of France. He is a private in the 106th regiment of the line. Jean Macquart, sobered by his experience in *La Terre*, is now a corporal in the same regiment. Tough and generous and sceptical, he represents the traditional French virtues. The two men are divided by their social class and by their symbolism. Yet circumstance has cast them together, and the human theme of the novel is that of their original hostility, and of their later deepening friendship.

This relationship needed to be assessed by a writer more concerned with the complexities of human love, the often irrational workings of the heart and mind; but Zola controlled his characters too firmly to let them live a life of their own. He could not make them behave according to some inner impulse, some spiritual continuity. He is a poor psychologist, and his characters are determined by literary necessity. So, at times, are events. At the end of the novel, Jean Macquart, now fighting with the army of Versailles, mortally wounds a Communard and finds that it is Maurice. The circumstance owes more to the need for a symbol than it does to Naturalism or to the precepts of Taine.

La Débâcle falls between the documentary and the work of fiction. The accumulation of eloquent detail still makes it an ineffaceable picture of war. The glory of battle has vanished; all that remains is immense, unnecessary suffering, the sacrifice of innocent, bewildered humankind for a purpose which they cannot comprehend. There are moments of panache. There are many days of pain and horror; there are incompetence, bitterness, corruption. The Emperor himself appears as the victim of circumstance. We see him at Courcelles, with his escort of Cent-Gardes; we see him again, at Bazeilles: 'He had certainly had himself made up, so as not to display, among his troops, the alarm of his wan mask, discomposed by pain . . . He had come, with the silent, mournful air of a phantom, his face touched up with rouge.'[4] The Emperor appears once more at Sedan: he is still courting death under shellfire. He re-appears, in his hired carriage, on his way to see the King of Prussia. Urged forward by the Empress-Regent, he is an expendable figure, a man who must suffer for the incompetence of the authorities, the lust of France for war, and the paramount ambition of his wife: that their son must reign, their dynasty survive. These visions of the rejected Emperor are a recurrent motif in *La Débâcle*, a repeated symbol of decline and fall; but, whatever Zola's contempt for the Second Empire, he sees the man himself as a tragic figure.

The crime which had distantly inspired *La Fortune des Rougon* had demanded expiation. The circle is now complete. But Zola does not blame the Emperor for the military defeat, or for the collapse of the régime. *La Débâcle* is a condemnation of the Empress and the Government, the Ministry of War and the High Command.

Edward Sackville-West observes that Zola's impressions of war lack the grandeur of Goya's; at best they recall the canvases of Gros and, at worst, those of Meissonier. *La Débâcle*, so he maintains, is not a great novel, but 'it is informed by a certain greatness of mind – the magnanimous integrity which made Zola the overt champion of Dreyfus'.[5] It is also informed by optimism. For all the horror Zola describes, his confidence in nature remains unshakeable, and the conclusion of *La Débâcle*, expressed by Jean Macquart, is that nature will reconcile man to man, and that life can only be good.

La Débâcle was predictably condemned by military critics in France. In a monograph, *Gloria Victis*, a captain in the army of Metz declared that Zola's book destroyed all feeling of honour and nobility.

The novel might well have been greater and more broadly realistic had Zola included more characters who were moved by patriotism. The religious element does not even exist in *La Débâcle*. But Zola has created an army which is the real hero of the novel, an army which lives and breathes and moves and is sacrificed as one. This is his achievement. Léon Daudet, son of Alphonse, assured him: '*La Débâcle* is more than a book, it is a philosophy of war.'[6] On 4 July, Verlaine wrote to him: 'I read and have just re-read *La Débâcle* . . . This is your masterpiece, and it has made me tremble and shudder with natural grief and with absolute admiration.'[7]

It was not perhaps true, as Maurice Dreyfous said, that Zola never wrote a line inspired by an interested thought. There were still times when his sales surprised him. On 8 July he assured Alfred Bruneau: 'The success of *La Débâcle* exceeds all my hopes, and I should be very happy if ever a man could be so.'[8]

He could not be happy. His domestic drama continued. Daudet suggested to Goncourt that Zola had asked a doctor for an injection to restore his sexual powers.[9] Goncourt continued to be malicious. Céard still attempted to advise both husband and wife. He was especially concerned about Alexandrine. She was thinking, seriously, of separation. On 2 August, when Mme Laborde was about to leave for Médan, Céard warned her:

To-morrow you will find a little more serenity down there. Yesterday, Monday, I went there and tried to calm things down . . . Our poor friend talked of leaving, of solitude, even of earning her living. I think that I managed to console her a little and to prevent her from deciding so quickly. But I quite see that life together is a perpetual agony and battle, and I am afraid it may be useless to try to soothe such broken hearts.[10]

Zola had sent Jeanne to Cabourg with the children. On 16 August he reminded her that he must continue to live with his wife.[11] But his heart was torn.[12]

For some years Zola had been tired of the Rougon-Macquart cycle, and he had wanted to do something different. During the 1880s and the early 1890s there was prolonged debate in France on the conflict between science and religion. It was the age of mysticism, Symbolism and anarchy, the age of social Catholicism, of neo-Christianity and a desire for social justice. When Jules Huret talked to him, Zola had declared that Naturalism must be enlarged to embrace all the confused wishes of the young. He had added: 'If I have time, I'll do what they want myself.'[13] Adolphe Retté, the poet and historian of Symbolism, recorded that Zola had asked him what he wanted to put in place of Naturalism. Retté had answered: 'We want to restore poetry to its rightful place in literature.' Zola had listened attentively. Then he had said: 'What you want to do, I shall do myself.'[14]

In 1891, while he and Alexandrine were visiting south-west France, they had found themselves, by chance, near Lourdes, and they had included it in their tour. They had spent a fortnight there, and Zola had recognised that Lourdes might inspire the sort of novel that he liked to write: a novel about a collective movement, driven by one impulse, and yet about a multitude of individuals, each with their personal burdens and needs. *Lourdes* was to satisfy the current interest in religion. It was also to be the first of his novels which was conceived as a work of propaganda.

In 1891 it had been too late to explore the theme. Zola had visited Lourdes in September, and the National Pilgrimage had taken place in August. Now, in 1892, he planned to return. On the afternoon of 18 August, fifteen trains of pilgrims left the Gare d'Orléans in Paris. That evening, Zola left for Lourdes, on the Pyrenees Express. Alexandrine was with him. They had taken rooms at the house of M. Dalavat, a clerk of the justice of the peace. Zola followed the pilgrimage so devoutly that some thought he was about to be converted.

After the pilgrims had departed, he stayed on in Lourdes, to work up the subject in detail. He had long been hostile to Catholicism. He was now predictably sceptical.

Nature often cures without medical aid [he explained to Sherard]. Certainly, many of the workings of nature are wonderful, but they are not supernatural . . .
I interviewed a number of people at Lourdes, and could not find one who would declare that he had witnessed a miracle . . .
Lourdes grew up in spite of all opposition, just as the Christian religion did, because suffering humanity, in its despair, must cling to something, must have some hope; and, on the other hand, because humanity thirsts after illusions. In a word, it is the story of the foundation of all religions.[15]

On 1 September Zola and Alexandrine left Lourdes. They travelled, unhurried, along the Côte d'Azur. For the first time since Sandrine had learned of her husband's betrayal, they found themselves on holiday together. Perhaps they had chosen to revisit the South of France in search of the sun. Perhaps they felt that its manifold associations would set their sorrow in a new perspective. It was a melancholy journey; the season was over, and the so-called winter towns were deserted. They went to Luchon, Aix itself – Plassans – and Cannes. Early that autumn, they were in Monte Carlo; and from here, on 25 September, Alexandrine wrote to her young cousin, Élina Laborde: 'I imagined that the gardens would be very beautiful, and full of flowers, but even the gardens are abandoned.'[16] From Monte Carlo Zola paid a rapid two-day visit to Genoa. It was the first time that he had been to Italy.

By mid October, after two months' absence, he was back in Paris. Once again he lost himself in work. *Lourdes* lay in the future. He wanted the 'terrible cycle' to be finished. He documented himself for *Le Docteur Pascal*.[17] On 7 December he began to write the twentieth and last of the Rougon-Macquart novels.

29

I have had only one faith, one strength, and that was work. What has sustained me has been the vast labour which I have imposed upon myself . . .

Let each of you accept his task, a task which should fill his life . . . It will make you live in health and happiness, it will free you from the torment of infinity.[1]

Zola made the confession on 18 May 1893, when he presided over the banquet of the Association générale des Étudiants. It was a poignant statement of the truth. He had not often enjoyed peace of mind, and he was increasingly disturbed by his belief in eventual annihilation.

It was not only the thought of death and infinity that disturbed him now. His domestic problems seemed insoluble. Only four days earlier, on 14 May, Goncourt had recorded:

This evening, at Daudet's, we were talking about the unhappy Mme Zola . . .

One evening, at Médan, after a violent argument between husband and wife, Mme Zola was packing her trunks and preparing to leave at once and for ever. Zola was shut up in his room, and he was letting her go. Céard happened to be at Médan ... He broke his diplomatic silence, and told Zola he was a pig and a brute if he let this woman go when she had shared the poverty of his bad years.[2]

Le Docteur Pascal was to be published in July. On 20 June Georges Charpentier and Eugène Fasquelle gave a banquet to mark the completion of the monumental work. It was held on the island in the lake in the Bois de Boulogne. Two hundred guests were invited to the *déjeuner*, which was 'abundant and delicious'.[3] Zola might attempt to diet, but no doubt he succumbed to what he happily called *la revanche du ventre*.

After the *déjeuner*, Charpentier proposed a toast to him. 'And now, my dear Zola, let me say that if this celebration is so dear to my heart, it is because it seems to me also the celebration of our friendship ... Allow me, my dear Mme Zola, to associate you with this toast: you, the courageous and devoted companion of former days – now happily distant! – of grief and poverty.'[4]

It was a bitter compliment. Earlier that month there had been yet another domestic crisis. It is difficult to judge what the 'new circumstances' might have been; but, on 5 June, Céard had written to Zola:

I have just had a visit from Madame Zola. Despite my efforts, and those of Madame Laborde, she feels that because of the new circumstances she has reached the end of her abnegation, and she is talking finally of separation.

[I was] faced with her clear and determined resolution. [I did not want her to] go to a lawyer who would have seen your misfortune only as the occasion for a sensational lawsuit. I thought of finding an intermediary who was also judicial and human, and capable ... of finding a means of conciliation ...

I thought of my good friend Jacquemaire [advocate at the Cour d'Appel] ... Would you like it if you and I went to talk to him tomorrow, Thursday, at 5 o'clock?[5]

The situation remained very grave. Alexandrine had conquered her feelings enough to attend the Rougon-Macquart banquet. Céard had felt unable to attend it.

As an old friend of the family [he explained to Mme Laborde], it would have been indispensable for me to speak ... I should of course have given the poor woman her rightful share in the present triumph, and my very compliments would only have wounded and grieved her . . .

What does the future hold for us? I cannot envisage it without sadness, for it seems to me that our poor friend's health is gravely affected.[6]

The storm passed; and, on 16 July, Céard invited himself to his usual Sunday *déjeuner* at Médan for the following day.[7] The Zolas were condemned to make one another suffer, but they could no longer be happy apart. It seems, however, that Céard broke with Zola at the end of this year, for that is when the correspondence ends.

On 14 July, some three weeks after the Rougon-Macquart banquet, Zola was promoted Officier de la Légion-d'honneur. He seemed to be accepted, now, and he was growing mellow. He wrote to Félix Albinet, who had asked him for a page on Hugo:' 'A page on Victor Hugo! A page! Good God, one would have to write a book! . . . Whatever legend says, I admired and loved Victor Hugo very much.'[8] On 7 July he paid, perhaps, a more wholehearted tribute when he spoke at the funeral of Maupassant. It was a tragic death. Maupassant was only forty-three; he had had venereal disease, and he had spent his last eighteen months in an asylum.[9] Zola had been fond of him since the days of the rue Murillo, and since the reading of 'Boule-de-Suif' he had recognised his powers. The respect had been mutual. Maupassant had asked him to speak at the inauguration of Flaubert's monument. 'I should be quite delighted,' he had written, '. . . to hear the greatest living novelist speak of one of the Revealers of the modern Novel.'[10]

On 4 July Robert Harborough Sherard, a great-grandson of Wordsworth, and the *Daily Graphic* correspondent in Paris, announced that he had been commissioned to write a life of Zola. 'I want to go off to Brittany and spend three whole months on it,' he told him. 'But before I leave I should certainly need a few minutes' conversation with you.'[11] The innocence – or impertinence – was astonishing. However, Zola answered Sherard by return of post, and offered his co-operation.

The book was published later in the year by Chatto & Windus. Sherard was, predictably, less than thorough in his

investigations. Zola's description of himself as a worthy bourgeois was, he decided, 'absolutely true'. It would be difficult to
find a more moral man in France.

Nobody ever heard the breath of a story about or against his conduct as a husband . . . Often when friends, chaffing him, have asked
him whether he has not in town some *petite amie*, he has always
answered with the greatest seriousness, and not without surprise:
'Another woman! But I am married. I live happily with my wife.
Why should I run after anybody else?'[12]

Zola had been evasive, but convincing.

On 7 July, the day of Maupassant's funeral, *Le Docteur Pascal*
had been published. 'To the memory of my mother and to my
dear wife I dedicate this novel, the summary and the conclusion of all my work.' So went the official dedication; and some
have seen it as a gesture of reparation to Alexandrine, a sign of
Zola's lasting attachment to her. On 20 June, the day of the
Rougon-Macquart banquet, Zola had inscribed another copy.

To my beloved Jeanne, – to my Clotilde, who has given me the
royal banquet of her youth and has made me, once again, thirty
years old with the gift of my Denise and my Jacques. For these dear
children I have written this book, so that one day they may know,
when they read it, how much I adored their mother, and with what
respectful affection they must later repay her for the happiness with
which she consoled me in my great griefs.[13]

In each of these dedications Zola is sincere; but Alexandrine
could hardly have borne to read *Le Docteur Pascal*. It is a passionate anthem to procreation. Here, in the Provence of his childhood, Zola describes the love that was consummated in the
rue Saint-Lazare. Doctor Pascal is Zola turned patriarch;
Clotilde, the impassioned mistress, is Jeanne.

Pascal Rougon is the brother of Eugène Rougon and Aristide
Saccard. He lives near Plassans, at La Souleiade. (Mistral used
the word *souleiade* to describe the moment when the sun emerged
from behind the clouds. Zola was no doubt conscious of the
symbolism.) Pascal has devoted his life to medicine and to the
study of the family heredity. He has adopted his niece Clotilde,
daughter of Aristide; she becomes his secretary. In the claustrophobic atmosphere of La Souleiade, uncle and niece fall violently

in love. Their love is fulfilled, but a sense of duty demands that Pascal lets his mistress go. She goes, and his health declines. On his deathbed, he learns that she is bearing their child. He adds the final touches to the genealogical tree of the Rougon-Macquart, inscribing the date of his own death. Under the name of Clotilde he writes, with confidence: 'Had a son in 1874, by her uncle Pascal.' Old Mme Rougon, Pascal's mother, burns his dossiers, and destroys the work of his life. The glory of the family has now, she feels, been saved. The conclusion of the Rougon-Macquart is not a logical result of Zola's scientific enquiry: it is a protest against the vision of life which science may give.

Le Docteur Pascal is a pretext for summarising the theories which have underlaid the Rougon-Macquart cycle; it is also a means of affirming Zola's current beliefs. Through Pascal's work, Zola restates the scientific basis of his novels. In the five generations of the Rougon-Macquart family assembled, awkwardly, in the asylum near Plassans, Pascal sees the whole unhappy line. Tante Dide, *la grande ancêtre*, is there, mad and bereft of speech; so is her great-great-grandson, who is also an inmate of the asylum. Charles, the illegitimate son of Maxime, is beautiful, haemophilic and subnormal. The line begins and ends in insanity, and the intervening generations are unsound. Antoine Macquart is so impregnated with alcohol that – in a famous and unfortunate passage – he dies of spontaneous combustion. Félicité Rougon, hard and ambitious even in her eighties, represents her dead husband. Maxime, threatened by ataxia, remains amoral in middle age.

The family has rarely known true goodness or enduring happiness. Now, in the early days of the Republic – for Zola has exceeded his time-scale – Eugène Rougon is a disheartened Deputy, still defending the discredited régime. Saccard has prudently turned Republican and become a Press magnate. Octave Mouret is already unfaithful to Denise. Serge Mouret lives on in obscurity, waiting for death. Pauline Quenu remains at Bonneville, devoting herself to Lazare's son – and Lazare, now a widower, has not married her, he has gone to seek his fortune in the New World. The good remain unhappy, and the unprincipled are still rewarded.

It is curious that the sense of sin and guilt ran strong in *La*

Curée, where the relationship was not in fact incestuous. Renée and her stepson, Maxime, were actually less immoral than Pascal and Clotilde. There is remarkably little sense of guilt in *Le Docteur Pascal*, where the love of uncle and niece is rewarded by the birth of a son. One can only explain the difference in atmosphere by events in Zola's private life. In his latest novel he forgot the implications of incest because he wrote of his love for his own Clotilde. 'Je ne suis rien, maître, si je ne suis pas tienne!' The words of Pascal's mistress were those of Jeanne.

Le Docteur Pascal is the most personal of the Rougon-Macquart novels; yet, strangely enough, it does not ring true. Clotilde is less living than Nana, Renée or Gervaise. Yet if *Le Docteur Pascal* is a literary failure, it remains an illumination of Zola's life, and of the beliefs which he had come to hold. In the debates between Pascal and Clotilde, Zola presents the contest between science and religion, between the need for knowledge and the need for faith. Religion is vanquished; but science, too, is finally defeated by life, by the overwhelming need to love and to create posterity. The son of Pascal and Clotilde gives promise of succeeding generations. 'Clotilde smiled at the child, which was still sucking, his little arm in the air, straight up, erect like a banner which was summoning life.' The brutal, tempestuous Rougon-Macquart series ends with a powerful symbol of Zola's confidence.

30

On 20 July, less than a fortnight after the publication of *Le Docteur Pascal*, Zola had announced to Van Santen Kolff:

I am leaving on my travels at the end of the month, and I shan't be back in Paris till the first days of October. The plan of *Lourdes* is more or less decided. All I have to do now is to write it. I had been held back a little because I didn't want to venture forth until I knew what *Rome* and *Paris* would be . . . All that is now elucidated, and . . . I have before me, on my desk, four years of a big new work which will interest me.[1]

He was, after all, to have no holiday during the summer of 1893. When they were about to start for Brittany, Alexandrine was once again unwell, and they decided to stay at Médan. On 29 July Zola wrote to Jeanne, who was with the children at Saint-Aubin: 'I should have liked to give you some pleasure in your youth, and not to force you to live like a recluse; I should have been so happy to be young with you, to grow young with your youth, and, instead of that, I am making you old, and making you continually sad . . . My greatest regret, in depriving myself of the sea, has been that I can't be a good papa to my dear children.'[2]

He stayed at Médan; but there remained a prospect of foreign travel. As President of the Société des Gens de Lettres, he had been invited to the annual meeting of the Institute of Journalists. It was to be held in London in September. He was considering whether or not to attend.

It was not an easy decision to make. His novels had disturbed Victorian England. In 1888 the Treasury had decided to prosecute the translator, Henry Vizetelly, and to suppress the books. The novels had been pronounced obscene, and Vizetelly had been sentenced to three months' imprisonment. Imprisonment had not changed his beliefs, and his son had taken up Zola's cause. However, 'it was as difficult to mention Zola's name in a public print in England as afterwards it became difficult to mention Oscar Wilde'.[3] Only with *La Débâcle – The Downfall –* had opinion begun to turn in his favour.

Now, in the summer of 1893, Zola invited Sherard to come and see him.

'What I want you to tell me,' he said, 'is first what is this Institute of Journalists? Has it any influence? . . . I have no wish to see London, and I have no desire to be fêted. If I consent to go, it will be with a view of advancing interest in my books in England . . . [Do you think that] it will be advisable for me to go?' I said: 'You certainly ought to go. People in England have been taught to consider you an obscene monster . . . You will be seen at this gathering by journalists from all parts of the Three Kingdoms. They will be proud and delighted to have met you, and they will make it known . . . what kind of man you are.' He said: 'Thank you; that is exactly what I wanted to be sure about. I shall accept this invitation.'[4]

He remained cautious. Early in August he wrote to Vizetelly's son: 'What is your view? Reply to me at once at Médan.'[5]

Ernest Vizetelly's answer was presumably satisfactory. Zola booked rooms at the Savoy Hotel.[6]

On 20 September he arrived in London. At Victoria Station Sir Edward Lawson, later Lord Burnham, read an address of welcome. Zola responded briefly, and drove off to the Savoy. Two days later he read a paper on anonymity to the journalists assembled in Lincoln's Inn Hall. It was, on the whole, well received.[7]

Although he was accompanied by several notable men, he soon became the centre of attention at every gathering. There was a dinner for the congress at the Crystal Palace, a reception at the Imperial Institute, and another reception, given by the Lord Mayor, at the Guildhall. 'It was strange indeed,' wrote Ernest Vizetelly, 'remembering all that had gone before, to see Zola and his wife marching in a kind of state procession, preceded by the City's trumpeters.'[8] Writing to Jeanne, Zola told her that four thousand people had applauded his entrance. Every day he sent notes to her, and told her about the receptions and banquets, even about the firework display in which his portrait appeared in lines of fire.[9]

Henry James had encountered Zola in the rue Murillo; meeting him again, he found his old opinion confirmed. He felt that nothing had happened to Zola but to write the Rougon-Macquart. Indeed, it was 'almost more as if Les Rougon-Macquart had written *him*, as he stood and sat, as he looked and spoke, as the long, concentrated, merciless effort had made and stamped and left him'.[10] Others were less critical. Vizetelly went every morning to help him with the applications for autographs and interviews. George Moore escorted him and Alexandrine to Greenwich. Andrew Chatto, Zola's English publisher, gave them 'a friendly luncheon'. Mr – afterwards Sir – Campbell Clarke acted as their cicerone at the National Gallery, and Dr Garnett showed them round the library at the British Museum. Under the guidance of George Petilleau, the French master at Charterhouse, they visited the French Club and the French Hospital. There was also

an excursion with Vizetelly and a fellow-journalist to County Council and Rowton lodging-houses, various sweaters' dens, sundry Jewish homes in Whitechapel, and Italian ones at Saffron Hill. On the whole, however, Zola was not impressed by what he saw of London poverty; he declared it to be nothing in comparison with what might be found in Paris . . .

At the National Gallery he was most interested in Turner, whom he called *la palette incarnée*, and whom he regarded as being far superior to Claude. And he greatly admired Turner's water-colour sketches in the little rooms in the basement of the building where he lingered for nearly a couple of hours. The British Museum Library also pleased him immensely, notably on account of its perfect arrangements, which were so superior, said he, to those of the Bibliothèque Nationale in Paris. However, what he admired in London most of all was the Thames, at Westminster, at Waterloo Bridge, and again at the docks and away towards Greenwich.[11]

Zola was naturally well pleased with his stay in London. The result, he said, could only be good. 'There would probably be less antagonism to his writings among English people in the future; but the point which interested him most of all was the effect which his reception might have in Paris, notably among the members of the French Academy.'[12]

PART SIX

LES TROIS VILLES
1893–1897

31

On 5 October, back at Médan, he began to write *Lourdes*. Whatever his polite attentions in London, George Moore now showed himself to be less than polite in print. During the last ten years, he said, in *The English Illustrated Magazine*, a striking resemblance had grown up between the Zola novel and a popular newspaper. Zola's true friends, his true admirers, had hoped that, with prosperity, he would widen his horizons,

that he would read and think and travel . . .; that he would cultivate that quality, which we knew was lacking in him, refinement of thought and the sentiment of literary expression. How have our hopes been justified? What bitter disappointment has not fallen upon us? What have we witnessed? The building of ridiculous towers at Médan, the purchase of hideous decorations, the arrival of translators from Paraguay, and the blowing of trumpets before the Lord Mayor of London in honour of *La Terre*, *La Débâcle*, *L'Argent*, and *Dr Pascal*. And we are menaced now by a novel on Lourdes, which is to be written in seven months, by a novel on Rome, and by another on the Russian Alliance . . .

Zola has sacrificed his genius for the sake of ephemeral conquest . . . For the sake of such conquest, I repeat, Zola has sacrificed the joy of life and the joy of art.[1]

While he was writing *Lourdes*, a young English artist came to draw his portrait. William Rothenstein found him wearing 'a kind of monk's habit, . . . and getting himself into the right frame of mind'. Goncourt had given Rothenstein an introduction. Perhaps this explained why Zola was less than cordial. 'I felt at the time,' wrote Rothenstein, 'that there was something ungenerous about Goncourt and Daudet – that they were both rather jealous, perhaps, of the phenomenal success of Zola's works.'[2] The lithograph portrait – a head of Zola, pensive and tight-lipped – appeared as the frontispiece to *Stories for Ninon*, published by Heinemann the following year.

On 21 June 1894, Zola finished *Lourdes*. On 11 August it was published in London, Paris and New York. The Americans had paid £800 for the serial rights alone. A Parisian publisher, wrote

Sherard, had recently offered Zola £20,000 for *Lourdes*, *Rome* and *Paris*, and Zola had rejected the offer.[3] The novel on the Russian Alliance was not to see the light.

In the Rougon-Macquart cycle, Zola had observed the Naturalist precept of impersonality. In Les Trois Villes he abandons his Naturalist spirit and technique. His hero – the Abbé Pierre Froment – will no longer be the creature of heredity and circumstance. He will be intelligent, determined and free, he will want to choose and act for himself.

Through Pierre Froment, Zola proposed to study the bankruptcy of faith, and then the rational philosophies which might perhaps supplant the old beliefs. *Lourdes*, *Rome* and *Paris* were to symbolise this examination of conscience, this profession of faith of the *fin de siècle*.[4] It is clear that Zola saw the social apostolate as the solution for collective faults and for individual disenchantments. Les Trois Villes were to reflect the spirit of the Third Republic, utilitarian and idealistic.

In the first of these novels, Pierre Froment accompanies Marie de Guersaint and her father to Lourdes. He is a young priest, troubled by his loss of faith. Marie is his childhood love, and, for years, she has been bedridden. He has renounced his manhood, she has never known her womanhood. Marie is cured (though perhaps by nature rather than by miracle); but the pilgrimage makes Pierre aware at last of his sexual needs.

He understood the omnipotence, the invincible will of life that must be. Love was stronger than faith, perhaps there was nothing divine but possession . . . For a moment, he was conscious of the abyss . . . He understood that, having given in to his reason, if he gave in to his flesh, he would be lost. All his pride in purity, all his strength, which he had put in his professional honesty, came back to him; and he vowed to himself again not to be a man, since he had chosen to cut himself off from the number of men.[5]

Pierre Froment is suffering from Zola's past predicament, and *Lourdes* contains a personal confession. However, since the advent of Jeanne, the birth of Denise and Jacques, Zola did not write of love and procreation with his former urgency. *Lourdes* is a verbose and lifeless novel. Yet as a documentary it has its interest. Zola records a world of commercial exploitation and religious mania. He catches the general hysteria of the place itself, he recognises the unethical behaviour of the doctors, the devotion of nuns and priests, the physical and emotional demands of the pilgrims. As for the actual pilgrimage, he sees it as a quest for the impossible.[6] One could expect no other conclusion from the author of *La Conquête de Plassans* and *La Faute de l'Abbé Mouret*.

Lourdes was duly put on the Index. 'I do not believe,' Paul Souday wrote in *L'Écho de Paris*, 'that, since *La Vie de Jésus* by Renan, any book has excited such anger in the Catholic world.'[7] The Abbé Joseph Crestey launched his *Critique d'un roman historique*. 'M. Zola,' he observed, 'did not go to Lourdes to enlighten his good faith, but to find real-life evidence to support his thesis ... Everything is denatured, presented in a false light.'[8] Four days after *Lourdes* was published, an outraged doctor presented his *Réponse complète au 'Lourdes' de M. Zola*. 'I think that your novel is nauseating,' Dr Moncoq informed the author. 'Like the harpies of the ancient poets, you soil everything you touch, and you touch everything.'[9]

Rodin disagreed. 'Let me make my humble protest and tell you how frank and impartial I find your book.'[10] On 25 August Verlaine, the poet of *Sagesse*, assured Zola: 'I find [your book] supremely interesting, both as a Catholic and as your admirer.'[11]

Whatever the fortunes of his work, Zola's private wretchedness continued. 'This sharing, this double life that I am forced to lead, is making me desperate,' he told Jeanne. 'I beg you to be good with me, and not to be cross when things don't go as I should wish them to.' In middle age he remained as romantic as he had been in his youth in Provence. He had refused to think of reality. 'I had dreamed of making everyone happy around me,' so he confessed, 'but I see quite well that that is impossible, and I am the first to be hurt.'[12] He might have reflected that Alexandrine suffered most of all.

Jeanne gave him touching love and admiration. 'I always dreamed about Prince Charming,' so she used to say. 'He came, and I loved him!'[13] She lived for him and for their children. She accepted the life of a recluse, and she saw only a few close friends. When Céard withdrew, for his peace of mind, only one friend of Zola's remained to her: Paul Alexis, the godfather of Jacques. Mme Alexis was godmother to Denise, and the Alexis daughters were the children's usual playfellows.

Denise herself was too young to be aware of the pervasive melancholy. She only recalled her father walking in the sunshine at Cheverchemont, near Médan, with a big grey parasol lined with green. In Paris, she and her mother and brother had moved to a larger apartment, at 8, rue Taitbout (later they moved to 3, rue du Havre). Zola sometimes came early, after *déjeuner*, and went out with Jeanne; sometimes they both went to fetch Denise from school. Usually he arrived at four, and the children waited eagerly for the sound of his key in the door. He had a favourite blue armchair. He used to sit there, take them on his knees, and tell them stories.[14]

Denise recorded their childhood in her biography of her father. It was recorded, too, by the camera. Zola, with his strong visual sense, had turned to photography. Since 1888 he had pursued the art – or science – with characteristic ardour. He had asked Nadar for instructions. He used five cameras, and three dark-rooms: one in Jeanne's apartment, one in the rue de Bruxelles, and one at Médan. His photographs catch the children – alert, intelligent and happy – gardening, or reading, or blowing bubbles. Denise, like her mother, has the beauty of a Greuze. Jacques looks exactly as Zola had done as a small boy in his family portrait.

32

In July 1893, Zola had written a summary sketch of *Rome*. The second volume of Les Trois Villes was to show the crumbling of the old Catholicism, the abortive attempt of neo-Catholicism to regain control of the world.

Zola's visit to Rome was intended to help his research; but, from the first, it assumed the proportions of a triumphal tour. On 30 October Henri Darcours, correspondent of *Le Matin* in

Rome, telegraphed home: 'M. Émile Zola will arrive by the
6.30 train tomorrow morning. A formal welcome has been
arranged. M. Luzzate and Comte Bertolelli, the director and
administrator of *La Tribuna*, will go to the station with the
correspondent of *Le Matin*, the Agence Havas and the *New York
Herald*.'

Next morning the reception party greeted the Zolas at the
railway station: all, that is, except the man from the *New York
Herald*. He had boarded the train at Civitavecchia so as to
question Zola before the rest. At the Grand Hotel, which Zola
had chosen for his stay, the visitors and journalists were waiting.[1]
On 10 November a Press telegram announced:

This evening, at the Hôtel de Rome, on the invitation of the Press
Association, a banquet was given in honour of M. Zola.

The room was splendidly illuminated. The table was decorated
with a profusion of flowers. A hundred places had been laid . . .

A magnificent bouquet was handed to M. Zola to be presented to
Mme Zola, who did not attend the dinner; at the same time, an
artistic goblet, containing the visiting cards of all the guests, was
presented to the French writer.

At dessert, M. Bonghi, President of the Press Association, proposed a toast to the illustrious representative of intellectual and
moral France.[2]

The title was impressive; but if Zola enquired about Naturalism – Verismo – in Italy, his journal bears no trace of his
interest. Always methodical, always in a hurry, he had planned
his schedule. He would give three days to topography, three to
the Vatican and the Pope, two to the economic and social
situation. The author of *Lourdes* was not accorded a Papal
audience, but he was received by the King of Italy, and then by
the Queen. As he left the Queen's presence he found himself
confronted by her next French visitor: the Catholic, anti-
Naturalist Ferdinand Brunetière.

On 5 December, Zola left for Florence. He went on to Venice,
where the municipality gave him a goblet in blue and gold
glass to mark his visit. On 10 December another banquet was
held in his honour. In his speech of thanks he recalled his
associations with the city:

When my father died I was seven years old, and then the links
with Italy were cut. Yet the memory of Venice has always been alive

in our family. How often my father said to my mother: 'I will take you there with the child!' Well, I am with you . . . It seems to me that I am almost with my kindred . . .

I drink to this magical city where my father was born, the city whose child I might perhaps have been.[3]

Zola's notes record that he found Venice isolated, moribund and stifling.[4]

On 15 December he returned to Paris, laden with presents for Jeanne and the children.[5]

He was a devoted father. When Denise went to school, he himself introduced her to the headmistress; when Jacques went to the Lycée Condorcet, he presented him to the principal. There was now a poignant relationship between the children and Alexandrine. She had asked to meet them, and she had grown fond of them. Once or twice a month, on Thursdays, they used to go for a walk with her and Zola. They were a little nervous of 'the lady', as they called her, although she watched them play with a kindly smile; but they were reassured by their father's presence. They were mystified because their mother was not with them, and no-one mentioned her; yet, again, they were reassured because she wore a wedding-ring engraved with the inscription: 'Hors cet annel, point n'est d'amour.' 'Outside this ring, there is no love.' The ring was a copy of St Louis' ring. It was also the same wedding-ring as Mme Charpentier wore, and – tolerant of his private life – she had lent hers to Zola, so that he could have it reproduced. Jeanne wore a necklace with seven pearls, Clotilde's necklace in *Le Docteur Pascal*. Zola had clasped it round her neck. She never took it off.

The rue de Bruxelles and Médan were sombre, full of depression and regret; Jeanne's apartment was bright, and full of happiness and serenity. Zola spoilt his children. Their every wish was granted. On anniversaries, he brought little presents out of his pockets. All the year round, he used to bring armfuls of flowers. Sometimes he astounded a flower-seller at the Gare Saint-Lazare: he bought her whole stock, and filled up his carriage with it. On New Year's Day he sent the children sweets, and put them, perhaps, in a little Chinese lacquer chest-of-drawers, or in a trinket intended for Jeanne. He loved Jeanne, Denise and Jacques with all the poetry that was in him.[6]

33

In April 1895, Zola had attended a banquet with the organic chemist Marcelin Berthelot. He had taken the occasion to acknowledge his debt to science, 'the good mother who has given me my freedom'.[1]

He was not entirely free. The author of the Rougon-Macquart still had certain inhibitions. In *Nana* he had touched on lesbianism. In *La Curée* he had suggested that Baptiste, the valet, was sexually perverted. But this was almost the only allusion in his work to male homosexuality. He could not bring himself to write about it at any length. In about 1887, a young Italian homosexual had sent him a confession: *Le Roman d'un inverti*. Zola had refused to use it. Perhaps his refusal was evidence of persistent guilt. Certainly he had been afraid of the scandal that would follow publication. He had kept the confession for some years before he gave it to Dr Saint-Paul, who (under the anagrammatic pseudonym of Dr Laupts) was studying homosexual behaviour. Zola discussed the subject with the doctor; he confessed that he disliked the sight of homosexuals, and especially physical contact with them. 'I have,' he said, 'met some of them socially, and shaking hands with them makes me feel an instinctive repulsion which I find it hard to control.' He had not forgotten the assault that had been made on him in his childhood.[2]

Robert Sherard was no doubt aware of his aversion. He had recently taken Oscar Wilde to call on him. From the first moment, Zola had shown 'his dislike for, and distrust of, Wilde'. He had shown 'all those signs of extreme nervousness which were to be observed in him when social observance was putting constraint upon him'.[3]

Zola tended to base morality on the observation of natural laws. 'What is healthy doesn't hurt him,' Dr Toulouse was to write. 'What is unnatural is, however, incomprehensible to him. It shocks him.'[4] This was indeed so. In this summer of 1895, he wrote the preface to *Tares et Poisons*, by Dr Laupts. 'An invert,' he ended, 'is a disorganiser of the family, the nation, humanity. Man and woman are here on earth only to produce children, and they are killing life when they no longer do what must be done to produce them.'[5]

As for Zola's liaison with Jeanne, it continued to be public property. On 10 November Goncourt noted sharply: 'Someone met the corpulent Zola in the Bois de Boulogne, cycling with his mistress, while his wife was travelling all alone, I don't know where.'[6] She was in fact in Italy; on 21 November Zola wrote to say that he would meet the train on her return. He had already ordered the menus for that day, and they included goose from Médan. His double life was inescapable. He needed Alexandrine just as he needed Jeanne and the children; and, refusing an invitation from Mme Henry Houssaye, he explained that his wife was coming home from Italy, and that all his evenings would be taken up in the 'slight stir' caused by her return.[7]

Goncourt remained in ignorance of Zola's complex feelings, and he continued to be malicious. Zola continued to be generous to him. Among the papers of Dumas *fils* is a letter, written this year, asking him to help organise a banquet in Goncourt's honour. 'It would be a good idea,' wrote Zola, 'to honour in him forty years of literature and labour. He has not been too favoured by success.'[8]

Late in May 1896, Goncourt sent Zola the latest volume of his *Journal*. 'What emerges from it,' Zola told him, 'and emerges with extraordinary clarity, is your sovereign passion for literature ... That is what I like in all the volumes of your *Journal*, and that is what gives it inestimable worth.'[9] It was the last letter Zola wrote to him. On 16 July Goncourt died. On 21 July, Zola delivered an oration at his funeral.

It was on 15 October that Zola addressed a letter to Édouard Toulouse. Dr Toulouse was director of the laboratory of experimental psychology at the École des Hautes Études in Paris. He was making what he pompously called a medico-psychological enquiry into intellectual superiority. For nearly a year he had been visiting Zola several times a week, to talk to him and to examine him. The novelist who believed in scientific accuracy in fiction carried his belief to the extreme. He now authorised the doctor to publish his findings.[10]

M. Zola [reported the doctor] is now 56. He is above the average height, robust and well-built. His chest is broad, his shoulders high and square, his muscles are rather voluminous, though unexercised. He has a certain *embonpoint* . . . His hair and beard were brown; they are now turning grey. There is a good deal of hair on his body, especially on his chest. His head is big, his face is large, his features rather marked. His expression is searching, gentle, and even made a little vague by short-sightedness. His whole physionomy expresses the habit of reflection and a certain emotivity.[11]

Zola, said the doctor, had inherited a nervous disposition from his mother, and his nervous troubles had become increasingly acute. A rather tight jersey might cause a painful oppressiveness in his chest. He could not even sleep in a tucked-up bed. Since he had no religion, he was a prey to morbid ideas, and among them was the idea of doubt. He was therefore in constant fear of being unable to finish a book. He never re-read his novels because he was afraid that he would make unfortunate discoveries in them.

Another of his morbid ideas is arithomania, or the need to count. M. Zola says that this is a sign of his instinct for order . . . And so he counts the gas-lamps in the street, the numbers on the doors, and especially the numbers on cabs, when he adds all the figures together . . . Some numbers seem to him to be unlucky. If the number on a cab, added up as I have mentioned, reaches this total, he doesn't take it . . . For a long time he believed in multiples of three; nowadays he is reassured by multiples of seven. And so he has often opened his eyes seven times, at night, to prove to himself that he was not dying.

Zola was afraid of the dark. Sometimes, on a train, he had been assailed by the thought of being caught in a tunnel, both ends of which collapsed. It was the kind of fear he had known when, as a boy, he had been delirious with typhoid fever; it was the fear he had conveyed in *Germinal* and in *La Bête Humaine*.

Dr Toulouse did not present an engaging portrait; nor did the *diseuse* Yvette Guilbert. She recalled Zola at the Charpentiers' in 1895 or 1896.

So that was the illustrious writer. The cold mask, the dull face, the hair brushed back, the tight, hermetic mouth, the thick glasses over the eyes: unchanging eyes which seemed without a light. A

terrible stubbornness appeared to be the characteristic feature of
Zola's face . . .

When he became my neighbour in the country, at Médan, . . . I
often had occasion to see him again on the roads, hunched up on
his bicycle, going along with the same fixed, cold glance, with the
same 'poor lawyer' look.[12]

Marie Belloc Lowndes recalled that Zola 'always looked ill and
unhappy, the expression of his face being what the French call
tourmenté'.[13]

Saint-Georges de Bouhélier called on him in 1896, and
recorded him with more sympathy. Zola's beard and pince-nez,
reflected the young Naturist poet, gave him a likeness to
Pasteur. His grave expression, his coarse grey hair, his lofty,
furrowed brow, suggested a scientist in his laboratory as much
as a man in his study.[14] Saint-Georges de Bouhélier was flat-
tered by his friendship, and by an invitation to his Thursday
evenings.[15]

It was on Thursday evenings, after dinner, that he always received his friends [Paul Brulat remembered]. He was one of those
rare men who gain by being known . . .

Émile Zola was eloquent only in intimacy . . .

But no-one, in intimacy, gave a clearer impression of his superior
nature.[16]

Zola had written the first line of *Rome* on 2 April 1895, his
fifty-fifth birthday, 'hoping that this would bring good luck to
the book'. *Rome* had been published in 1896. In this, the second
of *Les Trois Villes*, the Abbé Pierre Froment goes to the Eternal
City, taking his book on the future of Catholicism. He finds
himself confronted by an inflexible Vatican. A cardinal assures
him that Catholicism cannot change, that divine certainty,
absolute truth cannot be modified; the Pope himself condemns
the Abbé's work. Yet Pierre Froment remains convinced that
the renewal of religion lies in the search for social salvation, the
satisfaction of human charity. In a conclusion which recalls
Hugo's vision in *La Légende des siècles*, he foresees a future when
there will be no frontiers or wars. Zola goes further, and already
predicts a socialist world in which mankind will live by honest
toil and property will be fairly divided. Strongly anti-Catholic,
Rome looks back to *Lourdes* (and, indeed, to *La Conquête de*

Plassans, La Faute de l'Abbé Mouret). Strongly socialist, it recalls *Germinal*, and anticipates the theme of *Paris*. It is not only a *roman à thèse*, it is also a ridiculous and irrelevant *roman noir*; even Eugène Sue might have smiled at such Gothic melodrama as Benedetta entering the bed of the dying Dario, and herself dying in his embrace.

Lepelletier found *Rome* an amalgam of a Baedeker guide, a treatise on liberal Christianity, and a 'black' novel. Henry James dismissed it as a 'presumptuous volume, . . . superficial and violent'.[17] In March 1896, Rémy de Gourmont announced that Zola's work 'has, henceforth, all the signs of decay. It is vulgar and without style. It is an avenue de l'Opéra.'[18]

Zola was now preparing to write the last of Les Trois Villes. *Paris* was, predictably, to show the discovery of a human religion, the achievement of happiness through socialism. Zola had hardly needed to make a preliminary study. He had approached the subject as a direct observer. He had often taken Jeanne and the children on his explorations of the city. They had gone up the towers of Notre-Dame and the Trocadéro and, on the scaffolding at the Sacré-Cœur, he had discussed points with an architect, while Jeanne kept anxious watch on Denise and Jacques. Between the planks, they could see the void under their feet.[19]

The children already knew the titles of some of their father's novels, which had been pointed out in a shop window. On 15 February 1897, at the first performance of *Messidor*, at the Opéra, they first saw their father's work on stage. Not long before her death, Denise chanced to hear the music on the radio. It was during the German Occupation. Her son recalled how she sat, in silence, and tears flowed down her face.[20]

On 31 August 1897, Zola finished *Paris*; and next morning, wrote Alexandrine, 'as a treat, . . . I had to make him a good cup of chocolate, with many slices of toast and not a little butter'.[21]

PART SEVEN

THE DREYFUS AFFAIR
1894–1899

34

Late in September 1894 a document had come to light in the
offices of the French counter-espionage, then known as the
section de statistique. This undated letter, mistakenly described
as a *bordereau*, had been written by a well-informed French officer
who was prepared to sell military secrets to the Germans. On
6 October the writing was identified as that of Alfred Dreyfus,
a Jewish artillery captain who was attached that year to the
General Staff. Dreyfus was declared guilty, and sentenced to
deportation for life. On 5 January 1895, in the courtyard of the
École militaire, he was publicly degraded for high treason.
Then he was sent to Devil's Island.

Zola had been moved by the account of the degradation. He
had thought of using the scene in a novel. At the beginning of
the Affair, only the writer in him was stirred.[1] But at the time he
had been absorbed by Les Trois Villes. He had not paid much
attention when the Dreyfus family attempted to re-open the
captain's case.

Late in March 1896 Lieutenant-Colonel Picquart, the new
head of the *section de statistique*, began to make enquiries about
a Major Esterhazy, whose writing matched that on the *bordereau*. Esterhazy had frequent dealings with financial specu-
lators; he was living with a prostitute and sharing the profits
from a brothel with her. Picquart was discouraged from
pursuing his enquiries.

In 1895 *Le Figaro* had asked Zola to write a series of articles
in which he freely expressed his opinions on people and events.
These articles were later collected and published under the title
Nouvelle Campagne. The article 'Pour les Juifs' appeared on 16
May 1896, and in it Zola defended President Félix Faure
against the attacks of the anti-Semitic journalist Édouard
Drumont. Zola still believed that Dreyfus was guilty, he was not
especially pro-Semitic, but he did not tolerate intolerance.

It was in this frame of mind that he received a visit from
Bernard Lazare. Lazare – a contributor to *L'Aurore* – had published a book asserting Dreyfus' innocence, and demanding a

re-hearing of the case. He was also trying to interest celebrities in the cause. Zola was shaken by Lazare's arguments, but he was not convinced. Soon afterwards he had a conversation with the advocate Louis Leblois; from that moment he was sure of Dreyfus' innocence.

In October 1897, while Alexandrine was paying her annual visit to Italy, Zola dined with the Bruneaus. Towards the end of dinner, he said to his host: 'Do you remember that artillery captain who was condemned to deportation for life? . . . Well, *mon ami*, he is innocent. They know it, and they are leaving him on Devil's Island . . . I don't know what I shall do, but I shall certainly do something.'[2]

He was not writing a book at the time. He himself admitted that he did not know what he would have done if he had had a novel in preparation. Now the Dreyfus Affair coincided with the creed which he had recently expressed in *Paris*. It brought into question the *fin de siècle* religion of progress, justice and truth. Mr Martin Turnell maintains that Zola behaved like a Rougon with a love of power.[3] Yet one doubts whether Eugène Rougon would have risked his career to espouse Dreyfus' cause.

On 20 November Zola wrote to Scheurer-Kestner, Vice-President of the Senate, who had publicly affirmed his conviction of Dreyfus' innocence: 'No human drama has ever filled me with a more poignant emotion. It is the fight for truth, and that is the only good one, the only great one.'[4] A few days later, on 25 November, with an article in *Le Figaro*, 'Scheurer-Kestner', Zola entered the struggle. 'As you can imagine, I have been profoundly moved,' Scheurer-Kestner wrote to him. '. . . I draw new strength from your approval.'[5]

Zola still thought of the Dreyfus Affair in literary terms; he had now made 'the mental reservation of perhaps [writing] a drama'.[6] Gradually he turned from literature to action. On 30 November *Le Figaro* published facsimiles of the *bordereau* and of a letter from Major Esterhazy. These were virtual proof to every reader of the paper that there had been a miscarriage of justice; Esterhazy was protected from the law by the General Staff, but and by Saussier, the military governor of Paris. Reactionary critics declared that an international Jewish syndicate had been organised to save Captain Dreyfus, and to buy favour for

'the traitor'. In a second article, Zola refuted the legend of the
syndicate; or, rather, he insisted that a syndicate existed which
included all men of good will. In a third article he denounced
anti-Semitism. The readers of *Le Figaro* began to cancel their
subscriptions. Zola was obliged to leave the paper, and to have
recourse to brochures. *Lettre à la Jeunesse* was followed by *Lettre à
la France*. 'I shall dare to say everything,' he wrote, 'because I
have had one passion in my life, the truth.'[7]

'Rather like Tolstoy,' said Claretie, 'he wanted to put the
power of his mind at the service of the humble . . . He believed
in a duty, in his duty. He accomplished it.' Henry James touched
a more intimate truth. Zola's intervention in the Affair was,
he said, 'the act of a man with arrears of personal history to
make up, the act of a spirit . . . treating itself at last to a luxury
of experience'.[8]

Late in November Zola, Bourget and Maurice Barrès met for
déjeuner at the restaurant Durand, in the place de la Madeleine.
'One word greatly struck me,' wrote Barrès, 'coming as it did
from Zola . . .; that morning he had published an article (it
was in fact absurd) in favour of Dreyfus. And he said of his
demonstration: "It's scientific, it's scientific." . . . This was the
very word that I have heard used, so often, in the same sense, by
illiterates at public meetings.'[9]

The Dreyfus Affair was already beginning to set a strain on
friendships. On 1 December, when Barrès attended a second
déjeuner, he did so on condition that Dreyfus was not mentioned.[10]
On 7 December there was a dinner at the same restaurant.
Zola, Bourget and Barrès were present; so were Anatole France,
Coppée, Lemaître, Alphonse and Léon Daudet. Before the
evening was over, the guests had begun to discuss Captain
Dreyfus. Léon Daudet remembered: 'Immediately after the
soup, my father said: "Of course, in this affair we are going to
side with France and justice." At this declaration, Zola said
exactly the opposite . . . The atmosphere was icy, . . . the dinner
dragged on in futile and extremely sad conversation.'[11]

On 9 December, Sherard called on Daudet; he asked him
why Zola had set himself against public opinion.

He was dining here last night [Daudet replied], and seemed in a
state of the greatest irritation . . . He seems to have fancied that it

would be sufficient for him to say: 'Dreyfus is innocent!' for everybody to accept the fact. He has in the last year or two acquired a
greatly exaggerated view of his own importance . . .
    And then there is another cause. In Paris today no interest what-
ever is taken in anything but this *affaire* Dreyfus . . . Zola's feuilleton
[*Paris*], which is appearing in the *Journal*, might just as well not be
printed at all. Nobody is reading it; nobody is talking about it. That
is what Zola cannot stand.[12]

Daudet was, it seems, already alienated from Zola. Daudet had
long been gravely ill and, by a bitter chance, he died a few days
later. His funeral took place on 20 December. Sherard found
himself in the cortège behind Zola. 'He paced along, holding
one of the strings of Daudet's pall, amidst the jeers of the popu-
lace. He looked crushed, utterly dejected. I felt that he was risking his health, his reason, his very life in a matter where his
intervention was useless.'[13] Georges Gustave-Toudouze, the
son of Zola's friend, remembered that he and ten other young
men had followed Zola step by step, determined not to leave
him until he had safely returned to the rue de Bruxelles.[14]

As Daudet had noted, Zola's latest book was now being serialised in *Le Journal*. *Paris*, Zola had told Vizetelly, 'will be a
novel, full of action, on all the different "worlds" of Paris – the
political, the intellectual, the society, the working-class worlds'.[15]
He intended to paint the wretchedness of the common people,
suggest the dreams of the élites, the manifestations of anarchy,
the neo-mystical movement and socialism. It was a symbolic
city that he had to represent.
    Paris was a striking adaptation of contemporary events. One
could put a name to all seventy-five characters in the book.
Zola himself appeared in it, as he had done in *Pot-Bouille*. This
time he figured as 'a great observant writer, . . . the painter of
modern Paris'. The scientist Berthelot may be recognised in
Bertheroy, the anarchists Vaillant and Émile Henry in Salvat
and Victor Mathis, the socialist Guesde in Mège. Adrien
Hébrard, the editor of *Le Temps*, appears as Fonsègue, editor of
Le Globe, the *chansonnier* Aristide Bruant as Legras, and the journalist Drumont as Sanier. Some people wanted to see Sarcey
in 'the illustrious critic', but Sarcey vehemently refused to do
so. However, Brunetière was sure that Zola had had him in

mind, and he demolished *Paris* and reproached its author for
publishing his personal grudges.

The hostility was not surprising. In 1894 Brunetière had
been received by the Pope. Early in 1895 he had published an
article 'Après une visite au Vatican', in which he announced
that science was bankrupt, because it could not teach mankind
their origins or destiny, and because it could not found a moral
code. Brunetière had shown the need for a religion, and he
maintained that the Catholic Church was superior to the rest
because it provided discipline and authority. Zola must have
been angered by this article. *Paris* was strongly anti-Catholic.
He made it clear that Paris itself was synonymous with intellectual progress; the Sacré-Cœur symbolised superstition and
reaction.

Pierre Froment, the unbelieving priest, had gone to Lourdes
in search of miracles, and he had returned disillusioned. He had
gone to Rome, and found himself unable to accept contemporary Catholicism. Now, in Paris, disenchanted with past and
with present, he is concerned about the poor, disturbed by the
unconcern of the rich, and by the corruption of politics. Through
his brother Guillaume, a scientist, he begins to suspect the
existence of a new religion. In scientific progress there lies,
perhaps, the Utopia of the future.

Guillaume is wounded by an anarchist's bomb, and Pierre
takes in and tends his injured brother. Gradually they resume
the close relationship of childhood, and Pierre becomes one of
his brother's household. He falls in love with a new Marie, and
he is finally saved by his marriage to her and by the birth of
their child.

The Abbé Froment, like the Abbé Mouret, had been conquered by the flesh; but now the flesh was to overcome dogma
and spiritual death. Just as the Rougon-Macquart series had
ended with Clotilde breast-feeding her son, the sign of a hopeful
future, so Les Trois Villes end with Marie, wife of Pierre
Froment, showing Paris to their child, and giving him the city
to harvest. It is he who will reap truth and equity.

Paris is a laboured attempt to explain that modern religion
must be the religion of social justice. It emphasises that the
new order, the socialist future, is not to be achieved through
violence, but through persistent work and compassion. Life is

not to be dictated by Catholicism, but by acceptance of the laws of life. These simple creeds – or truisms – are presented at inordinate length, and in an inflated style. *L'Assommoir* had been a finer picture of social injustice. *La Faute de l'Abbé Mouret* had presented, with much deeper urgency, the human problem of the priest in love. The anguish of the Abbé Pierre Froment grows tedious. From the opening pages of *Lourdes* the solution had been inevitable, for his problem had been that of Zola himself. The value of *Paris* lies, in fact, in its patent autobiography, and in its extensive vision of the modern city. But a world divides this book from the Rougon-Macquart novels. It is not only that Pierre and Marie go for a bicycle ride, or that Monferrand, the Président du Conseil, talks to the Chief of Police by telephone. It is that Zola has largely lost his touch.

On 10 January 1898, Major Esterhazy appeared before a court martial; next day the military judges unanimously found him not guilty of the charges brought against him. On 12 January Saussier heard of the decision to arrest Picquart. On 13 January Scheurer-Kestner learned the effect of his support of Dreyfus, when he failed to be re-elected Vice-President of the Senate. The Dreyfus Affair might well have been silenced had Zola not already decided to rouse the public interest again.

Zola was well aware that the public did not know the whole of the Affair.[16] He saw that he must codify the fragments of truth, and set down a creed for the faithful. This would be his contribution to the cause.

He had asked to see the text of the law on the Press, which he knew that he would contravene. He knew the legal risks which he would be taking, the effect which his action would have on his career. All he wanted for himself was the Académie-Française. If he attacked the General Staff, he would destroy his remaining hopes at once, and for ever. He would also alienate his readers. He knew this, too, and he accepted it.

At first he had been indifferent to the Dreyfus Affair. Now, as Joseph Reinach remembered,

he wrote all day, without pause, in the fever of inspiration and anger; and the next day . . .; and again all the morning of the third day . . .

Towards the evening, he took his work to *L'Aurore*, and read it . . .

The editors, and a few visitors who were there, saw the drama, for the first time, in all its horror, and they burst into applause.[17]

On 13 January 1898, the paper published Zola's open letter to Félix Faure, the President of the Republic. It appeared on the front page with the banner headline: *J'accuse* . . .

Piece by piece, with the diligence which had helped him to build the Rougon-Macquart novels, Zola reconstructed the Dreyfus Affair. He presented the unstable Lieutenant-Colonel du Paty de Clam, who had determined to prove Dreyfus' guilt; he recalled how Lieutenant-Colonel Picquart, the head of the *section de statistique*, had found that Major Esterhazy was in touch with a foreign power. The *bordereau* on which Dreyfus had been condemned had been seen to be in Esterhazy's hand. The General Staff had been aware of Esterhazy's guilt, but they had demanded his acquittal, for his conviction would have meant the admission of Dreyfus' innocence. They had also encouraged a Press campaign to lead public opinion astray and to hide their own misdeeds. 'In making these accusations,' Zola ended, 'I am not unaware that I am exposing myself to articles 30 and 31 of the law on the Press of 29 July 1881. These make libel a punishable offence. I deliberately run this risk . . . What I am doing now is only a revolutionary act to hasten the explosion of truth and justice . . . I am waiting.'[18]

35

The Dreyfus Affair came at a time when France was slowly beginning to recover from the Franco-Prussian War. Despite the defeat, the army remained a symbol of national glory. To question the integrity of the General Staff was to question the honour of France; and, less than thirty years after the war, there could be no more hateful accusation than that of selling French military secrets to Germany. Anti-Semitism ran strong in France, as it does at times of insecurity, and the fact that Dreyfus was Jewish roused anti-Semitism in all its violence. Zola's open letter could not have touched a more vulnerable nation.

On 13 January 1898 three hundred thousand copies of

L'Aurore were sold. The presses had been unable to print more. The President of the Council, Jules Méline, hesitated to take legal action; but there was a stormy session in the Chamber of Deputies. Zola had the popular Press against him. His article alarmed the bourgeoisie; it stirred up the urban proletariat and the youth of the Écoles. Among his most ardent defenders was Maurice Le Blond, who published a pamphlet *Émile Zola devant les jeunes*. Le Blond was twenty-one, a friend of Saint-Georges de Bouhélier, with whom he founded the Naturist group of writers. He turned journalist at the time of the Affair. He collaborated with Georges Clemenceau on *L'Aurore*, and he became the head of his personal secretariat. He was later to be a sous-préfet.[1]

The publication of *J'accuse* . . . brought Zola fourteen thousand letters of support and congratulation. Every morning, the papers printed lists of Dreyfusards demanding a re-hearing of the case. Among them was the young André Gide, and among them, too, was Anatole France. The Affair had brought him down from his ivory tower. Pissarro reported to his son: 'Yesterday I had a card from Mirbeau, asking me to sign the protest [*sic*] with Monet, himself, and many others.'[2] On 14 January he had sent Zola a card to express his admiration 'for the nobility of your great character'.[3] Monet had deplored *L'Œuvre*, but he wrote to Zola: 'Once again I say bravo, and with all my heart, for your valour and your courage.'[4] 'I have always admired your genius,' Henri Barbusse assured him. 'Let me express this absolute admiration, and the deep and respectful sympathy which I feel for you as a man.'[5] 'I must write to you in this moment of peril,' added George Moore, crossing out the past, 'to assure you of all my sympathy and of my admiration for your courage.'[6] From Rome, on 15 January, Bjørnstjerne Bjørnson added: 'How I envy you to-day! How I should have liked to be in your place, to do such a service to my country and to humanity!'[7]

The Dreyfusards were attacked as bad Frenchmen, and derisively dismissed as 'intellectuals'. 'The list of intellectuals,' wrote Barrès, 'is mostly composed of fools.' University students were divided into two hostile factions. After the appearance of Zola's letter, families themselves were divided, and old friends ceased abruptly to see each other. The mayor of Aix-en-

Provence, where Zola had spent his childhood, chose to de-
nounce him; and many other mayors, anxious to flatter the
Government, followed his example. In Nantes, Rennes, Nancy,
Lille, Bordeaux and Angers, Zola and Dreyfus were burned in
effigy. In Paris there were public demonstrations, and posters
urging: 'Zola to the gallows! Death to the Jews!'

Some thought that Zola must be tried because he had insulted
the army; others felt that he must be tried in order that the
truth about Dreyfus should be published after a silence of four
years. Méline decided, finally, to take Zola to the Court of
Assizes, but he kept only fifteen lines of *J'accuse* . . . as a count
of indictment. He took proceedings against Zola and against
the manager of *L'Aurore* solely on the grounds of Zola's statement that Major Esterhazy had been acquitted by order. The
grounds for the prosecution were deliberately restricted so that
no-one touched the bottom of the Affair.

Zola had chosen his advocate: Fernand Labori, who had
defended the anarchist Vaillant. On 7 February 1898, his
trial opened in an atmosphere charged with hatred. After the
first day's hearing, when he left the Palais de Justice, the crowd
was so large and violent that the Prefect of Police himself was
obliged to intervene to ensure his passage.

Zola had been naturalised in 1862, as the son of a foreigner,
born in France. His mother had been French, but his father's
Italian origin was savagely brought home to him now. He was
not a true Frenchman, but a *métèque*. He was threatened with
murder, he was sent parcels of excrement. Peasants hurled
stones through his windows at Médan. Outside the Palais de
Justice, hired agitators shouted: 'Death to Zola!' Daniel
Halévy later said that the Nationalists had brought hired
assassins from Algeria. Zola was risking his life, and he knew it.
'They describe him coming out of the tribunal,' wrote Rosny,
'among the raised canes, the spitting and the jeers, an umbrella
under his arm . . . He was pale, he looked like a bourgeois who
had strayed into a savanna, but he was dignified, and, certainly,
very brave.'[8]

Except on two or three occasions when the rain fell in torrents [so
Vizetelly was to record], great precautions had to be taken for
Zola's safety . . . The carriage in which he drove to and from the
Palais de Justice was often pursued by a hostile mob, which the

police had to charge and disperse. On some occasions policemen mounted on bicycles escorted the carriage, and Zola was always accompanied by a little bodyguard of friends: M. Fasquelle, his publisher, M. Bruneau, the composer, and particularly M. Fernand Desmoulin, the accomplished engraver . . . Throughout the tumultuous period of the trial M. Desmoulin was invariably by his friend's side with a six-shooter in readiness.[9]

When Zola left the court he did not go back directly to the rue de Bruxelles. He used to visit different friends on the way, to put would-be assailants off the scent. His defenders used to draw up a plan of attack for the next day's hearing, and escort him and Alexandrine home late at night through the deserted streets.[10]

On 21 February he made his speech to the court. He insisted that Dreyfus was innocent. He had practised this final declaration with his arms held to his sides, to prevent any obvious trembling of his hands. 'If they saw me tremble,' he said, 'they would think that I was frightened.'[11] 'They may strike me here,' he ended his speech. 'One day France will thank me because I have helped to save her honour.'[12]

On 23 February he was inevitably found guilty on the charge brought against him.[13] He was given the maximum sentence: a fine of 3000 francs for libel, and a year's imprisonment. Arthur Meyer, the journalist, declared the verdict fortunate. 'One was afraid of very serious violence if the jury had acquitted M. Zola.'[14]

There were still those who gave him their moral support and expressed their admiration. 'I am ill and surrounded by invalids,' Monet wrote to him, 'and I could not attend your trial, and come and grasp your hand as I wished. None the less, I have passionately followed your trial in all its phases, and I want to tell you how much I admire your heroic conduct.' Two days later he added: 'I am among those who believe that you have just done a noble service to France . . . She will be proud one day that she gave birth to you.'[15]

François Coppée had supported Zola when he stood for the Académie; but he had been unable to support the author of *J'accuse* . . . On 2 March, in a letter to Zola, he explained himself:

I was troubled, but not at all convinced, by the approaches that were made to me about Dreyfus. Besides, I'm an old *Cocardier* [a lover of the army], and an enemy of revolutionary action. I could admire only your courage.

In defending the army, as I believed it my duty to do, I have been careful not to pronounce a word that could touch you. The friendship of your old champion at the Académie could not do more; but you see that it is intact, like my high and deep esteem for your talent and for your work as a novelist.

The affectionate inscription in your *Paris* – which I shall read with passion – proves to me that you have understood, and all that remains to us now is to grasp one another's hand – across an abyss.[16]

Zola had also sent a copy of the book to Mme Daudet. In a black-edged note she thanked him, and assured him of her 'old and faithful friendship'.[17]

Denise remembered how, after her father was sentenced to imprisonment, he had taken her and Jacques in his arms, and said: 'Be proud! I have been condemned because I wanted truth and justice.' Soon afterwards he gave them gold watches, engraved with their initials and the date: 23 February 1898.[18] He also sent a signed photograph of himself to his English publishers: a photograph which, they assured him, they 'considered as a treasure'. On 28 February, they wrote: 'We all congratulate you on the moral victory which you have won over injustice, and we express our admiration for your extremely brave and distinguished conduct, which is the admiration of the whole civilised world.'[19]

Zola had, however, appealed on legal grounds to the Cour de Cassation, which quashed his conviction and ordered a new trial. On 23 May the case re-opened: this time at the court of the Seine-et-Oise – the assize court at Versailles. The hearing was interrupted, once more on legal grounds; the Cour de Cassation rejected them, and it was decided to open the case yet again.

On 18 July, Zola and Desmoulin had *déjeuner* at the Charpentiers' in the avenue du Bois de Boulogne (now the avenue Foch). At quarter to ten, in a livery-stable brougham hired for fifty francs, they left for Versailles. After they had passed Viroflay, policemen on bicycles came out in search of them.

There were policemen on duty all along the avenue de Paris, there were sergents de ville every fifty yards. Zola and Desmoulin reached Versailles at about twenty past eleven.

The hearing was tempestuous. Labori raised a demurrer which was disallowed, and at this point Zola, his co-defendant – the manager of *L'Aurore* – and their counsel left the court, allowing judgment to go by default. The tumult in court was indescribable.

Outside, in the streets, the crowds were ready to lynch Zola. The chief of the municipal police asked for half-an-hour to organise police protection. Finally he announced that they could leave. Labori got into the brougham with Zola, and the two horses set off at full trot. As they left the palace, mounted police charged the angry crowds. Policemen on bicycles followed the brougham to keep off demonstrators. Finally they gave up their escort, and the brougham bowled on in solitude. Labori explained that they had gained a brief legal respite, but that Zola must leave France at once to avoid arrest and imprisonment. By doing so he would remain a threat to authority, free to come back when he chose and to have his revenge.

They returned to the avenue du Bois de Boulogne, where Georges and Albert Clemenceau gave Zola some final advice. It was decided that he must leave for London that evening. No doubt the decision saved him from imprisonment; it was the only means of gaining time. No-one, however, could claim that Zola went into noble exile. It was an inglorious escape from the consequences of *J'accuse* . . .

Desmoulin went to tell Alexandrine of his departure. She arrived in a state of emotion. She had not dared to pack a case, she had just brought a nightshirt and other essentials wrapped up in a newspaper. She and Zola took a cab to the Gare du Nord. Charpentier followed. He bought Zola's first-class ticket to London, and he and Alexandrine waited for the train to leave. They stood outside the carriage – the first after the engine – so that Zola could not be seen through the window. At nine o'clock, the express left for Calais.

Jeanne and the children were spending the summer, as usual, at Verneuil, near Médan. That afternoon Desmoulin had arrived with his cousin, Dr Larat. He had brought a letter from Zola. 'Chère femme, . . . I am obliged to leave for England this evening. Don't worry, wait quietly for my news. As soon as I can settle something, I shall let you know. I'm going to try to find a place where you can come and join me with the children ... Don't tell anyone in the world where I am going.'[20]

36

At half-past one next morning the Dover boat drew away from Calais. Zola remained on the bridge, watching the lights of France fade into the night.[1] Since it had been hot in Paris, he had not brought an overcoat; but he was still on the bridge as dawn was rising. As the boat came in to Dover, 'the gas-lamps in the little port were fading in the pale and growing light. I do not know a word of English,' Zola recorded. 'I am landing here, as if cut off from men, in a distant world.'[2]

It was nearly eight o'clock when he arrived in London. Clemenceau had advised him to stay at the Grosvenor Hotel, next to Victoria Station. They accepted him on payment of £1, explaining that this was the custom for travellers who came without luggage. Zola registered under the name of M. Pascal, and he was given a room on the fifth floor. The windows were barred by the openwork frieze outside the building. 'A foretaste of prison,' he noted.[3] That day he wrote to Vizetelly at Merton: 'Tell nobody in the world, and particularly no newspaper, that I am in London. And oblige me by coming to see me tomorrow, Wednesday, at the Grosvenor Hotel. You will ask for M. Pascal.'[4]

He waited impatiently for Desmoulin, who was to act as his interpreter. At seven o'clock next morning, Desmoulin arrived with Bernard Lazare. Vizetelly came at half-past twelve. They had lunch together: 'an omelette, fried soles, fillet of beef, and potatoes ... M. Desmoulin and myself ordered Sauterne and Apollinaris,' remembered Vizetelly, 'but the contents of the water bottle sufficed for M. Zola and the other gentleman.'[5] That afternoon they wandered to St James's Park; and there, as they sat beside the lake, Vizetelly produced an evening paper, and read 'an account of how M. Zola had sailed for Norway, ... and how he had been bicycling through the Oberland on

his way to some mysterious Helvetian retreat. Then we laughed,
. . . and fears were at an end.'[6]

Their fears were not yet over. The French authorities claimed
the right to serve process on French subjects throughout the
world, and it was clear that Zola must leave London as soon
as possible. 'His white billycock, his glasses, his light grey suit,
his rosette of the Legion of Honour, his many characteristic
gestures all attracted attention.'[7] That day, by chance, he had
been recognised by Mrs Percy Spalding, the wife of a director
of Chatto & Windus, as he walked in Buckingham Palace Road.
Mr Wareham, a solicitor known to Vizetelly, offered him
hospitality for a night. On the afternoon of Thursday, 21 July,
when Lazare returned to France, Vizetelly escorted Zola and
Desmoulin to Wimbledon.

Pending the arrival of Mr Wareham [Vizetelly was to remember],
we strolled hither and thither, peeped into the Free Library, and
down the Worple Road, walked up the Hill and back again, and
then along Broadway, Zola, meantime, taking stock of everybody
and everything . . .

That afternoon we all dined at Genoni's restaurant in the Hill
Road; and Mr Genoni, who speaks the French language and reads
French newspapers, speedily recognised Zola . . . [But] it was only
to me and to one other person that he spoke of what he had observed,
adding that he fully understood the position, and that we might
rely on his secrecy.[8]

Next day, 22 July, Zola took rooms at Oatlands Park Hotel,
near Weybridge. He admired the hotel in its handsome grounds,
and the English countryside.[9] When he was left to himself, his
anxieties took possession of him once again. On 26 July, the
Council of the Legion of Honour suspended him from his rank
in the Order. That day he wrote to Desmoulin, who was now
back in France:

It is ridiculous to think that I can live unknown in my present conditions, without any luggage, and not speaking the language of the
country, at the mercy of a meeting . . .

If Alexandre cannot come, will he send me a trunk at once, with
clothes and linen, but not manuscripts? He should send them to the
solicitor's address, and send the solicitor the key of the trunk in a
little box for the Customs.

I am going to be without money. Go and tell them to hurry up [at Charpentier's office] in the rue de Grenelle.[10]

'Alexandre has been much calmer these last two days,' Desmoulin reported. 'For the rest, his health is not bad, and he is still extremely brave. I go and see him every evening at six; we talk about you, and I take him news from outside. That keeps him happy for a little while . . .'[11]

The Alexandre of the letters was Alexandrine, and the Jean of other letters was Jeanne; and since the pseudonym Pascal seemed too obvious for Zola himself, he now assumed the name of M. Beauchamp. The naïve precautions continued. On 27 July he reflected: 'I have my most anxious moments in the big dining-room, because I can be recognised. They tell me that my portrait is displayed in many shop windows in London; but these English have this to be said for them: they pay no attention to anyone.'[12]

His 'exile' could have been more oppressive. In this high Victorian summer, at his comfortable hotel, he watched 'the game on the lawn, *le cricket*'; and his most serious complaint seems to have been that he disliked sash windows. Besides, he had already decided to rent a house nearby. On Monday, 1 August, he installed himself at Penn, Oatlands Chase.

Mrs Vizetelly had hired a maid, and Vizetelly's elder daughter, Violette, came to lodge with Zola so that she could be his interpreter. Even a bicycle was provided for him, and, when he was not working, he and Violette pedalled round Walton and Weybridge. Zola took a camera, and Vizetelly was to keep a collection of his photographs, 'little views of villages, commons, farms, churches, reaches of the Thames, glimpses of the Wye, Windsor Castle, the Crystal Palace, and so forth'.[13] Zola also found material for a story. He visited The Castle, a haunted house near Penn; he was told its history, transposed it into the setting of Médan, and wrote 'Angélique ou la Maison hantée'. It later appeared in his *Contes et Nouvelles*.[14] Nobody recognised him on his rambles. 'I even doubt,' wrote Vizetelly, 'if people, generally, thought him a foreigner.'[15] He had ceased to wear the rosette of the Legion of Honour – in fact he was not now entitled to wear it – and he had replaced his white billycock by an English straw hat. 'Towards the close of the fine weather he purchased a bowler, which greatly altered his appearance. Indeed, there is nothing like a bowler to make a foreigner look English.'[16]

On 1 August, Zola spent a peaceful evening at Penn. Desmoulin had already returned from Paris, bringing him a trunk of linen and personal belongings. Next day he unpacked, and found himself 'quite moved and happy at the little bit of my home it had brought me'.[17]

He organised his desk at once, and unpacked his manuscripts, but his ideas were still in disarray. 'I think I'll hover round my novel for a day or two before I begin to write it.'[18] That evening he went out: 'A wonderful night, an enormous bright full moon, all along the fine straight roads lined with venerable trees. There are endless parks, with broad lawns and deep verdures, majestic in their silence . . . Never did I have a stronger feeling of nature, opulent, mighty and serene.'[19]

On 3 August Desmoulin returned to France. He had been entrusted with a delicate mission. He had to find out if Alexandrine would come to see her husband, or if she would give place to Jeanne. Zola was loth to hurt his wife, but he longed to see his children. Alexandrine understood, and sacrificed herself. 'Your poor wife has now decided *to stay in Paris*,' Desmoulin reported in a letter dated 'Friday evening'. 'She has therefore asked me to *invite* you to have your children brought to you. She quite understands that you can't remain alone any longer.'[20] During the summer, in the stupefying heat, she chose in fact to stay at Médan, but she went to Paris three times a week for news.

Zola wanted now to go home, and to serve his year of imprisonment. 'If people think it advisable, if I should serve the cause like that,' he told Reinach, 'I am ready.'[21] But Labori insisted that he must not return until all hope of achieving justice by legal means was lost.[22]

On 13 August, Zola learned that the Court of Appeal in Paris had doubled his sentence. In *J'accuse* . . . he had attacked the three graphologists who had declared the *bordereau* to be in Dreyfus' hand. He had said that their sight and judgment were defective. They had now sued him for damages, and had had his furniture seized to ensure their payment. Fasquelle forestalled the sale. He bought Zola's work-table for 32,000 francs: the total sum that was claimed. Zola himself told Vizetelly that there were great financial demands on him, and that he had 'only a few hundred thousand francs, perhaps £12,000, put by. And more than once he had to draw on those investments'.[23]

On 11 August Jeanne and the children had arrived in England. On the 27th – perhaps because the owner wanted the house – they all left Penn, and moved, not far away, to Summerfield, a large house at Addlestone. Zola recorded 'the big garden, half abandoned to weeds, . . . the grass tennis-court, the wicker chaise-longue where I spent so many hours struggling with the *Daily Telegraph* and the *Standard*, not knowing a word of English, and trying to understand the despatches that came from France with the aid of forays into a dictionary'.[24] Charpentier arrived on a visit; and they all went to Windsor, where Denise marvelled at the deer in the Great Park, and at the flowers planted to represent the Crown of England.[25]

In October Jeanne and the children had to leave for France. Zola spent a few days with them in London. From 10 to 15 October he stayed at Bailey's Hotel in South Kensington. After they had left, he moved to The Queen's Hotel, in Church Road, Norwood.

In this unexpected setting he turned to another monumental enterprise. He intended Les Quatre Évangiles to be his philosophical testament. He also saw them as a source of his literary renewal. 'I can satisfy my lyricism,' he wrote in his *ébauche*,

throw myself into fantasy, allow myself all my leaps of imagination into dreams and aspirations. I should like a radiant optimism. This is the natural conclusion of all my work: after the long record of reality, a continuation into the future, and, in a logical way, my love of health and strength, of fruitfulness and justice, bursting out at last. And so I end the century, and enter the next century. *All this based on science*, the dream which is authorised by science. I am particularly glad to be able to abandon myself to all my lyricism and imagination.[26]

On 4 August, in the serenity of Penn, he had begun the first chapter of *Fécondité*. On 22 October Vizetelly imprudently made it clear that he was in touch with the wanted 'exile'. He announced in *The Athenæum*:

M. Zola has two books in hand; in the first place, one entitled *Fécondité*, which will be the first of a series of four novels . . . A large portion of *Fécondité* is now written . . .

With regard to L'Affaire Dreyfus, M. Zola certainly intends to write a book on it in due season, and has made many notes with that object . . . Meantime between the chapters of *Fécondité*, M. Zola has been preparing an account of his adventures, experiences, and observations in exile. This will be completely illustrated from photographs and sketches.

It was not in fact to be published. Zola never really 'felt' the subject. But he did intend to write a book when Dreyfus was finally rehabilitated. He kept a conclusion for it which seems peculiarly innocent and ironic. 'What a rôle for the French Republic, which has liberated the nations, if she teaches them justice! . . . She has been liberty itself. What a rôle to be justice, too, the initiator and the civilising influence of tomorrow!'[27]

Justice was far distant, now; the all-pervading Affair continued to occupy France. 'There's no possible doubt about it,' wrote Alexis on 30 November. 'Everyone, small and great, was more or less in an ivory tower, and now . . . you and the Affair are forcing us out of it. Such a change of habits is a little confusing.'[28]

It was in Norwood that Jean Jauèrs, the socialist politician, came to see Zola; and Zola spoke to him

with wonderful serenity about the comfort and joy which he found in work. 'Ah!' he said, '. . . what good this crisis has done me! . . . It has revealed life to me, it has shown me many problems at depths which I did not suspect. I want to give all my strength to the liberation of men . . . The time has come when it is no longer enough to dream and guess. We must know. We must specify the means of organisation and liberation . . .

'A friend has lent me Fourier, and I am dazzled by what I read. I don't know yet what will come of my researches, but I want to glorify work, and to oblige the men who profane it . . . to respect it at last.'[29]

Fasquelle had already come more than once to visit Zola; he accompanied Alexandrine when, on 30 October, she in turn arrived to see her husband. As usual, she was unwell. The climate did not suit her, and on 5 December she went home. Vizetelly recalled that, 'unless the weather was positively severe, Zola remained without a fire, simply casting little capes of his wife's over his shoulders, . . . while he sat at his window, writing for three or four hours at a stretch. Heat sapped one's energy, he said, cold spurred one on . . .' One local luxury he allowed himself. In Norwood he discovered a *pâtisserie suisse*, and he took a fancy to its 'very amusing little cakes'.[30]

Octave Mirbeau, too, had come to see him.

I should indeed have liked to stay with you longer, my dear friend [he wrote to him on his return to France]. And it was a painful impression for me when I touched French soil. One is no longer at home here, one is in some or other hostile foreign land . . .

Only recently, as I went to *L'Aurore*, along the boulevard, . . . I was booed and threatened by a group of anti-Semites. One soon won't be able to walk freely. Oh, I really envy you your retreat over there, especially now that I have seen it.[31]

Gustave Geffroy, the future biographer of Monet, also visited Zola in England. He remembered a discussion which illuminates *L'Œuvre*, a discussion about Manet, Monet, Cézanne and Impressionism.

The author of the Rougon-Macquart confessed his disappointment to me. In the work of these masters, which he did not see as a whole, he did not find the elements of composition which he affirmed were necessary to the work of art. I brought up the arguments which he had once used himself . . . He always came back to his need of composition, to his own way of constructing a book, he saw only sketches in [the work of] his old companion in art.[32]

His old companions felt strongly about him and Dreyfus. Renoir was anti-Dreyfus, and so was Cézanne. Someone spoke to Degas about Pissarro, whose painting he professed not to like. They reminded him that he had once admired him. 'Yes,' he said, 'but that was before the Affair.'[33]

Monsieur Pascal had become M. Beauchamp, M. Rogers and, now, M. Jean Richard. 'I am here, and weary of being in peace and security,' Zola told Alexis on 11 December. 'But when I express a wish to go home, our friends in Paris send me terrified letters . . . So here I am tied down for another few weeks in my cloister.'[34]

George Moore, in turn, tried to lighten the monastic seclusion. It is not clear how he learned where Zola was living, but on 15 December he wrote to him: 'You could count on my discretion, and perhaps it would not displease you to break

your silence by talking to an old friend.'[35] It did not displease
the 'exile'. In the next letter in Zola's papers, dated simply
'Tuesday', Moore continued: 'Certainly, with the greatest
pleasure ... Till Thursday.'[36] Georges Clemenceau, too,
remembered Zola. On 29 December, on the eve of a visit to
Admiral Maxse, at Dorking, he wrote to him, discreetly:

I met Madame ..., who had just left you, on a visit to Picquart.
She told me that you were determined to come back as soon as
possible. Your presence could only complicate a situation which is
already terribly complex, while your arrival after the verdict of the
Cour de cassation will completely demonstrate your triumph. Be
patient, then, for a little longer, and above all do not think that you
are absent from the fight. You would be the only one to think so.

Next week I shall probably spend a few days with some friends in
England. If you would like me to pay you a brief visit, let me know.[37]

Zola seems to have written at once. In a note dated 'London,
Friday,' Clemenceau told him: 'I got your welcome letter in
Paris this morning just as I was leaving. It will give me great
pleasure to come and have a talk. I'm going down to the country
tomorrow, and I expect to spend three or four days there. Write
and tell me how to meet you.'[38]

Throughout the winter, Zola tried to re-make his life as it was
in France; but on certain days he did not speak to anyone,
even to the servants. A mouse used to prowl round his waste-
paper basket while he was working. He missed it when it stopped
its visits. 'And to think [this to Mme Charpentier] that perhaps,
one day, I shall regret this great calm, which now makes me
fret myself away!'[39] On 6 January 1899 he reflected on events
in France, and he wrote to Reinach: 'That unhappy country is
very sick, it is showing all the signs of acute dementia. How
shall we ever restore it to health?'[40]

In February, he was more than ever weary of the slowness of
events. 'If I had to make a bold decision, in a clear-cut situation,
I should make it in two hours,' he explained to Bruneau, 'and
I should come to terms with my fate ... What is exhausting is
this ignorance of tomorrow.'[41] His courage sometimes seemed
to fail him. He begged Jeanne to bring the children again. They
spent some of their Easter holidays at The Queen's Hotel.

Zola's devotion to his second household did not lessen his affection for Alexandrine. On 14 March he asked the ever-obliging Charpentier to buy a sixty-franc basket of flowering plants. This was to be sent to her on Friday, 17 March, between three and four o'clock. Perhaps, as Professor Hemmings suggests, Zola's relationship with her had begun early in 1865. Perhaps they had first met on 17 March. It was certainly an anniversary of particular importance to them both.[42]

Zola's need of France had now become overwhelming. He was apprehensive but determined. The Cour de cassation had still not decided if the Dreyfus Case would be re-heard; but whatever they decreed, whatever prudence dictated, his 'exile' must end.[43] On 27 May he finished *Fécondité*. Soon afterwards he wrote to Labori: 'Nothing in the world would keep me here an hour longer. If they were to arrest me at the frontier, I should come back all the same.'[44]

In fact Fasquelle and his wife had come to England to fetch him home. That day, 3 June, there was a farewell dinner at The Queen's Hotel.

The Fasquelles, having been to the Oaks on the previous day, began to talk of Epsom, and the scene . . . which the famous race-course presents during Derby week. M. Zola half regretted that he had missed going. 'But I will go everywhere and see everything,' he repeated, 'the next time I come to England . . . Oh, it won't be till after the Paris Exhibition, that is certain; but I have written an oratorio for which Bruneau has written the music, and if it is sung in London, as I hope, I shall come over and spend a month going about everywhere. But of course,' he added, with a twinkle in his eyes, 'I have about two years' imprisonment to do as things stand, so I must make no positive promises.'[45]

That day, in Paris, the Cour de cassation quashed the judgement of 1894 which had condemned Captain Dreyfus, and demanded a re-hearing of the case. Next day, Sunday, 4 June, at nine o'clock in the evening, Zola left Victoria Station. The following morning he arrived in Paris.

PART EIGHT

LES QUATRE ÉVANGILES
1899-1902

37

'My good friend, I have just arrived . . . How happy I shall be to embrace you!'[1] So went Zola's telegram to Desmoulin. Labori was convalescing from typhoid fever, and he was too weak to come and greet him;[2] but Bruneau, his wife and daughter were already in the rue de Bruxelles, where an unknown admirer had strewn the pavement with roses.[3]

That day, the day of his return, Zola published an article in *L'Aurore*. 'I have,' he explained, 'only been the good citizen who resigns himself to exile, even to total disappearance, the citizen who agrees no longer to exist in order that his country may be appeased.'[4] All he wanted was to resume his place in the life of France. He waited serenely to learn the decree of the Court of Assizes at Versailles; but the sentence passed on him was now ignored. There was no arrest and no imprisonment.

On 9 June Captain Dreyfus left Devil's Island; he was brought back to France, to be judged a second time. On 4 July, in the military prison at Rennes, he first read the accounts of the Zola trial of 1898, the enquiry of the criminal chamber, and the debates at the Cour de cassation.[5] The re-hearing of his case began on 8 August. It ended on 9 September with a second condemnation. 'When the complete account is published,' wrote Zola in *L'Aurore*, 'there will be no more execrable monument to human infamy!'[6]

Once again he proclaimed his belief in the innocence of Dreyfus, and the despair into which the verdict had cast him. Writing to Reinach, he insisted: 'We must win, and win at once, before the century ends, before the world comes to our [International] Exhibition.'[7] He remained despondent; in a letter to Labori, he confessed: 'I am not at all in a state of mind to celebrate our Exhibition, to sing the glory of our *fin de siècle*.'[8] When, on 19 September, President Loubet had signed Dreyfus' pardon, Zola published another open letter in *L'Aurore*. This time it was addressed to Mme Dreyfus. 'The innocent man, twice condemned,' he assured her, 'has done more for the brotherhood of nations, the idea of solidarity and justice, than a hundred years of philosophical discussions and humanitarian theories.'

Cher maître [wrote Dreyfus himself to Zola on 30 September],
. . . My pen is powerless to express all that I feel, to tell you all the words that rise from my heart to my lips. I should like to make you understand, in conversation, the profound emotion that I felt in reading you. I felt it first when I went through your first letter, 'J'accuse . . .', that heroic deed which you performed with such tranquillity of soul, with such simplicity. When the passion of battle has died away, when history has recorded it, its grandeur will remain beyond compare . . . Ah! dear Master, if only I had a poet's pen with which to praise you, to tell you how you have warmed my heart! And, with your great voice, how many other voices have come to me, voices which are all equally dear to me, because they are the very soul of our beloved France, that land of equity and goodness which has sheltered us for so long.

It will be your eternal honour to have been able to see far above me, to have known that, above the personal question, there was one that was much higher, much nobler, a question of Justice and Humanity.[9]

Few men can have shown such greatness of heart.

It was, apparently, soon afterwards that Dreyfus spoke to Zola. The Bruneaus dined with Dreyfus and his wife at the rue de Bruxelles.

An extraordinary emotion caught hold of us [Bruneau remembered] when, all at once, the door of the salon opened . . . Through the sudden flood of our tears we saw them emerge from the shadow of the vestibule. They seemed to come, a phantasmagoric vision, from a fabled land . . . During this unforgettable and moving evening, Dreyfus told us about his stay on Devil's Island with a kind of austere detachment . . . He understood wonderfully that his 'affair' went beyond his own personality.[10]

In May 1900, the proposed law of amnesty was laid before the Senate. Zola protested against this gesture which absolved the innocent and guilty, the criminals and judges alike.

The official rehabilitation of Dreyfus was to take place on 12 July 1906. Zola was not to live to witness it.

October 1899 saw the publication of *Fécondité*. There had been some difficulty about the English version, which Vizetelly had for once felt unable to undertake. On 12 October Percy Spalding came to Paris to discuss the matter. Zola agreed to a sum of £500 for the English translation of the book (the previous year he had received £400 for the English version of *Paris*).[11]

Fécondité, as its title suggests, is an anthem in praise of fruitful love. Mathieu Froment, a son of Pierre and Marie, is profoundly in love with his wife Marianne. With Biblical fecundity, Marianne conceives and gives birth. She and Mathieu are rewarded for their twelve children. Their diamond wedding celebration is attended by 'one hundred and fifty-eight children, grandchildren and great-grandchildren, not to mention a few infants of the fourth generation'. The Froments now own the Beauchêne factory, where Mathieu had worked, and their once barren land is now fruitful through their toil.

Fécondité is the first of Les Quatre Évangiles, but it is a curious secular scripture. Malthusian theory and the question of *familles nombreuses* are openly debated. Mathieu Froment, Zola's spokesman, deplores the disastrous influence 'of a literature which professed hatred of life, a passion for nothingness ... He himself had the religion of fecundity. He remained convinced that a people who no longer believed in life were a dangerously sick people.' *Fécondité* concerns us chiefly as a statement of Zola's own preoccupations, and as a proof of his literary decline.

Zola had long emphasised the significance of names in his novels, and his choice here was naïve and inevitable. Three of the sons of Pierre Froment, Mathieu, Marc and Luc were to be accorded their Évangile. Only Zola's death prevented Jean from being the apostle of *Justice*. Yet Les Quatre Évangiles were to prove less spiritual than one might suppose. Like the Rougon-Macquart series, they concern the rise and domination of a family. As Charles Péguy rightly observed: 'Far from being a book about humanity, about solidarity, *Fécondité* is a book about the conquest of mankind by the Froments. It is, in a sense, a much more dangerous new beginning – because it appears moral – of certain Rougon-Macquart histories. This is really *La Fortune des Froment*.'[12]

Fécondité is much too long. It is the expression of a creed, too frequently repeated; and a sermon cannot inspire a work of fiction. A kind of lifeless symbolism marks all the post Rougon-Macquart novels. Les Quatre Évangiles were intended to satisfy the current need for apostolic literature. They also satisfied Zola's need to express his aspirations. 'All this is very Utopian,' he confessed to Mirbeau, 'but . . . I have been dissecting for forty years, you really must let me dream a little in my old age.'[13]

He remained a dreamer. This year, in an article 'Sur la Guerre', he wrote:

> If France wants to rediscover her rôle as a great nation in Europe, she must have the signal courage to abandon her ancient warlike ideal. She must create herself the soul of a lover of justice, and work for the emergence of the society to be . . . I should like to see her take the lead in this socialist movement, in this reorganisation of work which, in my opinion, will be the great fact of the next century.[14]

The struggles of the Dreyfus Affair, far from casting him down, had inspired Zola with new purpose. Saint-Georges de Bouhélier recalled that he exuded formidable energy. He was steadfast, proud, intransigent. 'His talk was solid and sensible, and it gave you courage. His soul was like a rock.'[15] Albert Laborde saw that Zola's natural kindness masked an inflexible determination.[16]

On his return from England he had set to work on *Travail*. The distance between *Germinal* and *Travail* is enormous. Zola's cycle of life and work had revolved from science to conscience, from natural to social history, and from observation to action. He wanted, now, to illustrate Fourier's theories of social and economic reform. Among the books he read was *Cent ans après, ou l'an 2000*: the French translation of a work by Edward Bellamy. It described a society in which industry and commerce were controlled by the state, and the principle of universal and compulsory military service was applied to civil professions. 'A vast barracks,' wrote Zola. 'Oh no, never! [This] creates a mortally uniform, regimented society . . . I must keep life, progress, freedom, all the cherished ideas which we owe to Greece and Rome, the Renaissance and the French Revolution.' He suspected Bellamy of preaching collectivism. 'There seems to be a movement towards the levelling of conditions and minds,' he continued, 'but that isn't what I want . . . The dream of collectivism, no!' Marie Belloc Lowndes recalled: 'He regarded it as certain that State socialism would be established in time all over the world. He told me he was glad he would be dead when that came to pass, as he valued freedom far above everything.'[17]

He sketched out several plans for *Travail*. At first he thought of taking a glassworks as his factory. He finally chose the steel-works at Unieux, in the Loire, which provided shells and cannon for the army. They had been founded by Jacob Holtzer, a humble wire-drawer from Alsace. One of Holtzer's daughters was the mother of Mme Ménard-Dorian, who was well known in literary circles. M. Ménard-Dorian opened the doors of the steelworks to Zola. He spent several days at Unieux and brought back a mass of technical notes.

Denise also remembered how attracted her father was by the gallery of machines in the Champ-de-Mars, during the Exhibition of 1900. She remembered, too, that one day he had shown her the belvedere near the Jardin des Plantes where, as a young man, he had lived in poverty. He had laughed as he remembered the hardships of his youth.[18] Léon Bloy recorded that Zola now earned 400,000 francs a year.[19]

On 15 March 1900 he began to write *Travail*, and on 3 December, before he had finished the novel, *L'Aurore* began to serialise it. Since the paper was then in financial trouble, he refused payment.

That month he began to collect notes for the fourth of his Évangiles. *Justice* was not to be written, but the embryonic dossier remains. It seems to have been assembled from December 1900 to April 1901. Then Zola was absorbed by *Vérité*, and he abandoned it.[20]

The newspaper cuttings suggest his current – and very modern – preoccupations: peace, arbitration, disarmament, and the reconstruction of Europe. Zola, like Victor Hugo, had a francocentric vision of the world. He saw France as 'Messiah, redeemer, queen'. In his notes he repeats the theme of his article 'Sur la Guerre': 'Let the belief in the god of slaughter and conquest crumble, let work and wealth be redistributed ... If France is truth and justice, she has only to blazon the idea, the nations will be sure to follow her, the democratic movement will be complete, and a new era will begin for the world that she has taught.'[21]

These notes reveal the general theory of *Justice*: one might almost say, again, the meaning of the sermon, for Zola seems to be preaching to himself the Crusade which he is going to narrate. To these notes one must add the first notes for Les Quatre Évangiles, which must have been written towards the end of 1897. '*Justice*,' wrote Zola, 'will give me . . . the summit, by creating humanity above the frontiers . . . The United States of Europe. The alliance of all the nations . . . And the great kiss of peace.'[22]

I really think that, for *Justice*, I shall plunge right into Utopia [he confessed to Adolphe Retté]. Yes, it will no doubt be a dream of beauty and goodness, the lyrical apotheosis of humanity marching on to more and ever more civilisation. I shall put in it all my hopes and all my optimism. In short, I shall write a great prose poem, full of light and sweetness. And then perhaps they won't accuse me any more of insulting humankind . . . After that, I shall rest. I shall have earned the right to do so, shan't I? I dream of living in the Balearic Islands . . . I shall try to forget that I was somebody . . . I shall spend my last years warming myself in the sun.[23]

38

Fécondité had been a hymn in praise of the family; *Travail* – which appeared in May 1901 – is a hymn in praise of the city of the future. Luc Froment, brother of Mathieu, finds himself in Beauclair as the strike at the local steelworks is ending. He becomes aware of the social bitterness, the dormant violence, the widespread suffering. He sees, too, that the world could be changed for the next generation. He becomes more personally involved in the social problem when he finds a young girl, Josine, cast out on the streets by her drunken lover.

If some superhuman power had made him omnipotent, he would have changed the city rotten with egoism into a happy City of solidarity, so that she might be happy there. And then he really felt that this dream within him came from far away, that he had always dreamed it, ever since he had lived in a poor neighbourhood in Paris, among the unknown heroes and the pitiful victims of work. It was like an inner anxiety about a future which he did not dare to specify, it was a mission which he felt within him.[1]

Josine is the symbolic victim of society; she is also the love that is essential for the happiness of the City that is to be. It is, ultimately, for Josine that Luc founds a workers' co-operative. Inevitably he becomes her lover. They produce a large family, and, in time, they establish a socialist Utopia. The forces of opposition have long since met their end. The Catholic priest dies in the débris of his ruined church; the bourgeois, who have been concerned only with their own prosperity, die in their blazing house.

There are moments of drama in *Travail* which might have come from a Rougon-Macquart novel; but the preaching far outweighs the action. *Travail* is only a cumbersome fictional framework for the expression of Fourier's creeds.

The whole doctrine of Fourier revealed itself [to Luc]. The stroke of genius was to use the passions of men as the very forces of life. The old, disastrous error of Catholicism came from having wanted to subdue them, from having tried to destroy the man in man . . .

And then there was the other stroke of genius, the new respect for work. Work had become the public function, the pride, the health, the happiness, the very law of life.[2]

The Revolution of 1789 had only brought the bourgeoisie to power; another hundred years had brought power to the common people. The religion of humanity might take centuries to become established, but then it would evolve continually.

Zola's vision is socialist; some might call it communist. It reflects his personal struggle to establish himself, his sympathy for the underprivileged, and his search for truth and justice. In *Travail*, as in many other works, his passion leads him astray; he sees little virtue in the upper classes of society, and he sees almost none in the bourgeoisie. Zola the Naturalist had attributed neuroses to heredity; Zola the socialist considers them to be characteristic of a bored and over-privileged caste. His idea of social justice is simply to destroy privilege. It is the idea of the parvenu, the outsider with a lifelong grievance; and it comes strangely from the man who had earned a fortune and lived in luxury. Zola – like Hugo – did not practise his creed. Zola – like Hugo – was a man of unchangeable prejudice. But, unlike Hugo, Zola was constructive. In his idea of co-operatives, of a workers' city, he looked into the twentieth century.

Jaurès considered Zola's espousal of socialism as an event of capital importance. 'The social revolution,' he declared, 'has found its poet.'[3] The Fourierists and the working men's associations organised a banquet to mark the publication of *Travail*. Zola himself did not attend. Since the Dreyfus Affair he had refused all public appearances.

On 27 July, two months after *Travail* was published, he began to write *Vérité*: the third of the Quatre Évangiles. It was, he told Retté, firmly, to be based on science. 'Yes, on science, for I still believe in science. It is science ... which will give us the morality and the aesthetic of the society which is to be. It will give us more prosperity, a broader conception of life and less hatred between men ... I am going to show that it is the very base of fruitful labour for humanity. When you have a scientific conception of the world, you are well and happy. Do you think that if I had not been imbued with this conviction I could have gone on writing in spite of the mockery, the calumnies and insults with which they pursued me?'[4]

In June 1902 Maurice Le Blond went to visit Zola in the rue de Bruxelles. Zola confessed that he was weary of his way of life. Once again he indulged in fantasy, and dreamed of living on the shores of the Mediterranean. No-one would even know his name. He would call himself Pascal or Durand. He had already imposed this sort of incognito on himself in London, and he had (so he now maintained) delighted in obscurity. His Mediterranean retreat would enable him to undertake the series of dramas which he had in mind; after nearly forty years, he was tired of writing novels.[5]

Soon after this conversation, he left for Médan.

We have been here, now, for nearly three weeks [he told Bruneau on 2 July] ... I have been working hard, but I don't expect to finish *Vérité* until about the end of the month. It is terribly long ... I am very tired, and I greatly need a little rest. I hope not to do very much in August ...

I am spending delightful afternoons in my garden, watching everything living around me. As I grow older, I feel everything departing, and I love everything with more passion.[6]

He was only sixty-two, but at times he felt a growing solitude. A year ago, on 28 July 1901, Paul Alexis had died. Zola had not been so grieved since the death of Flaubert.

Now, in the summer of 1902,

his great concern was to finish *Vérité* so that he could begin *Justice*,
the last of Les Quatre Évangiles. He told me [remembered Maurice
Le Blond] that he thought of writing a novel on Zionism. He was
excited by the theme of a new Jerusalem . . . Only, as he said, he
would have to document himself on the spot, and the sedentary
Zola was a little apprehensive at the thought of a long journey . . .

He talked a great deal about this plan. For a long time I believed
that Zionism was to be the great theme on which he would build
Justice.[7]

Albert Laborde recalled a conversation in the billiard-room at
Médan. Zola mentioned going to Jerusalem to study the place
in which Christ had lived. It was clear that the subject already
enthralled him.

In the meanwhile, he was writing *Vérité*. On 14 July Chatto
& Windus acknowledged receipt of the first four chapters,
presumably proofs or cuttings of the serial version. 'We have,'
they wrote, 'handed the printed slips you sent us to Mr Vizetelly,
he is fully alive to the importance of translating [the work]
without delay.'[8]

Zola finished *Vérité* on 7 August. The following day he told
Bruneau: 'I am expecting the Charpentiers at the beginning of
next week, and I hope to rest during their stay . . . Then, in
September, I shall think about you, I shall settle down to one of
the poems.'[9] 'Yes, of course,' answered Bruneau, 'you must rest
a little before you settle down to the poem you choose from
the three. I shall be happy to begin to set it on our return to
Paris.'[10]

Sardou ironically recorded a comment that Zola was said
to have made to Alexandrine: 'When [my novel] is finished,
I shall rest. *I shall do some theatre.*'[11] Le Blond recorded, more
precisely, that Zola meant to write a series of dramas called
La France en marche. 'I want,' so Zola wrote, himself, 'to do for
the Third Republic what I have done for the Second Empire.
[I want to write] a series of works in which people will find the
natural and social history of the age. But these works will be
dramas instead of novels . . . Each drama may be incarnated in
a type: *the Teacher, the Priest, the Magistrate, the Scholar* . . .'[12]
He had lost none of his energy. He still kept his feeling for the
monumental.

H

Fécondité had been a hymn in praise of the family; *Travail* had been an anthem in praise of the city. In *Vérité*, Zola turned to the future of the nation. He transposed the Dreyfus Affair to the world of teaching, and set it in a small provincial town.

Every figure in the Affair reappears as a character in the novel, involved in equivalent adventures; but *Vérité*, as Zola said, is 'terribly long', and it seems contrived. The characters are only symbols, the mood is theatrical, the work is clearly a *roman à thèse*. Zola had long been anti-Catholic; his antipathy had grown with the years. In *La Conquête de Plassans* he had suggested the corrupt and ruthless ambition of the priesthood; in *La Faute de l'Abbé Mouret* he had shown how Catholicism killed love and life itself, and ran contrary to natural laws. In *Paris* he had dreamed of blowing up the church of the Sacré-Cœur, the monument to religious bigotry. In *Vérité*, where the murderer is a priest and sodomite, Zola reveals the vice and violence that may be concealed beneath the cleric's robes; he shows the clergy more concerned with appearances than with the pursuit of truth or justice. He concludes that the Catholic nations are being destroyed by the Church, and that Catholic education is propagating ignorance and superstition. This ignorance is largely responsible for all moral ills.

Zola's final novel is the product of a tired intellect. As Henry James observed, he had buried the felicity of his past under a great flat leaden slab. His imagination had run dry. It had come to its end in deep desert sand.[13] But Zola ends by insisting on the need for truth; and so it is that *Vérité*, his last published work, is linked with the Rougon-Macquart, indeed with the early novellas, and that it finds a place in his career. 'No! Happiness had never lain in ignorance. It lay in knowledge, which was going to change the dreadful field of material poverty into a vast and fruitful earth.' Marc Froment is Zola himself; and in him Zola's love of truth, his belief in Fourier, his socialist vision meet at last.

August 1902 was spent, as usual, at Médan, and Zola paid frequent visits to Jeanne and the children at Verneuil.

On 20 September, Denise was thirteen. On 25 September, Jacques was eleven. Zola's troubled domestic life was now settled and complete. Yet he himself was still not entirely happy. For

many years his sleep had been disturbed. He had woken suddenly during the night, and had woken full of terror. These
crises had recently become more frequent. He always locked
his bedroom door; Saint-Georges de Bouhélier wondered if
he did so in order to forestall some unseen peril.[14] The danger
was real. Since the beginning of the Affair, Zola had known
that his life was in danger.

On 25 September, anxious about his health as ever, he told
Bruneau: 'I have had terrible toothache ... However, it is
quietening down a little; I am waiting to go to Paris to have it
attended to. We shall be there on Sunday evening. I believe my
wife will be leaving for Italy on Friday 3 or Saturday 4
October.'[15] Jerusalem lay in the more distant future. He had
hoped, himself, this autumn, to go to Greece. Georges Gustave-
Toudouze was now at the École Française Archéologique in
Athens; he had expected him late in September. At the last
moment Zola postponed his departure for a few weeks.[16] He
had work to do for Bruneau, and he wanted to begin *Justice*.

On 27 September [remembered Denise], he came to embrace us
at Verneuil, we were all to return to Paris next day. I do not remember now why we did not go back with him, as usual, up to a hundred yards of his house, through those village streets where, so often,
during the Affair, people had thrown buckets of dishwater on the
wheels of our bicycles as we passed. We stayed in front of the carriage
gate. We watched him go away and turn round towards us, one
last time, before he disappeared at the street corner.[17]

Next day, 28 September, it was still fine at Médan; but Zola
and Alexandrine returned to the rue de Bruxelles. In Paris it
was cold, and a wind was blowing; and soon the rain fell.
Zola asked for a fire to be lit in their bedroom. Jules Delahaye,
the valet, saw that the fire would not catch alight; he lowered
the trapdoor in the stove and opened the bedroom window. He
later came to look at the fire, and found that it was burning.
He raised the trapdoor and then, as usual, he shut the window.
At nine o'clock that evening, as soon as they had dined, Zola
and Alexandrine went to bed.

At about three in the morning, Alexandrine felt violently
sick, and for a few minutes she left the room. Zola complained
of a headache; he, too, felt nauseated, almost suffocated. His

extraordinary sense of smell had deserted him. He dismissed their ailments as some passing gastric disorder, and he refused to wake a servant in the small hours. He got up to open the window, and to escape the discomfort which had now begun to overpower him. Then he collapsed. Alexandrine opened her eyes to see him on the floor; but her vision was confused, and she became unconscious. Next morning, when the servants called them, there was no answer. A locksmith forced the door. They found Alexandrine still in bed, in a critical condition. Zola lay at the foot of the bed. He was asphyxiated, but not yet dead.[18]

Alexandrine was taken to a clinic at Neuilly, where she recovered consciousness some hours later. Albert Laborde arrived at the rue de Bruxelles between half-past nine and ten. Zola lay on a couch in the bedroom. Doctors and friends were attempting artificial respiration, but their faces showed increasing despair. At about ten o'clock, Zola died.[19]

Antoine heard the garbled news from a scene-shifter at the theatre. He hurried to the rue de Bruxelles. Charpentier, overwhelmed with grief, confirmed the facts to him.[20] At about two o'clock that afternoon, Fasquelle and Desmoulin arrived, unexpectedly, at the rue du Havre. 'Oh, my mother's cry!' recalled Denise. 'She understood everything, but she imagined that someone had killed Zola!'[21]

That evening the news began to spread through Paris. There was a feeling of incredulity. There was a mean absurdity about the death which was an insult to the man himself.[22] 'What Zola was, above all,' wrote Reinach, 'was a force. The dominant quality of his vast work . . . is force. When he enters public life, it is like a force, an unleashed force which shakes everything in its passing. And this force lay there, for want of a pane of glass smashed in time, a window through which life would have returned.'[23]

There was an immediate investigation into the cause of Zola's death. The police forbade the use of the chimneys and the heating apparatus. They left some animals in the bedroom to test the atmosphere. The animals survived, and the commission of enquiry concluded that Zola's death had been accidental.

Maurice Le Blond accepted the conclusion as 'irrefutable'.[24]

In 1953, in *Libération*, Jean Bedel discussed the evidence. He decided that only one theory could explain why on one day the chimney had given out a lethal amount of carbon dioxide, and on the next the animals had survived. The chimney must have been blocked on the day of Zola's return, and unblocked on the following morning. Bedel's enquiry prompted a reader of *Libération*, a Monsieur Hacquin, to state his conviction that Zola had been murdered. Before the First World War, M. Hacquin had come to know a chimney-sweeping contractor. In 1927, the man – now dead – had confessed to him: 'Zola was deliberately asphyxiated. It was we who stopped up the chimney in his apartment . . . They were repairing the roof and chimneys of a neighbouring house. We took advantage of the constant coming and going in this building to mark out Zola's chimney, and block it up. We unblocked it very early on the following morning. No-one saw us.'[25]

It would have been quite possible to mark out Zola's chimney, but – unless the contractors knew the interior of the *hôtel* – they could hardly have been aware that it led to his bedroom. There seems an element of chance in the affair. Yet Zola's son found Bedel's hypothesis 'extremely probable'. The theory of suicide had, he said, been suggested by his father's enemies. Some people even said that Zola had been poisoned by Alexandrine. Zola's friends had accepted the verdict of accidental death, and they had not sought to go further. But even if this verdict could not be corroborated, the Government had been grateful to accept it. If it had been possible to prove that Zola was murdered, the passions roused by the Dreyfus Affair would have been revived. Indeed, the examining magistrate might well have been requested not to pursue his enquiries. Jacques concluded that 'the theory of political murder holds better than the official theory of accidental asphyxiation'.[26] With Zola's son, with Jean Bedel and Armand Lanoux, one must accept at least the possibility of murder. It had been Jeanne Rozerot's first instinct when she had learned of Zola's death.

The Bruneaus were spending the summer of 1902 in Brittany. On 29 September they received a telegram: 'Terrible tragedy. Émile dead, Alexandrine saved. Desmoulin.' They left that night for Paris, and next morning, on their arrival, they went at once to the rue de Bruxelles.[27] They were followed by Jules Claretie and the Mirbeaus.

A servant in livery received us, took us to the salon [Claretie recorded] ... Round a long table, under the portraits of Zola and Mme Zola, in front of the bronze bust which was already decorated with flowers, the table had been laid, and ten or so friends were having *déjeuner*; there were Bruneau, and Desmoulin, the engraver; doctors in white hospital coats and caps, Dr Laborde and Dr Larat. Only one woman, hatless, in a woollen dress: Mme Charpentier,with Charpentier, very red-faced ... 'Can you imagine it?' repeated Mme Charpentier. 'They only had to open the windows! And they didn't do it! It's too absurd!'[28]

The autopsy had shown that Zola's organs were sound; he might have lived to a venerable age.

Bruneau and Desmoulin organised the vigil. They were joined in turn by Georges Charpentier, Eugène Fasquelle, Frantz Jourdain, Dr Larat, Théodore Duret, Octave Mirbeau, Picquart, Maurice Le Blond, Saint-Georges de Bouhélier and Paul Brulat.[29] Alfred Dreyfus went every morning to meditate by the deathbed of the man he had much loved.[30] Zola's face had been made up by the embalmers. Under the electric lights, he looked like a saint of the Byzantine School.

The cold had become acute [Bruneau remembered], and, as the Prefecture of Police forbade the use of the heating apparatus and the chimneys, ... we assembled in the salon, wrapped in thick blankets, with our feet on hot-water bottles, while Zola lay in the study, the door of which remained open. Towards midnight, the sounds of the city gradually died away, and silence reigned outside: a heavy, respectful and solemn silence. But, at dawn, Paris ... slowly awoke, and soon we heard the strong breathing, the enormous clamour of the Paris which Zola had sung so splendidly, the Paris he would never see again. Never did the contrast between life and death appear to me so striking and so moving.[31]

I kept watch, for a whole night, over the mortal remains of Émile Zola [Paul Brulat recalled]. No dead man had seemed to me so full of serenity. His countenance bore no trace of anxiety or suffering ... He seemed already to have reached the city of happiness and brotherly peace which, in his lifetime, he had glimpsed in the distance of his dreams.[32]

Zola's children were allowed to see him for the last time. Denise remembered that he looked as if he were serene about the vast labour that he had accomplished.[33] 'You have heard of Zola's death,' wrote Pissarro to his son. 'It is a great loss for France . . . I don't think I'll be able to go to the funeral; at my age [he was seventy-two] I shan't dare to follow the hearse.'[34] Cézanne learned from his gardener of Zola's brutal death. He shut himself up in his studio all day, alone with grief.[35]

Zola had been a free-thinker, a lifelong anti-clerical, and there was to be no religious service. On 4–5 October, the night before the funeral, Alexandrine kept watch by her husband's body. With her were Mme Laborde, Octave Mirbeau and Alfred Bruneau; and with her, too, at his own request, was Alfred Dreyfus. Alexandrine was too ill to go to the Cimetière Montmartre. Mme Laborde and her daughter stayed with her in the rue de Bruxelles. Lost in the crowd outside, Jeanne, Denise and Jacques saw Zola's coffin being borne away.[36]

Since he had been an officer of the Légion-d'honneur, a company of the 28th regiment of the line, commanded by Captain Ollivier, paid him final honours as the coffin left the rue de Bruxelles. The military honours caused general surprise, for, at the time of the Affair, Zola had been suspended from the Order; he had refused to have his name restored.[37]

Since it was Sunday, all Paris was free to attend his funeral. Édouard Rod remembered: 'He was carried to his last resting-place followed by an excited mob, guarded by an army, through streets lined with the whole force of the police . . . In front the funeral cars were hung with wreaths from all the corners of the earth; behind [came] a mixed troop of friends, reporters, colleagues and curiosity-mongers; workmen's deputations were brandishing their red-ribboned wreaths like banners.'[38] 'We considered Émile Zola as one of ourselves,' explained a young working man, Léon Jouhaux. '. . . This feeling was almost general among working men; and many of them, some of them come from distant provinces, attended his funeral . . . I therefore found quite natural the presence, in working clothes, of the miner from Denain and the blacksmith who came with him.'[39]

At the Cimetière Montmartre, Chaumié, the Minister of Public Instruction, represented the Government, and spoke beside the grave. Anatole France delivered an oration. 'In the crowd, near me,' recalled Antoine, 'Dreyfus stood motionless, with that impassible face which has always surprised his warmest partisans.'[40] He looked impassible, but he recorded his 'indescribable grief', his 'irreparable loss'; he also recorded his emotion at the words of Anatole France.

Let us not pity [Émile Zola] because he endured and suffered. Let us envy him. Raised up on the most stupendous accumulation of insults which stupidity, ignorance and spite have ever erected, his glory has reached an unattainable height.

Let us envy him: he honoured his country and the world by a vast work and a great deed. Let us envy him, his destiny and heart gave him the noblest fate. He was, for a moment, the conscience of man.[41]

When Captain Ollivier had saluted Zola's coffin, he was struck in the face by a fellow-officer. For some, the moment of conscience had still not come.

POSTSCRIPT

POSTSCRIPT

Vérité was published in February 1903, with a black-edged cover. Maurice Le Blond founded an annual pilgrimage to Médan – a pilgrimage which some called le Saint-Zola. On 29 September, the first anniversary of his death, a multitude of friends and admirers went to pay homage to him. Alexandrine received them, with Denise and Jacques. She felt increasing affection for 'her two children', as she called them; and Pierre Paraf, a schoolfriend of Jacques, sometimes met 'the great lady whom they called Bonne Amie'.[1] She fulfilled her husband's wish, and authorised Denise and Jacques to adopt the surname Émile-Zola. She watched devotedly over their upbringing and their education, and she became reconciled with Jeanne.[2]

In March 1903, Alexandrine had sanctioned a sale of Zola's possessions;[3] and in time she moved from the rue de Bruxelles to 62, rue de Rome, where she held a literary *salon*.[4] In the spring of 1904 she made a pilgrimage to the scene of Zola's childhood, the birthplace of his Rougon-Macquart. 'Your nice postcard . . . reached us yesterday while Denise was with us,' Bruneau told her on 5 April. '. . . [Denise] filled our apartment with that familiar gaiety of hers, mingled with sadness . . . It makes us love her so much, as you know . . . We are following you from place to place in Aix, that city where at every step you find such living memories of the man we mourn.'[5]

In the summer of 1905 Alexandrine had all the contents and livestock of Médan sold by auction. She gave the property itself to l'Assistance publique, and on 1 October 1907 la Fondation Zola was inaugurated. The rooms where Goncourt had lamented the absence of children were now turned into wards where nurses attended ailing foster-children from Paris. The memory of Zola was also kept alive by the foundation of the Association Émile Zola. Alexandrine drew up the 'charter' in her own hand.[6]

On 12 July 1906, the Cour de cassation had finally acknowleged Alfred Dreyfus' innocence, and Dreyfus – promoted major – was reinstated in the army. It was Zola's posthumous triumph.

Next day a Deputy suggested in the Chamber that Zola should be reburied in the Panthéon. The honour was intended for the citizen, rather than the novelist, and the motion was carried, without debate, by a majority of nearly two to one. It was supported in the Senate by Georges Clemenceau, now President of the Council of Ministers; and, though it was contested by several centre and right-wing Senators, it was adopted on 11 December. Next day Alexandrine wrote to an unidentified correspondent: 'Yes, I am proud and happy, and I fully appreciate the great tribute which they have paid to my husband. He well deserved it, whatever those gentlemen in the Senate say . . . Clemenceau truly earned my deep gratitude yesterday, because one really has to admit that this vote would not have happened without him. And I, too, am making a great sacrifice for my friends, for France, in separating from my dear beloved. If the vote had not happened yesterday, I was going to write to the Senate, and send them my irrevocable refusal, because I was so indignant at their tergiversations . . .'[7] The proposal to rebury Zola in the Panthéon became law on 15 December. The Government asked for a credit of 35,000 francs to cover the cost of the ceremony. Maurice Barrès, now a Deputy, remained antagonistic. In March 1908, when the Chamber debated the proposal, he observed: 'We shall never have a better occasion to economise.'[8]

It was finally arranged that the reburial should take place on 5 June 1908. A police officer predicted that the day would not pass without pistol shots.[9] The authorities were indeed afraid of hostile demonstrations. On the evening before the ceremony, the gates of the Cimetière Montmartre were locked against demonstrators and sightseers, and Zola's friends kept vigil as the gravediggers opened his tomb. The coffin was taken to the Panthéon after dark, through deserted streets. Desmoulin, Fasquelle and Bruneau escorted it. There had been threats that the hearse would be overturned into the Seine. The threats proved empty, but demonstrators shouted insults as the coffin was borne up the steps of the Panthéon. The demonstrations continued all night.[10]

Next day, a formidable number of policemen held the crowds in check. The President of the Republic, Armand Fallières, attended the ceremony; so did Clemenceau. Alexandrine came with Jeanne, Denise and Jacques, the Bruneaus and the Fasquelles. With her, too, against her advice, was Dreyfus. Gaston Doumergue, the Minister of Public Instruction, one day to be President of the Republic, read the customary panegyric, and he spoke of Zola's intervention in the Affair. He recalled how,

suddenly, this solitary, this timid man, had abandoned his ivory tower, his books and his work, to throw himself into party politics, into the midst of that crowd of which he had a sort of instinctive apprehension: not to flatter it, not to pay it homage, certainly not to serve its passions and associate himself with its movements, but to clash with it, resist it, oppose his effort and his breast to its insults, its violence and its blows.[11]

That violence had not died away. Now, in the Panthéon, in the presence of the Head of State, while a detachment of Gardes républicains mounted guard over Zola's coffin, a Nationalist fanatic made an attempt on Dreyfus' life. Dreyfus was only slightly wounded, but the ceremony was marred by a moment of horror and anguish.

Then Zola's intimates went down into the vault where, opposite Victor Hugo, a stone sarcophagus awaited him.

Four months later, on 14 October, with 'unconcealed delight',[12] Alexandrine attended the wedding of Denise and Maurice Le Blond, the young man of letters whom she had met at Médan and in the rue de Rome. It was a perfect literary marriage. Denise wrote a life of her father. She contributed a biographical sketch as a preface to a volume of his œuvres complètes. These were edited by her husband. They filled fifty volumes, and it was calculated that they contained more than forty million words.

On 22 May 1914, Jeanne Rozerot died after an operation in a nursing home in the rue de la Chaise. She was forty-six. She had asked to keep the necklace with the seven pearls which Zola had given her, and she was buried, wearing it, in her native Rouvres-sous-Meilly.[13] 'The death of the children's mother,' wrote Alexandrine, '. . . shook me profoundly, because of the great grief which they felt.'[14] She made Denise and Jacques her sole heirs.

Jacques married in 1917. Alexandrine lived on in the rue de
Rome. In her second-floor apartment she reconstructed the
study in the rue de Bruxelles. The portraits by Manet (which
she was to leave to the Louvre), the table, inkstand, pen and
paperknife, the tall old silver lamp were found in their customary places. Friends gathered there on Thursday evenings, as
they had done in the rue de Bruxelles. Michel Robida, as a
child, was oppressed by the profusion of knick-knacks, the
suffocating darkness everywhere.[15] Alexandrine gave the
manuscripts of Les Trois Villes to the Bibliothèque Méjanes,
at Aix-en-Provence. She gave most of the manuscripts and
dossiers for the Rougon-Macquart novels to the Bibliothèque
Nationale. (The manuscript of *Nana* found its way to the
J. Pierpont Morgan Library, and some of the material for
Le Docteur Pascal is now in the Bibliothèque Bodmer, in Geneva.)
Alexandrine also presented her husband's correspondence to
the Bibliothèque Nationale, but she apparently removed everything that related to Jeanne. She lived long enough to see a
plaque unveiled at 10 *bis*, rue Saint-Joseph, to commemorate
Zola's birthplace. She saw the inauguration of his monument.
This was unveiled at the corner of the avenue Émile-Zola on
15 June 1924.[16] (In 1942 it was melted down by order of the
Vichy Government.)

Alexandrine died on 26 April 1925. She was eighty-six. She
was buried in Zola's former grave at the Cimetière Montmartre.[17] Dreyfus died on 12 July 1935: twenty-nine years to
the day after his innocence had been acknowledged.

40

Novels demand the study of human nature, and Zola had a
remarkably limited knowledge of life. He had had an obscure
provincial childhood, a youth of bitter hardship, and a marriage
which had brought him years of cloistered domesticity. His
circle of friends was restricted, he rarely left Médan unless his
literary work demanded it. Few men of letters in his day took
less advantage of the cultural and social life of Paris. It was
not surprising that he chose to write almost entirely about the

bourgeoisie and the working class; it was not surprising that his characters often had no spiritual existence.

Zola depended too heavily on documents when he created them; he also depended too much on theories which he felt obliged to make them prove. But human beings cannot be mathematically explained, they do not always behave in a rational manner. They may act on impulse, on a sudden inexplicable whim. They are influenced for good by religion (a fact which Zola did not recognise); they are stirred by patriotism (a fact which he hardly considered even in *La Débâcle*). They are moved by altruism, and by affection. When they make love, they are not moved exclusively by lust; they can be happy without being euphoric. Zola's characters do not seem to experience average sensations; they too often feel emotional extremes. They are unsubtle, they do not mature. One cannot often imagine them existing beyond the confines of their particular novels. They exist to serve a purpose. This is clear in the early novels, and in the Rougon-Macquart cycle, and it is even clearer in Zola's later work. It is a serious criticism of any novelist that he should create so many characters, and that so few of them should be convincing.

There are, as we have seen, some memorable exceptions: Renée, Gervaise, Nana, Pauline Quenu. These are three-dimensional figures, they dominate their respective novels, and they continue to exist outside them. There are flashes of life, too, in Eugène Rougon, and in the later Octave Mouret; both of them largely reflect their creator.

We come here to a point which can hardly be over-emphasised. Zola's early books had been relatively impersonal. The Rougon-Macquart cycle, the *massif central* of his achievement, was – as he himself confessed – a *déversoir* for his own deeper feelings. Sometimes deliberately, sometimes unconsciously, the novels reflected his personal ambitions and regrets, his resentments and his longings, over a quarter of a century.

Zola patently resented the premature death of his father, which had darkened so much of his life. There is no satisfactory father in the early works or even in the Rougon-Macquart cycle. Rougon, the husband of Tante Dide, dies soon after the birth of his son; Macquart is an alcoholic vagabond. Pierre Rougon is solely concerned with his own ambitions, Saccard

sends his daughter away, and sets a poor example to his son.
Lantier deserts Gervaise and their offspring. Hélène Grandjean's husband dies before the opening of *Une Page d'Amour*.
Fathers are absent, cruel or indifferent. They bring no security
or happiness. Nor do their wives and mistresses show genuine
concern for their young. Madeleine Férat takes little interest
in her daughter; and the child dies when Madeleine surrenders
to her lover, just as Jeanne dies when Hélène surrenders to
Henri. Gervaise, perhaps, is the mother who shows most
affection for her children; but Nana neglects her son, and
Mme Josserand is ambitious rather than understanding.
Jacques, the deformed child of Christine and Claude, is given no
parental love. In Zola's early novels, and in the Rougon-
Macquart cycle, children are ignored and victimised.

Zola's novels reflect his disappointment in his father, his
need and perhaps resentment of his mother, his endless bitterness about his early years. They reflect the child who had been
aware of poverty and the social stigma it brought with it; they
reflect a man who still remembered the misery and frustration
of the declassed. They recall the unhappiness and insecurity of
the provincial in Paris. Zola's novels remind us of the assertive
opportunist, determined to overcome his weaknesses, determined to impress himself on a hostile world by virtue of his
labour and his talent. Above all, they reveal the unhappy
husband of Alexandrine: a man who longed for love and for
posterity. The Rougon-Macquart novels show not only that
disturbing family, but the heart and soul, the spiritual progress
of their author.

Havelock Ellis recognised that Zola's outlook had been
conditioned by his adolescence. 'His soul seems to have been
starved at the centre, and to have encamped at the sensory
periphery. He never tasted deep of life . . . Zola's literary methods are those of the *parvenu* who has tried to thrust himself in
from outside, who has never been seated at the table of life,
who has never really lived.'[1]

When these comments were first published in 1898, they
were already, in one respect, untrue. Zola was then the lover
of Jeanne, and the father of two children. He was no longer
starved at the centre. But he had also died as a novelist. For if
some authors must store up emotional experience, others need

to sublimate desires. Zola's love-affair had brought the end of his creative literary powers. Claude Roy maintains, no doubt correctly, that it was Freud who offered the key to the Rougon-Macquart. It was not, as Zola had believed, the theory of heredity, but sublimation; Zola had rediscovered life because he had refused it, and this life of art deserted him when real life took hold of him.[2] For Zola, the appearance of Jeanne also coincided with the decline of Naturalism. It catalysed the romanticism which he always struggled to repress. After the Rougon-Macquart he had fallen into literary decline. The later novels, like the early works, are interesting only because they were written by the author of *Nana* and *Germinal*.

Nana had shown the demi-monde of the Second Empire; *Germinal* had presented a mining community. One of Zola's best claims to remembrance is his unequalled portrayal of groups and institutions, his understanding of mass psychology. No-one else has the same skill in describing a crowd and the people who compose it; no-one else understands, like Zola, how to marshal masses of human beings and yet remain concerned with the individual.

> He is [wrote Paul Brulat] the psychologist of the multitudes . . . His characters are not at all exceptional beings, they are general types, incarnating collectivities, the miseries, the state of mind and soul of a whole category of individuals, of a whole social class. It is there that Zola's work, rough as the breath, the smell exhaled from the crowds, is a formidable democratic epic.[3]

This opinion was shared by Paul Bourget. 'One has only to open one's eyes to see the functioning of the great social organisms which absorb man and make him into one of their cells. It is Zola's great merit that he showed this social fact and showed it with extreme power in his novels.'[4]

Unanimism was an art form concerned with collective life, the life of a group. Forty years before Jules Romains had established the formula, Zola had applied the theories in *Le Ventre de Paris*. Unanimism must count Zola among its ancestors. Georges Chennevière asserted that, with the aid of Zola's novels, one could formulate a theoretical psychology of crowds. Zola, he wrote, 'is the first in a literature which is beginning; he has seen and understood modern life. He has seen and understood groups from the smallest gathering to the huge crowd. He has seen cities; he has seen the modifications which are made to individual sensibility by collective life. . . . It has been said of Loti that the sea moved between all the lines of his novels. With Zola it was the crowd, "like the sea".'[5] The real proletariat of the towns and the countryside had made its first appearance in Zola's novels; and while the novel had once revolved round individual people, it now embraced collective characters seen from the outside. It is true that the interior richness of human beings lost by the change; but poetry gained by it.

'I am never tired of learning facts.'[6] So Zola had confessed. He had made facts the stuff of his fiction; and Georges Lote predicted in 1918 that, when political hatreds had died away, and Zola had found his true place in French literature, the Rougon-Macquart would still keep 'the echo of spent passions and the memory of a forgotten reign'.[7]

The reign was hardly to be forgotten; but one must repeat that Zola's mirror had always been the mirror of his own temperament. What captivates us in the Rougon-Macquart is not simply the documentation of social 'climate' and individual behaviour during the Second Empire; it is a vision of man, a powerful sense of Nature in opposition to Society. The Rougon-Macquart world is indeed a world of its own: an independent creation. 'Such is the alchemy,' wrote Robert Margerit. 'From the real which serves him as his material, Zola draws the quintessence, that is to say the elements of poetry, . . . and his lyricism, his visionary imagination push this creation to the point where, in a personage, it becomes the man, and in a life it incarnates all life.'[8] Zola, decided Guy Robert, was not a great creator of souls. The processes of his powerful art often remained elementary. But his work 'moves in turn on the level of realism and on that of poetic vision, it expresses, simultaneously, demands of a logical, a lyrical and an epic order. It imposes the presence of a singular world, which bears the marks of its creator'.[9]

The Rougon-Macquart cycle is more than a record of a Second Empire family, more than a microcosm of French life. It breaks the framework and definitions originally imposed. As the series continues, the themes become grander, the figures grow symbolic, and we recognise the underlying struggle between good and evil, light and darkness, life and death. *La Faute de l'Abbé Mouret* is a hymn to nature and to creation. *Au Bonheur des Dames* asserts the author's buoyant belief in progress. *Germinal* offers the hope of social justice. Even *La Débâcle* concludes with an affirmation that France must be reborn. *Le Docteur Pascal* ends with a portent of Zola's faith in the future.

> We are accused of not believing [he had once explained]. I should like to rise and proclaim my faith.
> I believe in my century . . . Only the believers are strong. Whoever does not believe in his time, in politics or in literature, falls into error and powerlessness . . .
> I believe in science, because it is the tool of the century, because it brings the only solid formula for the politics and literature of tomorrow . . .
> I believe in the day which is passing, and I believe in tomorrow, . . . having put my passion in the forces of life.[10]

In an article on Taine, Zola had confessed: 'In every historian, every philosopher, . . . there is a man, a temperament made of mind and flesh, which sees the philosophical truths and the historical facts in its fashion . . . We feel the need of truth and, as we do not find the whole truth anywhere, we compose one for our especial use.'[11] Taine's theory had seemed to him the basis for a new kind of novel. It did in fact inspire him to write one of the grandest works in nineteenth-century French fiction. It also proved untenable, and the study in social mathematics was gradually forgotten as literature asserted itself. Zola, like Saccard in *L'Argent*, was too passionate to remain detached; and, as Havelock Ellis said, 'these growing piles of large books are the volcanic ejecta of an original and exuberant temperament.'[12]

Zola needed Naturalism because he needed a banner. He needed a creed in order to preach. He needed a system to impose on his romantic nature. Yet no writer of fiction can be impersonal; even a Naturalist must sometimes follow his instincts and the dictates of his heart. The truth had already been recognised in Zola's lifetime. The Vicomte de Voguë, after reading *La Débâcle*, declared that Zola 'remains the last in date and not the least of our great Romantic poets. He is an epic and visionary builder, sometimes better informed of reality than his elders, but equally the slave of his imagination.'[13] Maupassant had written: 'The son of the Romantics, a Romantic himself in all his proceedings, he bears within himself a tendency to the poem, a need to enlarge, to magnify, to make symbols out of people and things ... His teachings and his work are in eternal disaccord.'[14] Anatole France agreed:

M. Zola is less faithful to his doctrines than he says or believes. He has not managed to suppress his robust imagination ... M. Zola's instincts rebel at direct observation. Of all worlds, it is his own which he seems to know least. He divines, and he seems to enjoy divination. He has the visions, the hallucinations of a solitary ... From the depths of his retreat, he evokes the soul of the masses. It is at Médan that there hides the last of the Romantics.[15]

Zola owed more than most novelists to documentation; but he drew his inspiration from the tensions of his private life. His inspiration also sprang from the tensions between his creed and his nature, between the Naturalism which he professed and the Romanticism which had informed his nature from his youth. Zola needed the theories of Lucas and Taine, the family-tree of the Rougon-Macquart, the dossiers of facts for his fiction. Yet, from the beginning, he began to break the confines which he had created, to turn types into symbols, to turn prosaic facts into poetry. Accuracy is not enough. The impersonal fails to move us. Naturalism alone cannot inspire a work of literature. By a paradox, Zola's achievement begins where Naturalism ends.

NOTES

Abbreviations:

B.N. – Bibliothèque Nationale, Paris
Corr. – *Correspondance*
Z – Émile Zola

Zola's works have been quoted from the Le Blond edition, unless otherwise stated.

I

1 This account of Zola's family is largely based on Ternois: 'Les Zola. Histoire d'une famille vénitienne.' (*Les Cahiers naturalistes*, No. 18, 1961, pp. 49 sqq.)
2 Vizetelly: *Émile Zola*, 15–16
3 Chabaud: 'Un épisode inconnu de l'enfance d'Émile Zola.' (*Mercure de France*, 1 March 1929, p. 508)
4 Zola et Le Blond: 'Une enquête sur l'éducation (textes retrouvés).' (*Les Cahiers naturalistes*, No. 21, 1962, p. 215)
5 Topin: *Romanciers contemporains*, 244–5; Seillière: *Émile Zola*, 20
6 Michel: *La Petite Patrie*, II, 226
7 Rod: *À propos de 'L'Assommoir'*, 32
8 Vizetelly: op. cit., 40
9 Le Blond-Zola: *Émile Zola raconté par sa fille*, 7–8
10 19 June 1892. Michel: op. cit., I, 225
11 To Paul Alexis, 30 December 1896. Z: *Corr.*, 784–5
12 Xau: *Émile Zola*, 16
13 Z: *Corr.*, 8
14 Z: *La Faute de l'Abbé Mouret*, 425

2

1 3 December 1859. Z: *Corr.*, 18–19
2 Ibid, 23–4
3 Ibid, 29–30
4 Ibid, 32
5 Ibid, 40
6 Ibid, 47
7 25 March 1860. Ibid, 53

8 Ibid, 70, 71
9 Ibid, 84, 86
10 Ibid, 141, 146
11 Ibid, 155
12 Ibid, 187, 188
13 Ibid, 55
14 Ibid, 187, 188
15 Xau: op. cit., 28

3

1 5 February [1862]. B.N. N.A.Fr. 24524 f 43
2 Z: *Corr.*, 235
3 Brisson: *l'Envers de la gloire*, 74 sqq.
4 To Valabrègue, 6 February 1865. Z: *Corr.*, 266
5 Ibid, 267
6 Ibid, 271–2
7 Ogden mss.
8 Deffoux: *Le Groupe de Médan*, 32
9 Mitterand: *Zola journaliste*. 56–7
10 Mme Victor Hugo to her husband, 15 March 1866. (Maison de Victor Hugo)
11 B.N. N.A.Fr. 24520 f 310. On 21 May 1869 Hugo sent Zola a signed copy of *La Voix de Guernesey* (N.A.Fr. 24520 ff 301–8)
12 2 March [1866]. B.N. N.A.Fr. 24524 ff 44–5
13 Ogden mss.
14 Z: *Mon Salon*, 225, 226, 230
15 Ibid, 232
16 Z: *Mes Haines*, 24 sqq.
17 Ibid, 55 sqq.

4

1 Lepelletier: op. cit., 143–4
2 Silvestre: *Au pays des souvenirs*, 158–9
3 Z: *Mes Haines*, II, 94–5
4 Quoted in Adhémar: *Zola*, 12–13
5 Robert: '*La Terre*' *d'Émile Zola*, p. 13, note
6 For the most complete account of Alexandrine see Laborde: *Trente-huit années près de Zola. Vie d'Alexandrine Émile Zola*
7 Hemmings: 'The Present Position in Zola Studies' (*French Studies*, April 1956, 102–3)
8 26 July 1866, Z: *Corr.*, 285–6

5

1 Le Blond-Zola: op. cit., 37; Z: *Œuvres complètes*, ed. Guillemin, tome X, 280, 281
2 Z: *Corr.*, 532
3 Ibid, 295
4 Ibid, 296
5 Ibid, 305
6 Z: *Thérèse Raquin*, 237
7 Ibid, 237, 239; Vizetelly: op. cit., 103–4
8 Z: *Thérèse Raquin*, 240
9 B.N. N.A.Fr. 24524 f 238
10 Z: *Thérèse Raquin*, 252
11 Undated. B.N. N.A.Fr. 24524 ff 46–7
12 8 May 1867. Z: *Corr.*, 392
13 Grand-Carteret: *Zola en images*, 7
14 15 April 1868. Quoted in *Madeleine Férat* (Guillemin edition), 520, 522
15 16 September 1872. Z: *Mélanges*, 107–8
16 Z: *Documents littéraires*, 226
17 Lepelletier: op. cit., 149
18 14 December 1868. Goncourt: *Journal*, VIII, 154–5

6

1 Ogden mss.
2 Z: *Les Mystères de Marseille*, ix sqq.
3 Z: *Mes Haines*, 168–9
4 18 May 1882. Letter-preface to Villas: *Un Amour avorté*, ii
5 Sherard: *Émile Zola*, 90–2
6 Ibid, 88–90
7 Mitterand: 'Histoire indiscrète d'une œuvre'; Adhémar, op. cit., 110
8 Lepelletier: op. cit., 268–9
9 James: *Notes on Novelists*, 23

7

1 4 July 1860. Z: *Corr.*, 113
2 Z: *L'Œuvre*, 106
3 Z: *Corr.*, 360
4 Goncourt: *Journal*, IX, 24–5
5 Z: *Corr.*, 361
6 Ogden mss.

7 Ogden mss.
8 Ibid
9 Ibid
10 Ibid
11 B.N. N.A.Fr. 24510 ff 52–3
12 Ibid, f 384
13 Z: *Corr.*, 377
14 Republished in Z: *Mélanges*, pp. 9 sqq.
15 Alexis: *Émile Zola. Notes d'un ami*, 173–4
16 Deffoux: 'EZ et la sous-préfecture de Castelsarrasin en 1871.'
   (*Mercure de France*, 15 October 1926, p. 344)
17 Quoted in Z: *La Curée*, 313
18 Z: *Corr.*, 279

8

1 Ogden mss.
2 B.N. N.A.Fr. 24545 ff 54–5
3 17 May 1870. B.N. N.A.Fr. 24839 à 594
4 Z: *La Curée*, 308
5 Ibid, 344; Brisson, loc. cit.
6 Dreyfous: *Ce qu'il me reste à dire*, 283, 285
7 Ibid, 297

9

1 Z: *Les Romanciers naturalistes*, 212
2 Ibid, 148–9
3 Z: *Une Campagne*, 261
4 Z: *Les Romanciers naturalistes*, loc. cit.
5 Goncourt: *Journal*, X, 171
6 Alphonse Daudet: *Trente Ans de Paris*, 320 sqq.
7 Z: *Le Ventre de Paris*, 335–6
8 Ibid, 326; and Alexis: op. cit., 97
9 Z: *La Conquête de Plassans*, 371 sqq.

10

1 Z: *La Faute de l'Abbé Mouret*, 409 sqq. For the origins of the novel,
   see Hemmings: 'The Secret Sources of *La Faute de l'Abbé
   Mouret*' (*French Studies*, July 1959, pp. 226 sqq.)
2 Hertz: 'Émile Zola, témoin de la vérité' (*Europe*, November–
   December 1952, p. 33)
3 Alexis: op. cit., 101

4 Faure: *Pèlerinages passionnés*, 2e série, 196–7
5 [1875] B.N. N.A.Fr. 24522 ff 41–2
6 20 April [1875]. B.N. N.A.Fr. 24524 ff 48–9
7 22 July 1883. Pissarro: *Lettres à son fils Lucien*, 56

11

1 Alexis: *Naturalisme pas mort*, 55 sqq. Alexis' somewhat romantic-
  ised account of events appeared in *L'Aurore* on 5, 6 and 7 February
  1898. His letters to Zola are in the Bibliothèque Nationale, but
  Zola's letters to Roux, among the Ogden Papers, are published
  here for the first time
2 Alexis' letters to Zola about his imprisonment may be found in
  the Bibliothèque Nationale. N.A.Fr. 24510 ff 56 sqq.
3 Alexis: loc. cit.
4 Ogden mss.
5 Ibid
6 Goncourt *Journal*, X, 230
7 Ibid, XI, 14
8 5 May 1876. Ibid, XI, 90
9 Quoted by Louis de Robert in Franzen: *Zola et 'La Joie de Vivre'*,
  228
10 To J.-K. Huysmans, 29 October 1887. Quoted by Girard:
  'Deux lettres inédites de Zola à Huysmans' (*Revue d'Histoire
  littéraire de la France*, 1958, pp. 372–3). To Georges Charpentier,
  16 May 1895. Z: *Corr.*, 774–5
11 Z: *Corr.*, 429
12 7 August 1875. Ibid, 430
13 Ibid, 431
14 B.N. N.A.Fr. 24524 f 161
15 Z: *Corr.*, 431
16 Ibid, 432
17 Ibid, 436

12

1 Z: *L'Assommoir*, 461–2, 469, 471
2 Roux: *Évariste Planchu*, 321, 325
3 Deffoux: *La Publication de 'L'Assommoir'*, 28–9; Lepelletier, *Écho
  de Paris*, 1 October 1902; Alexis: op. cit., 107, 108; Dreyfous:
  Ce qu'il me reste à dire, 292
4 Z: *Corr.*, 439
5 Sherard: op. cit., 151
6 3 June 1872. Goncourt: *Journal*, X, 94–5

7 Lonergan: *Paris by Day and Night*, 146

8 Amicis: pp. cit., 211 and *passim*

9 Montrenaud: 'Un journaliste russe chez Zola' (*Les Cahiers natural-istes*, 1975, pp. 86, 87)

10 Vicaire: 'L'Esthétique d'Émile Zola' (*Revue des Deux Mondes*, 15 June 1924, pp. 812, 815)

11 Mitterand: 'La genèse et la publication de *Son Excellence Eugène Rougon*' (*Mercure de France*, August 1961, pp. 679–80); Alexis: *Émile Zola. Notes d'un ami*, 105

12 Reproduced in Grand-Carteret: *Zola en images*, 100

13 22 April 1876. James: *Parisian Sketches*, 135

14 1 July 1876. Z: *Corr.*, 444

15 2/9 December 1876. Halperine-Kaminsky: *Ivan Touguéneff d'après sa correspondance avec ses amis français*, 97

16 Goncourt: *Journal*, XI, 130

17 Moore: 'My Impressions of Zola' (*English Illustrated Magazine*, Vol. XI, 1894, p. 484)

18 Quoted in Deffoux: op. cit., 100

19 Ibid, 76–7

20 February 1877. Flaubert: *Trois Contes. Correspondance 1876–1877*, 306–7

21 Deffoux: op. cit., 109

22 2 February 1877. B.N. N.A.Fr. 24511 ff 284–5

13

1 Adhémar: op. cit., 68

2 Mitterand: 'Le regard de Zola' (*Europe*, April–May 1968, p. 187)

3 Hertz: op. cit., 32–3

4 Adhémar: 'La myopie d'Émile Zola' (*Æsculape*, 1952, p. 197)

5 Z: *Corr.*, 474

6 *Le Figaro*, 30 September 1881

7 Z: *Corr.*, 477–8

8 Ibid, 478–9

9 17 August 1877. Ogden mss.

10 Ogden mss.

11 Z: *Corr.*, 492, 493

12 [April 1878] Flaubert: *Carnets et Projets . . .*, 161

13 26 April 1878. Quoted in ibid, 357–8

14 24 April 1878. B.N. N.A.Fr. 24522 ff 46–7

14

1 Sherard: op. cit., 212–13
2 Ibid; Le Blond: 'Zola acquéreur de biens' (*Europe*, April–May 1968, pp. 65, 70)
3 Gosse: 'The Short Stories of M. Zola'. Introduction to Z: *The Attack on the Mill*, 24–5
4 Céard: op. cit., 141
5 Ogden mss.
6 Z: *Corr.*, 506–7
7 Vizetelly: 'Some recollections of Émile Zola' (*Pall Mall Magazine*, Vol. XXIX, January–April 1903, pp. 71, 72)
8 Z: *Contes à Ninon*, II, 660
9 Speech of 25 May 1896 to the Société Protectrice des Animaux. Z: *Mélanges*, 318–19
10 B.N. N.A.Fr. 24520 ff 133–4
11 Sherard: op. cit., 215–17
12 Ibid
13 Ibid, 222, 223–4
14 Goncourt: *Journal*, XV, 233–4
15 Field: op. cit., 162
16 16 August 1886. Z: *Corr.*, 659
17 Laborde: 'Émile Zola à Médan' (*Les Cahiers naturalistes*, No. 38, 1969, pp. 147, 148)
18 *L'Événement*, 14 March 1903
19 Belloc Lowndes: *Where Love and Friendship Dwelt*, 181
20 See Burns: 'Henry Céard and his relations with Flaubert and Zola.' (*French Studies*, October 1952); Deffoux et Xavie: *Le Groupe de Médan*, 11–12
21 *L'Aurore*, 4 March 1905
22 Léon Daudet: *Études et milieux littéraires*, 56–7

15

1 Z: *Corr.*, 488
2 Auriant: *La véritable histoire de Nana*, 18 and *passim*; Field: *Things I shouldn't tell*, 162
3 Halévy: Carnets (*Revue des Deux Mondes*, 15 December 1937, p. 819)
4 Z: *Nana*, 442–3; Robida: *Les grandes heures du salon Charpentier*, 129
5 Z: *Corr.*, 505
6 Du Camp: *Paris*, III, 460

7 Z: *Corr.*, 506–7
8 Ibid, 507–8
9 Maupassant: *Lettres inédites à Gustave Flaubert*, 68
10 21 January 1879. Goncourt: *Journal*, XII, 10, 11
11 Montrenaud: op. cit., 93, 99
12 Z: *Corr.*, 511
13 Ibid, 512
14 Ibid, 513
15 Rod: *À propos de 'L'Assommoir'*, 27 sqq.
16 Alexis: op. cit., 178
17 Rod: op. cit., 74
18 B.N. N.A.Fr. 24516 ff 16–17
19 B.N. N.A.Fr. 24516 ff 21–2
20 Halévy: *Carnets*, loc. cit., 821–2
21 22 January 1879. Flaubert: *Carnets et Projets* . . ., 298
22 Deffoux: op. cit., 131 and 131, note; Grand-Carteret: op. cit., 123 sqq., 130
23 Z: preface to *Théâtre* (1891), viii; dated I June 1878
24 B.N. N.A.Fr. 24511 ff 162–3
25 Halpérine-Kaminsky: op. cit., 109
26 B.N. N.A.Fr. 24521 f 348
27 Le Blond: 'Le Centenaire d'Alfred Bruneau' (*Les Cahiers naturalistes*, No. 7, 1957, p. 171); and Vizetelly: op. cit.
28 Strindberg's correspondence with Zola (B.N. N.A.Fr. 24524 ff 3 sqq.) dates from 29 August 1887
29 Antoine: op. cit., 162, 163, 181

16

1 Maupassant: *Lettres inédites à Gustave Flaubert*, 67, 69
2 B.N. N.A.Fr. 24524 ff 83–4. For further details about Flaubert's accident, see Richardson: 'Unpublished Letters of Flaubert' (*Times Literary Supplement*, 13 June 1968)
3 23 December 1878. B.N. N.A.Fr. 24516 ff 21–2
4 Kanes: 'Zola, Flaubert et Tourguéniev: autour d'une correspondance' (*Les Cahiers naturalistes*, No. 36, 1968, p. 180)
5 17 February 1879. Z: *Corr.*, 525
6 [3 March 1877] Flaubert: *Trois Contes* . . ., 316; [3 April 1876]: ibid, 158–9. Albalat: *Gustave Flaubert et ses amis*, 233
7 Dreyfous: *Ce qu'il me reste à dire*, 279–80
8 Z: *Les Romanciers naturalistes*, 148–9
9 24 February 1879. Maupassant: op. cit., 84
10 B.N. N.A.Fr. 24516 ff 39–40
11 Auriant: op. cit., 80 sqq.

12 B.N. N.A.Fr. 24510 f 105
13 Z: *Corr.*, 533; Auriant: op. cit., 88–9, 100
14 B.N. N.A.Fr. 24516 ff 70–1
15 Quoted in Auriant: op. cit., 72–3
16 Z: *L'Œuvre*, 46
17 Z: *Corr.*, 537–8
18 Ibid, 539
19 B.N. N.A.Fr. 24516 ff 85–7
20 B.N. N.A.Fr. 24516 ff 88–9
21 Z: *Lettres inédites à Henry Céard*, 84,
22 Ibid, 84, note
23 1 February 1880. Goncourt: *Journal*, XII, 61, 62
24 15 February 1880. Flaubert: *Carnets et Projets . . .*, 591
25 June–July [1887] Z: *Letters to Van Santen Kolff*, 15
26 15 February 1880. B.N. N.A.Fr. 24520 ff 336–7
27 Z: *Nana*, 442–3

17

1 Antoine: loc. cit.
2 Z: *Les Romanciers naturalistes*, 17
3 Z: *Documents littéraires*, 45
4 Ibid, 49–50
5 14 December [1876]. Flaubert: *Trois Contes. Correspondance, 1876–1877*, 260
6 8 [December] 1877. Ibid, 444–5
7 Artinian et Maynial: *Lettres inédites de Guy de Maupassant à Émile Zola*, 133, 134
8 Vicaire: *L'Esthétique d'Émile Zola*, 818
9 Rod: 'The place of Émile Zola in literature' (*The Contemporary Review*, December 1902, pp. 629, 630, 631)
10 Mme Alphonse Daudet: *Souvenirs autour d'un groupe littéraire*, 53–4
11 Robida: op. cit., 42, 98–9
12 Rosny: *Torches et lumignons*, 36–7, 48
13 Bruneau: op. cit., 116–17
14 Mme Daudet: op. cit., 120 sqq.

18

1 Goncourt: *Journal*, XII, 69–71
2 Z: *Les Romaniers naturalistes*, 137 sqq.
3 8 May 1880. B.N. N.A.Fr. 24520 f 207; for Goncourt's arrangements for the funeral, see Richardson: 'Claudius Popelin and

his correspondents', II. (*French Studies*, Vol. XXIII, No. 3, p. 259)

4 9 May 1880. Z: *Corr.*, 545
5 Z: *Les Romanciers naturalistes*, loc. cit.
6 Céard: 'Zola intime' (*Revue illustrée*, 1887, pp. 146–7)
7 Z: *La Joie de Vivre*, 362; Alexandrine Zola to Mme Laborde, 8 December 1880 (Laborde: op. cit., pp. 78–9)
8 Laborde: loc. cit.

19

1 Z: *Corr.*, 558–9
2 Ibid, 560
3 Moore: *Confessions of a Young Man*. Preface, xiii
4 Goncourt: *Journal*, XII, 119, 120
5 Ogden mss.
6 Z: *Lettres inédites à Henry Céard*, 30
7 Z: *Corr.*, 562
8 Z: *Lettres inédites à Henry Céard*, 32
9 Ogden mss.
10 Mme Daudet: op. cit., 210
11 Mme Adam: *Mes Angoisses et nos luttes*, 358
12 *Revue des Deux Mondes*, 15 May 1882

20

1 Z: *Au Bonheur des Dames*, 467–8
2 Recollections published in *La Phare de la Loire*, 19 March 1883. Quoted in Z: *Au Bonheur des Dames*, 461–2
3 Matthews: *Les Deux Zola*, 61; Z: *Au Bonheur des Dames*, 465–6
4 Z: *Corr.*, 585
5 6 July 1882. Goncourt: *Journal*, XII, 184
6 Z: *Corr.*, 588
7 Ibid., 590
8 Michel: op. cit., II, 230

21

1 Zakarian: *Zola's 'Germinal'*, 35
2 6 October 1889. Z: *Letters to Van Santen Kolff*, 33
3 Z: *Corr.*, 611
4 *Le Matin*, 7 March 1885
5 22 March 1885. Z: *Corr.*, 637
6 Z: *Germinal*, 557

7 14 June 1884. Z: *Corr.*, 618
8 Z: *Lettres inédites à Henry Céard*, 45
9 B.N. N.A.Fr. 24516 ff 215–17
10 Z: *Corr.*, 627
11 Ibid, 631–2
12 Ibid, 632
13 Psichari: 'Zola et la misère humaine' (Cercle Parisien de la Ligue Française de l'enseignement. No. 75, pp. 56, 57 and *passim*)
14 Z: Germinal, 557
15 *Le Figaro*, 6 June 1896
16 14 March 1885. Quoted in Tieghem: *Introduction à l'étude d'Émile Zola. 'Germinal'*, 9
17 24 February 1885. B.N. N.A.Fr. 24522 ff 219–20
18 12 November 1885. B.N. N.A.Fr. 24520 ff 364–5
19 'Palermo. Vendredi soir'. B.N. N.A.Fr. 24522 ff 69–70

                                      22

1 Quoted in Robert: op. cit., 127
2 Z: *L'Œuvre*, 417
3 Ibid, 417; Niess: 'Another view of Zola's *L'Œuvre*' (*The Romantic Review*, Vol. XXXIX, December 1948, pp. 287, 288, 300); Lanoux: 'Cézanne et Zola' (*Revue de Paris*, October 1966, p. 75)
4 Niess: *Zola, Cézanne and Manet. A study of 'L'Œuvre'*, 159 and *passim*; Z: *L'Œuvre*, 409
5 Z: *L'Œuvre*, 196, 198
6 Goncourt: *Journal*, XIII, 215, 229
7 Z: *Corr.*, 643
8 Mitterand: 'Un projet inédit d'Émile Zola en 1884–5' (*Les Cahiers naturalistes*, No. 10, pp. 401 sqq.)
9 Z: *Lettres inédites à Henry Céard*, 52
10 Z: *Corr.*, 647
11 Ibid, 655–6
12 8 February 1887. Antoine: *Mes Souvenirs sur le Théâtre Libre*, 21
13 Z: *L'Œuvre*, 427
14 2 May 1886. B.N. N.A.Fr. 24511 f 8
15 Z: *L'Œuvre*, 406
16 Rewald: *Cézanne*, 6, 7
17 Pissarro: *Lettres à son fils Lucien*, 93, note, 99, 100
18 B.N. N.A.Fr. 24522 ff 225–6
19 Moore: 'My Impressions of Zola' (*English Illustrated Magazine*, Vol. XI, 1894, p. 489)
20 Retté: *Le Symbolisme*, 191–3
21 Robida: op. cit., 124, 127

22 'Le Critique d'art', in Adhémar: op. cit., 53 sqq.; Hemmings: 'Zola, Manet and the Impressionists' (1875–80)' (PMLA, Vol. LXXIII, 1958, pp. 407 sqq.)
23 Z: *Corr.*, 655–6

23

1 Vizetelly: 'Some recollections of Émile Zola' (*Pall Mall Magazine*, Vol. XXIX, January–April 1903, pp. 72–3)
2 'Chez M. Émile Zola' (*Le Parti National*, 22 August 1887)
3 Z: *Corr.*, 658
4 To M. Bonnet, 25 October 1894. Z: *Corr.*, 768
5 Z: *La Terre*, 521
6 Z: *Letters to Van Santen Kolff*, 12
7 Ibid, 14
8 Z: *Corr.*, 677
9 Undated. B.N. N.A.Fr. 24522 ff 79–80
10 *Le Figaro*, 18 August 1887
11 Undated. B.N. N.A.Fr. 24517 f 306
12 19 November 1887. B.N. N.A.Fr. 24545 ff 22–3
13 Quoted in Robert: op. cit., 444
14 Z: *Letters to Van Santen Kolff*, 18

24

1 Sherard: *Twenty Years in Paris*, 119
2 Robida: op. cit., 129
3 B.N. N.A.Fr. 10323, ff 217–18, 221–2
4 28 January 1878. Goncourt: *Journal*, XI, 178
5 For Goncourt's spiteful comments on Zola at this time, see *Journal*, XIV, 108–10, 197–8, 205, 220, See also Laborde; op. cit., 92
6 Goncourt: *Journal*, XIV, 89
7 4 November 1888. Ibid, 176–7
8 13 January 1860. Z: *Corr.*, 29–30
9 Le Blond-Zola: op. cit., 165–6
10 Toulouse: *Émile Zola*, 261
11 Lonergan: *Paris by Day and Night*, 143, 144
12 Lonergan: *Forty Years of Paris*, 102, 103; Quilter: *Is Marriage a Failure?*, 102–4
13 Lonergan: *Paris by Day and Night*, 147
14 Ibid, 144–5; Lanoux: *Bonjour, Monsieur Zola*, 221
15 16 July [1888]. B.N. N.A.Fr. 24517 f 248
16 Vizetelly: op. cit., 101–2; Le Blond-Zola: op. cit., 163–4

17 Blavet: *La Vie Parisienne* (1888), 214 sqq.
18 14 July 1888. Z: *Corr.*, 699
19 Ibid, 699–700
20 Deffoux: *Chronique de l'Académie Goncourt*, 29, 44, 45
21 B.N. N.A.Fr. 24545 ff 26–7
22 B.N. N.A.Fr. 24545 ff 28–9
23 22 January 1888. Z: *Letters to Van Santen Kolff*, 20
24 Kahn: 'Anatole France et Émile Zola' (*La Grande Revue*, July 1926, p. 47)
25 Z: *Letters to Van Santen Kolff*, 25

25

1 Z: *Letters to Van Santen Kolff*, 26–7
2 Z: *Corr.*, 708; Lonergan: *Paris by Day and Night*, 153
3 Z: *La Bête Humaine*, 375 sqq.
4 Kanes: op. cit., 38, 39, 41; Antoine: op. cit., 141
5 Z: *La Bête Humaine*, 383–4
6 Ibid, 389
7 Z: *Corr.*, 709
8 Ibid, 711
9 Z: *Letters to Van Santen Kolff*, 28–30
10 Z: *Corr.*, 713–15
11 Z: *Travail*, II, 349
12 Guillemin: *Émile Zola*, 40
13 *Le Matin*, 8 March 1890. Quoted in Z: *La Bête Humaine*, 393. See also Doumic: *Études sur la littérature française* and *Portraits d'écrivains*.
14 Z: *La Bête Humaine*, 395, 396
15 Ibid
16 B.N. N.A.Fr. 24511 f 10
17 10 March 1890. B.N. N.A.Fr. 24520 ff 197–8
18 Mallarmé: *Dix-neuf lettres de Stéphane Mallarmé à Émile Zola*, 55
19 Quoted by Kaye, in introduction to Marmier: *Journal*, I, 49
20 Vizetelly: *Émile Zola*, 309–10 and 310, note; Ibrovac: *Heredia*, 164 and note, 165
21 Sherard: *Émile Zola*, 259
22 Ibid, 288
23 To Halpérine-Kaminsky, 4 November 1891. This letter served as preface to the French edition of Tolstoy's *L'Argent et le Travail*.

I

26

1 Z: *Letters to Van Santen Kolff*, 37
2 Z: *L'Argent*, 437–8
3 Grant: 'The Jewish Question in Zola's *L'Argent*' (PMLA, Vol. LXX, December 1955, 962–3, 966, 967)
4 Z: *Letters to Van Santen Kolff*, 35
5 Chennevière: 'Émile Zola' (*Europe*, 15 December 1927, p. 93)
6 20 March 1891. B.N. N.A.Fr. 24520 ff 139–40
7 Claretie: 'Souvenirs d'un Académicien' (*Les Œuvres libres*, January 1934, pp. 14 and *passim*)
8 Ibid
9 Peter: 'Zola et l'Académie' (*Mercure de France*, 1 March 1940, p. 572, note)
10 Papiers Alexandre Dumas *fils*. B.N. N.A.Fr. 24639 ff 666–7
11 B.N N.A.Fr. 24518 f 121
12 Claretie: loc. cit.
13 'Lundi'. B.N. N.A.Fr. 24517 f 290
14 Papiers Alexandre Dumas *fils*. B.N. N.A.Fr. 24639 f 674
15 Claretie: loc. cit.
16 Claretie: *La Vie à Paris, 1901–3*, 137
17 Z: *Letters to Van Santen Kolff*, 40

27

1 France: *La Vie littéraire*, I, 75–7
2 Quoted in Vizetelly: preface to *The Downfall*, vi, vii
3 Ibid, vii
4 Z: *Letters to Van Santen Kolff*, 58–9
5 Barrès: *Cahiers*, II, 266
6 Quoted by Sisley Huddleston in *Bohemian Literary and Social Life in Paris* (Harrap, 1928), p. 216; Rhodes: 'The Sources of Zola's medical references in *La Débâcle*' (*Modern Language Notes*, February 1930, pp. 110–11)
7 Huret: *Enquête sur l'évolution littéraire*, 169, 188
8 For an account of the religious revival, see Fraser: *Le Renouveau religieux d'après le roman français de 1886 à 1914*
9 Z: *Letters to Van Santen Kolff*, 41–2
10 Burns: 'Henry Céard and his relations with Flaubert and Zola' (*French Studies*, October 1952, pp. 26 sqq); Le Blond-Zola: op. cit., 197. According to Lanoux: op. cit., 227, Zola was in Lourdes when Jacques was born
11 Burns: loc. cit; Laborde: op. cit., 92–3
12 Goncourt: *Journal*, XVI, 177

13 Burns: loc. cit.
14 Laborde; loc. cit.
15 Laborde: op. cit., 93

28

1 Quoted in Vizetelly: introduction to Z: *The Downfall*, viii
2 Ibid, x
3 Ibid, xi
4 Z: *La Débâcle*, 208
5 Sackville-West: *Inclinations*, 200, 202
6 B.N. N.A.Fr. 24517 ff 314–15
7 B.N. N.A.Fr. 24524 f 529
8 Z: *Corr.*, 749
9 13 July 1892. Goncourt: *Journal*, XVIII, 215
10 Laborde: op. cit., 98
11 Le Blond-Zola: op. cit., 167
12 Ibid
13 Huret: loc. cit.
14 Retté: *Le Symbolisme*, 177–8
15 Quoted in Vizetelly: op. cit., ix, x
16 Laborde: op. cit., 99
17 Z: *Letters to Van Santen Kolff*, 47–9

29

1 Discours au banquet de l'Association des Étudiants. Z: *Mélanges*, 291–3
2 Goncourt: *Journal*, XIX, 112–13
3 *Le Journal*, 22 June 1893. Quoted in Z: *Le Docteur Pascal*, 352–4
4 Ibid
5 Céard: *Lettres inédites à Émile Zola*, 410–11
6 Laborde: op. cit., 101–2
7 Céard: op. cit., 412
8 Zola had long criticized Hugo. On Hugo's death in 1885, he had addressed a public letter to his grandson, affirming his admiration for Hugo's genius. This demonstration had incurred the displeasure of Daudet
9 For details, see Thomas: *La Maladie et la Mort de Maupassant*
10 Undated. B.N. N.A.Fr. 24522 ff 97–8. The monument was inaugurated on 23 November 1890, but Zola seems to have left the speech to Goncourt
11 B.N. N.A.Fr. 24523 ff 449–50

12 Sherard: op. cit., 157–8
13 Reproduced in Z: *Le Docteur Pascal* (ed. Guillemin), 140

30

1 Z: *Letters to Van Santen Kolff*, 52
2 Le Blond-Zola: op. cit., 168
3 Sherard: *Twenty Years in Paris*, 466
4 Ibid, 468–9
5 Vizetelly: *Émile Zola*, 324
6 Z: *Corr.*, 759
7 Vizetelly: *Émile Zola*, 329–30
8 Ibid, 332
9 24 September 1893. Le Blond-Zola: op. cit., 190
10 James: *Notes on Novelists*, 24
11 Vizetelly: op. cit., 334–7
12 Ibid

31

1 Moore: 'My Impressions of Zola' (*English Illustrated Magazine*, Vol. XI, 1894, p. 485)
2 Rothenstein: *Men and Memories*, I, 162–3; Marie Belloc Lowndes, who went to Paris in 1888, said that Daudet and Zola were both reported to earn 300,000 francs a year (*Where Love and Friendship Dwelt*, 170)
3 Sherard: op. cit.
4 Z: *Lourdes*, 548–9
5 Ibid, 434–5
6 Ibid, 542–3
7 Quoted in ibid, 552
8 Crestey: *Critique d'un roman historique*, 5–6
9 Moncoq: *Réponse complète au 'Lourdes' de M. Zola*, 7
10 24 September 1894. B.N. N.A.Fr. 24523 f 329
11 B.N. N.A.Fr. 24524 f 530
12 13 July 1894. Le Blond-Zola: op. cit., 169
13 Le Blond-Zola: quoted in Z: *Contes à Ninon*, 30–1
14 Ibid

32

1 Z: *Rome*, 689
2 Ibid, 694–5
3 Ibid, 697

4 Ternois: *Zola et son temps*, 290–1
5 Le Blond-Zola: op. cit., 200
6 Ibid, 171 sqq.

33

1 Z: *Mélanges*, 314
2 Laupts: *L' Homosexualité et les types homosexuels*, 431
3 Sherard: *Twenty Years of Paris*, 463, 464–5; on 1 March 1891, Sherard had written to Zola, asking if he might bring Wilde next day. B.N. N.A.Fr. 24523 ff 447–8
4 Toulouse: *Émile Zola*, 249
5 Z: *Mélanges*, 263
6 Goncourt: *Journal*, XXI, 130
7 Salvan: 'Quatre lettres de Zola à sa femme (1895)' (*Les Cahiers naturalistes*, No. 41, 1971, pp. 83, 85). 6 December 1897; George: 'Some Unpublished Correspondence of Émile Zola' (*Symposium*, Vol. X, No. 2, Fall, 1956, p. 275)
8 Undated. B.N. N.A.Fr. 24639 ff 675–6
9 30 May 1896. Z: *Corr.*, 782
10 Toulouse: op. cit., v–vii
11 Ibid, 127–8; the following quotation is taken from the same work
12 Guilbert: *La Chanson de ma vie*, 156 sqq.
13 Belloc Lowndes: op. cit., 183
14 Bouhélier: *Le Printemps d'une génération*, 289 sqq.
15 Ibid, 326
16 Brulat: *Histoire populaire de Émile Zola*, 104, 105
17 James: op. cit., 38
18 De Gourmont: *Épilogues, 1895–8*, 33
19 Le Blond-Zola: op. cit., 201–2
20 Le Blond: 'Le Centenaire d'Alfred Bruneau' (*Les Cahiers naturalistes*, No. 7, 1957, p. 341); Denise Le Blond-Zola died on 12 December 1942.
21 Laborde: op. cit., 115

34

1 Kayser: 'J'accuse!' (*Europe*, January 1948, p. 11)
2 Bruneau: op. cit., 112
3 Turnell: *The Art of French Fiction*, 105
4 Z: *Corr.*, 792
5 B.N. N.A.Fr. 24523 f 424
6 Kayser; op. cit., 12

7 Z: *Lettre à la France*, 4, 5
8 Claretie: *La Vie à Paris, 1901–3*, 135–6; James: op. cit., 24
9 Barrès: *Cahiers*, I, 223–4
10 Ibid, 224
11 Léon Daudet: *Études et milieux littéraires*, 170–1
12 Sherard: *Twenty Years in Paris*, 473–4
13 Ibid, 475
14 Gustave-Toudouze: 'Quelques Souvenirs' (*Les Cahiers naturalistes*, I, 1955, p. 26)
15 11 December 1896. Vizetelly: *Émile Zola*, 429
16 Reinach: *Histoire de l'Affaire Dreyfus*, III, 220, 221–2
17 Ibid
18 Ibid, 223, 229

35

1 Maurice Le Blond was born in Niort on 26 February 1877; he died on 14 January 1944. For an appreciation, see Mitterand: 'Souvenir de Maurice Le Blond' (*Les Cahiers naturalistes*, No. 27, 1964, p. 116)
2 Pissarro: op. cit., 463, where it is wrongly dated 19 November 1898
3 14 January 1898. B.N. N.A.Fr. 24523 f 90
4 14 January 1898. B.N. N.A.Fr. 24542 f 230
5 B.N. N.A.Fr. 24511 f 14
6 27 January 1898. B.N. N.A.Fr. 24522 ff 375–6
7 B.N. N.A.Fr. 24511 ff 174–6
8 Rosny: op. cit., 169–70. See also Saint-Georges de Bouhélier: *L'Affaire Dreyfus*; Paleologue: *Journal de l'Affaire Dreyfus*; Sévérine *Vers la Lumière*
9 Vizetelly: *Émile Zola*, 453–4
10 Psichari: 'Le rôle social d'Émile Zola' (*Les Cahiers naturalistes*, No. 12, 1959, pp. 490 sqq.)
11 Bruneau: op. cit., 129
12 Sévérine: op. cit., 175
13 Ibid, 210–11
14 Meyer: *Ce que mes yeux ont vu*, 149
15 24 February 1898. B.N. N.A.Fr. 24522 ff 231–2; 26 February 1898. B.N. N.A.Fr. 24523 f 91
16 B.N. N.A.Fr. 24517 f 246. There is undated correspondence from François Coppée, but this is the last dated letter from him among Zola's papers.
17 7 March [1898]. B.N. N.A.Fr. 24517 ff 312–13
18 Le Blond-Zola: op. cit., 222

19 Chatto & Windus Archives
20 Le Blond-Zola: op. cit., 224

36

1 Z: *Pages d'exil* (*Nottingham French Studies*, III, 1 and 2, 1964, p. 27)
2 Ibid, 28
3 Ibid, 29, 30
4 Vizetelly: *Émile Zola*, 465–6
5 Vizetelly: 'Émile Zola at Wimbledon', 20
6 Ibid, 29–30
7 Ibid, 28–9
8 Ibid, 88–91
9 Z: *Pages d'exil*, 33, 34
10 Z: *Corr.*, 802
11 'Jeudi soir'. Otherwise undated. B.N. N.A.Fr. 24517 ff 457–8
12 Z: *Pages d'exil*, 37
13 Vizetelly: *Émile Zola*, 408–9
14 Z: *Contes et Nouvelles*, 667
15 Vizetelly: *With Zola in England*, 153–4
16 Ibid
17 Z: *Pages d'exil*, loc. cit.
18 Le Blond-Zola: op. cit., 231–3
19 Z: *Pages d'exil*, 43
20 'Vendredi soir'. Otherwise undated. B.N. N.A.Fr. 24517 ff 463–4
21 Reinach: op. cit., V, 40, note
22 Z: *Pages d'exil*, loc. cit.
23 Le Blond-Zola: op. cit., 239 sqq. Vizetelly: 'Some recollections of Émile Zola' (*Pall Mall Magazine*, Vol. XXIX, p. 72)
24 Le Blond-Zola: loc. cit.
25 Ibid
26 Le Blond: 'Sur Émile Zola' (*Mercure de France*, November–December 1913, p. 12). Ibid: 'Projets littéraires d'Émile Zola au moment de sa mort' (*Mercure de France*, 1 October 1927, p. 11)
27 Guillemin: *Éclaircissements*, 285
28 B.N. N.A.Fr. 24510 ff 345–7
29 Quoted in Z: *Œuvres complètes*, ed. Guillemin, tome 8, p. 977
30 Vizetelly: 'Some recollections of Émile Zola' (*Pall Mall Magazine*, Vol. XXIX, January–April 1903, pp. 75, 76)
31 B.N. N.A.Fr. 24522 ff 194–5
32 Geffroy: *Claude Monet*, 204–5
33 Robida: op. cit., 156
34 Z: *Corr.*, 818

35 B.N. N.A.Fr. 24522 ff 396–7
36 B.N. N.A.Fr. 24522 ff 398–9
37 B.N. N.A.Fr. 24517 ff 224–5
38 B.N. N.A.Fr. 24517 ff 228–9. Clemenceau had given Zola an introduction to Admiral Maxse in London (B.N. N.A.Fr. 24517 ff 222–3); he also gave him the admiral's Dorking address
39 Z: *Corr.*, 819
40 Correspondance de Joseph Reinach. B.N. N.A.Fr. 24899 ff 105–6
41 1 February 1899. Z: *Corr.*, 825
42 Salvan: 'Vingt-deux lettres et billets d'Émile Zola' (*Les Cahiers naturalistes*, No. 37, p. 73); Hemmings: 'Zola's apprenticeship to journalism (1865–1870)' (PMLA, Vol. LXXI)
43 Reinach: op. cit., V, 42
44 Z: *Lettres à Maître Labori*, 29
45 Vizetelly: *With Zola in England*, 214–15

37

1 [5 June] 1899. Z: *Corr.*, 843
2 Marguerite-Fernand Labori: *Labori. Ses notes manuscrites. Sa vie*, 78
3 Bruneau: op. cit., 155–6
4 *L'Aurore*, 5 June 1899
5 Dreyfus: *Cinq années de ma vie*, 326–7
6 *L'Aurore*, 12 September 1899
7 25 September 1899. Correspondance de Joseph Reinach. B.N. N.A.Fr. 24899 ff 116–17
8 15 March 1900. Christie: 'Zola, Labori, et "La Grande Revue" ' (*Renaissance and Modern Studies*, Vol. IV, p. 44)
9 B.N. N.A.Fr. 24518 ff 125–6
10 Bruneau: op. cit., 164–6
11 Chatto & Windus Archives. Letters of 14 February 1898, 9 October 1899, 11 May 1900
12 Quoted in Z: *Fécondité*, 713
13 Z: *Corr.*, 855
14 Z: *Mélanges*, 173, 177
15 Christie: 'Deux manuscrits inédits de Saint-Georges de Bouhélier' (*Les Cahiers naturalistes*, No. 37, p. 86)
16 Laborde: 'Laissons parler Zola' (*Les Cahiers naturalistes*, No. 38, p. 169)
17 Belloc Lowndes: op. cit., 182
18 Le Blond-Zola: loc. cit.
19 12 July 1901. Bloy: *Lettres à René Martineau*, 62
20 Z: *Vérité*, II, 685, 686
21 Ibid, 688–9

22 Quoted in Le Blond: *Projets* . . ., 10
23 Retté: op. cit., 189–90

38

1 Z: *Travail*, I, 155
2 Ibid, 157
3 Quoted in ibid, II, 615; and see Angell: op. cit., 139
4 Retté: op. cit., 188–9
5 Le Blond-Zola: op. cit., 255–6
6 Antoine: op. cit., 190, 191
7 Le Blond: 'Projets . . .', 7, 8
8 Chatto & Windus Archives
9 Bruneau: op. cit., 180–1
10 12 August 1902. B.N. N.A.Fr. 24512 ff 283–4. On 16 September Bruneau added: 'Let me thank you without more ado for working for me like this. How delighted I am at the thought of knowing the whole of your poem when I return to Paris, and how happy I shall be when I begin to set it!' (B.N. N.A.Fr. 24512 ff 285–6)
11 [Sardou]: *Les Papiers de Victorien Sardou*, 445
12 Le Blond: op. cit., 20–1, 22
13 James: op. cit., 39
14 Saint-Georges de Bouhélier: 'La Fatalité dans la mort d'Émile Zola' (*Revue bleue*, 28 March 1908, p. 415)
15 Bruneau: op. cit., 182, 183
16 Gustave-Toudouze: op. cit., 26
17 Le Blond-Zola: op. cit., 256
18 Claretie: 'La Mort de Zola' (*Revue de France*, 15 October 1922, p. 856); Reinach: op. cit., V, 198
19 Laborde: op. cit., 173, 174
20 Antoine: op. cit., 226, where the date is wrongly given as 1904
21 Le Blond-Zola: op. cit., 259
22 Romains: 'Zola et son exemple' (Discours de Médan), p. 12
23 Reinach: op. cit., VI, 198
24 Le Blond: 'Projets . . .', 5
25 Lanoux: op. cit., 372–6. The subject had been discussed in *Libération* on 1–7 October 1953
26 Ibid
27 Bruneau: op. cit., 185 sqq.
28 Claretie: 'La Mort de Zola', 853–4, 856
29 Bruneau: op. cit., 188–9
30 Dreyfus: op. cit., 335
31 Bruneau: loc. cit.
32 Brulat: op. cit., 103–4

33 Le Blond-Zola: loc. cit.
34 3 October 1902. Pissarro: op. cit., 494
35 Rewald: op. cit., 334
36 Dreyfus: op. cit., 336–7; Laborde: op. cit., 123–4, 176
37 Antoine: op. cit., 226–7
38 Rod: 'The place of Émile Zola in literature' (*The Contemporary Review*, December 1902, pp. 617–18)
39 Jouhaux: 'Zola et la classe ouvrière', in Angell: op. cit., 158
40 Antoine: loc. cit.
41 Dreyfus: loc. cit.

39

1 Preface to Laborde: op. cit., 7
2 Laborde: op. cit., 195, 204
3 Duret: op. cit., 171
4 Laborde: op. cit., 184
5 B.N. N.A.Fr. 24512 ff 288–9
6 B.N. N.A.Fr. 24508 ff 92 sqq.
7 B.N. N.A.Fr. 24508 f 81
8 Barrès: *Cahiers*, VI, 271 sqq.
9 Ibid, VII, 123
10 Letters of 14 July, 26 August 1902. Chatto & Windus Archives; Bruneau: op. cit., 225
11 Quoted by Denise Le Blond-Zola in Z: *La Vérité en marche*, 250
12 Laborde: op. cit., 213–14
13 Le Blond-Zola, quoted in Z: *Contes à Ninon*, 30–1
14 Laborde: op. cit., 219
15 Bruneau: op. cit., 222–3; Robida: op. cit., 123
16 Monet: op. cit., 211–12
17 Laborde: op. cit., 232

40

1 Quoted in Angell: op. cit., 140, 141–2
2 Quoted in Adhémar: op. cit., 169, 170
3 Brulat: loc. cit.
4 Bourget: *Études et Portraits*, I, 276
5 Quoted by Rufener: *Biography of a War Novel*, 90; and Chennevière: 'Émile Zola' (*Europe*, 15 December 1927, p. 101)
6 Z: Preface to Blavet: op. cit., vii
7 Lote: 'Zola: historien du Second Empire', 87
8 Quoted in Angell: op. cit., 89, 91
9 Robert: *Émile Zola*, 179–80

10 Z: *Une Campagne*, 308
11 Z: *Mes Haines*, 157, 158
12 Havelock Ellis: *Affirmations*, 2nd edition, 137
13 15 August 1892. Vicomte E.-M. de Voguë: *Heures d'histoire*, 14–15
14 *La Revue politique et littéraire*, 10 March 1883, pp. 289 sqq. This appreciation was later included in *Célébrités contemporaines*
15 France: *La Vie littéraire*, I, 75–7

SELECTED BIBLIOGRAPHY

English books are published in London, French books in Paris, unless otherwise stated.

Adam, Mme (Juliette Lamber) *Mes Angoisses et nos luttes, 1871–1873*. (Lemerre. 1907.)

Adhémar, Jean (*et al.*) *Zola* ('Génies et Réalités'. Hachette. 1969.)

Albalat, Antoine *Gustave Flaubert et ses amis*. (Plon. 1927.)

Alexis, Paul *Émile Zola. Notes d'un ami*. Avec des vers inédits d'Émile Zola. (Charpentier. 1882)

'*Naturalisme pas mort*'. Lettres inédites de Paul Alexis à Émile Zola, 1871–1900. Présentées et annotées avec de nombreux documents par B. H. Bakker. (Toronto. University of Toronto Press. 1971)

Alméras, Henri d' *Avant la Gloire. Leurs Débuts*. Ire série. (Société Française d'imprimerie et de librairie. 1902.)

Amicis, Edmondo de *Studies of Paris*. Translated from the Italian by W. W. Cady. (N.Y. G.P. Putnam's Sons. 1879.)

Angell, N. (*et al.*) *Présence de Zola*. (Fasquelle. 1953.)

Antoine, André *Mes Souvenirs sur le Théâtre-Libre*. (Fayard. 1921.)

Mes Souvenirs sur le Théâtre Antoine et sur l'Odéon. (*Première Direction*.) (Grasset. 1928.)

Aragon, Louis *La Lumière de Stendhal*. (Denoël. 1954.)

Auriant *La Véritable Histoire de 'Nana'*. (Mercure de France. 1942.)

Baillot, Alexandre *Émile Zola. L'Homme, le Penseur, le Critique*. (Société française d'imprimerie et de librairie. 1924.)

Baldick, Robert *The Life of J.-K. Huysmans*. (Oxford. The Clarendon Press. 1955.)

Barbusse, Henri *Zola*. (N.R.F. Gallimard. 1932.)

Barrès, Maurice *Mes Cahiers. 1896–1923*. 14 tomes. (Plon. 1929–1957.)

Le Départ pour la vie (Plon. 1961.)

Belloc Lowndes, Marie *Where Love and Friendship Dwelt*. (Macmillan. 1943.)

Bergerat, Émile *Souvenirs d'un Enfant de Paris. Les Années de Bohème*. (Charpentier. 1911.)

Bernard, Marc *Zola par lui-même* ('Écrivains de toujours'. Éditions du Seuil. 1952.)

Blanche, J.-E. *Portraits of a Lifetime.* Translated and edited by Walter Clement. (Dent. 1937.)

Bloy, Léon *Lettres à René Martineau, 1901–1917.* Avec une préface d'Hector Talvart. (Éditions de la Madeleine. 1933.)

  Le Mendiant ingrat. (Journal de l'auteur, 1892–1895.) (Bruxelles. Deman. 1898.)

  Je m'accuse . . . (Édition de 'La Maison d'Art'. 1900.)

Bonnamour, Georges *Le Procès Zola.* Impressions d'audience. (Pierret. 1898.)

Bonnières, Robert de *Mémoires d'aujourd'hui.* 2e série (Ollendorff. 1885.)

Bouhélier, Saint-Georges de *Le Printemps d'une génération* (Nagel. 1946.)

Bourget, Paul *Études et Portraits.* I. (Lemerre. 1889.)

Brady, Patrick *'L'Œuvre' d'Émile Zola.* Roman sur les arts. Manifeste, autobiographie, roman à clef. (Genève. Droz. 1967.)

Braibant, Charles *Le Secret d'Anatole France.* (Denoël et Steele. 1935.)

Brisson, Adolphe *La Comédie littéraire.* Notes et impressions de littérature. (Armand Colin. 1895.)

  L'Envers de la gloire. Enquêtes et documents inédits. (Flammarion. n.d.)

  Portraits intimes. Ire série. (Armand Colin. 1894.) 2e série (1896). 3e série (1897).

Brulat, Paul *Histoire populaire de Émile Zola* (La Librairie mondiale. 1908.)

Bruneau, Alfred *À l'ombre d'un grand cœur.* Souvenirs d'une collaboration. (Charpentier–Fasquelle. 1932.)

Burrows, Herbert *Zola.* (Swan Sonnenschein. 1899.)

Busnach, William, et Gastineau, Octave *L'Assommoir.* Drame en 5 actes et 9 tableaux, avec une préface d'Émile Zola. (Charpentier. 1880.)

Carpuat, l'Abbé E. *Zola et Paris.* (Montauban. Imprimerie Prunet frères. 1898.)

Carter, Lawson A. *Zola and the theater.* (Paris. Presses Universitaires de France. 1963.)

Céard, Henry *Lettres inédites à Émile Zola.* Publiées et annotées par C. A. Burns. Avec une préface de René Dumesnil. (Nizet. 1958.)

Cézanne, Paul *Correspondance.* Recueillie, annotée et préfacée par John Rewald. (Grasset. 1937.)

Claretie, Jules *La Vie à Paris, 1881.* (Victor Havard. n.d.)

  La Vie à Paris, 1898. (Charpentier, 1899.)

  La Vie à Paris, 1901–3. (Charpentier. 1904.)

Crestey, l'Abbé Joseph *Critique d'un Roman Historique.* Le 'Lourdes' de Zola. (Roger et Chernoviz. 1894.)

Daudet, Alphonse *Trente ans de Paris*. (Marpon & Flammarion. 1888.)

Daudet, Mme Alphonse *Souvenirs autour d'un groupe littéraire*. (Charpentier. 1910.)

Daudet, Léon *Études et milieux littéraires*. (Grasset. 1927.)

Fantômes et vivants. (Grasset. 1931.)

Paris vécu. 1re série. (N.R.F. Gallimard. 1929.)

Deffoux, Léon *Chronique de l'Académie Goncourt*. (Librairie de Paris. Firmin Didot. 1929.)

La Publication de 'L'Assommoir'. (Société Française d'Éditions Littéraires et Techniques. 1931.)

Deffoux, Léon, et Xavie, Émile *Le Groupe de Médan*. (Crès. 1924.)

Delhorbe, Cécilé *L'Affaire Dreyfus et les écrivains français*. (Attinger. 1932.)

Deraismes, Maria *L'Epidémie naturaliste*. (Dentu. 1888.)

Desprez, Louis *L'Évolution naturaliste*. (Tresse. 1884.)

Lettres inédites de Louis Desprez à Émile Zola. Introduction et Notes de Guy Robert. (Société d'Édition Les Belles Lettres. 1952.)

Dessignolle, Émile *La Question sociale dans Émile Zola*. (Clavreuil. 1905.)

Doumic, René *Études sur la littérature française*. 2e série. (Perrin. 1898.)

Portraits d'écrivains. (Delaplane, n.d.)

Dreyfous, Maurice *Ce qu'il me reste à dire*. (Ollendorff. 1912.)

Dreyfus, Alfred *Cinq années de ma vie (1894–1899)*. (Charpentier. 1901.)

Lettres d'un inconnu. (Stock. 1898.)

Souvenirs et correspondance. Publiés par son fils. (Grasset. 1936.)

Dubois, Jacques *'L'Assommoir' de Zola*. Société, discours, idéologie. (Larousse. 1973.)

Du Camp, Maxime *Paris. Ses organes, ses fonctions et sa vie dans la seconde moitié du XIXe siècle*. 6 tomes. (Hachette. 1869–1876.)

Dumesnil, René *L'Époque réaliste et naturaliste*. (Tallandier. 1945.)

La publication des 'Soirées de Médan'. (Société Française d'Éditions Littéraires et Techniques. 1933.)

Dupuy, Aimé *1870–1871. La Guerre, la Commune et la Presse*. (Armand Colin. 1959.)

Duret, Théodore *Histoire des peintres impressionistes*. (Floury. 1906.)

Ellis, Havelock *Affirmations*. 2nd. edition. (Constable. 1915.)

Euvrard, Michel *Émile Zola*. (Éditions Universitaires. 1967.)

Faure, Gabriel *Pèlerinages passionnés*. 2e série. (Charpentier. 1922.)

Field, Julian Osgood *Things I shouldn't tell*. (Eveleigh Nash & Grayson. 1924.)

Flaubert, Gustave *Trois Contes. Correspondance 1876–1877*. Préface et notes de Maurice Nadeau (Lausanne. Éditions Rencontre. 1965.)

Carnets et Projets. Correspondance 1878–1880. Préface et notes de Maurice Nadeau. (Lausanne. Éditions Rencontre. 1965.)

France, Anatole *La Vie littéraire.* 4 tomes. (Calmann-Lévy, n.d.)

Franzen, Nils-Olof *Zola et 'La Joie de Vivre'.* La Genèse du roman; les personnages; les idées. (Stockholm. Almqvist & Wiksell. 1958.)

Fraser, Elizabeth M. *Le Renouveau religieux d'après le roman français de 1886 à 1914.* (Société d'Édition Les Belles Lettres. 1934.)

Geffroy, Gustave *Claude Monet.* Sa vie, son temps, son œuvre. (Crès. 1922.)

Goncourt, E. & J. de *Journal.* Mémoires de la vie littéraire. (Monaco. Les Éditions de l'Imprimerie Nationale. 1956.)

Goncourt, J. de *Lettres.* (Charpentier. 1885.)

Gourmont, Rémy de *Épilogues.* Réflexions sur la vie 1895–1898. (Société du Mercure de France. 1903.)

Épilogues. Réflexions sur la vie. 3e série. 1902–1914. (Société du Mercure de France. 1905.)

Grand-Carteret, John *Zola en images.* (Juven. 1905.)

L'Affaire Dreyfus et l'Image. (Flammarion. 1898.)

Grant, Elliott M. *Zola's 'Germinal'.* A critical and historical study. (Leicester. Leicester University Press. 1962.)

Grant, Richard B. *Zola's 'Son Excellence Eugène Rougon'.* An historical and critical study. (Durham, North Carolina. Duke University Press. 1960.)

Guilbert, Yvette *La Chanson de ma vie.* Mes Mémoires. (Grasset. 1927.)

Guillemin, Henri *Zola: légende et vérité.* (Julliard 1960.)

Éclaircissements. (N.R.F. Gallimard, 1961.)

Présentation des Rougon-Macquart. (N.R.F. Gallimard. 1964.)

Émile Zola. Sa. Vie. Le Sens de son œuvre. (Bruxelles. Centre d'éducation populaire. 1971.)

Guyot, Yves *Affaire Dreyfus.* Analyse de l'enquête. (Stock. 1899.)

Halpérine-Kaminsky, E. *Ivan Tourguénieff d'après sa correspondance avec des amis français.* (Charpentier. 1901.)

Hemmings, F. W. J. *Zola.* (Oxford University Press. 1970.)

The Life and Times of Émile Zola. (Elek. 1977.)

Hermant, Abel *Discours.* (Société d'Éditions littéraires et artistiques. Ollendorff. 1903.)

Souvenirs de la vie mondaine. (Plon. 1935.)

Herriot, Édouard *Esquisses.* (Hachette. 1928.)

Hoche, Jules *Les Parisiens chez eux.* (Dentu. 1883.)

Huret, Jules *Enquête sur l'évolution littéraire.* (Charpentier. 1891.)

Huysmans, J.-K. *En Marge.* Études et Préfaces réunies et annotées par Lucien Descaves. (Lesage. 1927.)

Lettres inédites à Émile Zola. Publiées et annotées par Pierre

Lambert avec une introduction de Pierre Cogny. (Genève. Droz. 1953.)

Ibrovac, Miodrag *José-Maria de Heredia*. Sa vie – son œuvre. (Les Presses Françaises. 1923.)

Jagmetti, Antoinette. *'La Bête Humaine' d'Émile Zola.* Étude de stylistique critique. (Genève. Droz. 1955.)

James, Henry *Notes on Novelists.* With some other notes. (Dent. 1914.)

Parisian Sketches. Letters to the *New York Times,* 1875–1876. Edited with an Introduction by Leon Edel and Ilse Dusoir Lind. Hart-Davis. 1958.)

The House of Fiction. Essays on the novel. Edited with an Introduction by Leon Edel. (Hart-Davis. 1957.)

Johnson, Douglas *France and the Dreyfus Affair.* (Blandford Press. 1966.)

Josephson, Matthew *Zola and his Time.* (Gollancz. 1929.)

Kanes, Martin *Zola's 'La Bête Humaine'.* A Study in Literary Criticism. (Berkeley and Los Angeles. University of California Press. 1962.)

L'Atelier de Zola. Textes de journaux 1865–1870. Recueillis et présentés par Martin Kanes. (Genève. Droz. 1963.)

Kranowski, Nathan *Paris dans les romans d'Émile Zola.* (Presses Universitaires de France. 1968.)

Laborde, Albert *Trente-huit années près de Zola.* Vie d'Alexandrine Émile Zola. Préface de Pierre Paraf. (Les Éditeurs Français réunis. 1963.)

Labori, Me Fernand *Affaire Zola.* Plaidoirie de Me Fernand Labori. Audiences de février 1898. (Charpentier & Fasquelle. 1898.)

Labori, Marguerite-Fernand *Labori.* Ses notes manuscrites. Sa vie. (Attinger. 1947.)

Lafargue, Paul *Critiques littéraires.* Introduction de Jean Freville. (Éditions sociales internationales. 1936.)

Lanoux, Armand *Bonjour, Monsieur Zola.* (Amiot-Dumont. 1954.)

Laporte, A. *Le Naturalisme, ou l'immoralité littéraire.* Émile Zola, l'homme et l'œuvre. (No publisher given. 1894.)

Larguier, Léo *Avant le déluge.* Souvenirs. (Grasset. 1928.)

Lasserre, Henri *Les Lettres de Henri Lasserre à l'occasion du roman de M. Zola.* Avec Pièces justificatives, Démenti et Défi. (Dentu. 1895.)

Laupts, Dr [G. Saint-Paul] *L'Homosexualité et les types homosexuels.* Nouvelle édition de *Perversion et perversité sexuelles.* Préface d'Émile Zola. (Vigot. 1910.)

Lazare, Bernard *Figures contemporains.* Ceux d'aujourd'hui, ceux de demain. (Perrin. 1895.)

Une erreur judiciaire. La Vérité sur l'Affaire Dreyfus. (Stock. 1897.)

Le Blond, Maurice *La Publication de 'La Terre'*. (Société Française d'Éditions Littéraires et Techniques. 1937.)

Le Blond-Zola, Denise *Émile Zola raconté par sa fille*. (Fasquelle. 1931.)

Lepelletier, Edmond *Émile Zola. Sa Vie – Son Œuvre*. (Mercure de France. 1908.)

Levin, Harry *The Gates of Horn. A Study of Five French Realists*. (New York. Oxford University Press. 1963.)

Lonergan, W. F. [Anglo-Parisian] *Paris by Day and Night. A book for the Exhibition*. (Ward & Downey. 1889.)

Forty Years of Paris. (T. Fisher Unwin. 1907.)

Mallarmé, Stéphane *Dix-neuf lettres de Stéphane Mallarmé à Émile Zola*. Avec une introduction de Léon Deffoux. Un Commentaire de Jean Royère. (Bernard. 1929.)

Marmier, Xavier *Journal* (1848–1890). Établissement du texte, présentation et notes de Eldon Kaye. 2 tomes. (Genève. Droz. 1968.)

Martino, P. *Le Naturalisme français, 1870–1895*. (Armand Colin. 1923.)

Le Roman réaliste sous le Second Empire. (Hachette. 1913.)

Massis, Henry *Comment Émile Zola composait ses romans*. D'après ses notes personelles et inédites. (Charpentier. 1906.)

Matthews, J. H. *Les Deux Zola*. Science et personnalité dans l'expression. (Minard. 1957.)

Maupassant, Guy de *Célébrités contemporaines. Émile Zola*. (Quantin. 1883.)

Lettres inédites à Gustave Flaubert. Publiées par Pierre Borel. (Éditions des Portiques. 1929.)

Max, Stéfan *Les Métamorphoses de la grande ville dans les Rougon-Macquart*. (Nizet. 1966.)

Meyer, Arthur *Ce que mes yeux ont vu*. (Plon-Nourrit. 1911.)

Ce que je peux dire. (Plon-Nourrit. 1912.)

Michel, Sextius *La Petite Patrie*. Notes et documents pour servir à l'histoire du mouvement félibréen à Paris. (Flammarion. 1894.)

Mirbeau, Octave *Les Écrivains*. 1re série. (Flammarion. 1925.)

Mitterand, Henri *Zola journaliste*. De l'affaire Manet à l'affaire Dreyfus. (Armand Colin. 1962,)

Monnier, Marc *Un Détraqué*. Roman expérimental. (Calmann Lévy. 1883.)

Moore, George *Confessions of a Young man*. By George Moore, 1886. Edited and annotated by George Moore, 1904. (Werner Laurie. 1904.)

Niess, Robert J. *Zola, Cézanne and Manet. A Study of 'L'Œuvre'*. (Ann Arbor. University of Michigan Press. 1968.)

K

Paléologue, Maurice *Journal de l'Affaire Dreyfus*, 1894–1899. L'Affaire Dreyfus et le Quai d'Orsay. (Plon. 1955.)

Pissarro, Camille *Lettres à son fils Lucien*. Présentées, avec l'assistance de Lucien Pissarro, par John Rewald. (Albin Michel. 1950.)

Pritchett, V. S. *Books in general*. (Chatto & Windus. 1953.)

Psichari, Henriette *Anatomie d'un chef-d'œuvre: 'Germinal'*. (Mercure de France. 1964.)

Quilter, Harry (ed.) *Is Marriage a Failure?* (Swan Sonnenschein. 1888.)

Ramond, F.-C. *Les Personnages des Rougon-Macquart*. Pour servir à la lecture et à l'étude de l'œuvre de Émile Zola. (Fasquelle. 1901.)

Reinach, Joseph *Histoire de l'Affaire Dreyfus*. 6 tomes. (Éditions de la Revue Blanche, 1901–1908.)

Renard, Jules *Journal, 1887–1910*. Texte établi par Léon Guichard et Gilbert Sigaux. (N.R.F. Bibliothèque de la Pleiade. 1960.)

Retté, Adolphe *Le Symbolisme*. Anecdotes et Souvenirs. (Messein. 1903.)

Rewald, John *Cézanne*. Sa vie – son œuvre – son amitié pour Zola. (Albin Michel. 1939.)

Richardson, Joanna *Théophile Gautier: His Life and Times*. (Reinhardt. 1959.)

Verlaine. (Weidenfeld & Nicolson. 1971.)

Victor Hugo. (Weidenfeld & Nicolson. 1976.)

Robert, Guy *Émile Zola*. Principes et caractères généraux de son œuvre (Société d'édition Les Belles Lettres. 1952.)

'La Terre' d'Émile Zola. Étude historique et critique. (Société d'édition Les Belles Lettres. 1952.)

Robida, Michel *Les grandes heures du Salon Charpentier*. (Éditions Rencontre Société co-opérative. 1958.)

Rod, Edouard *A propos de 'L'Assommoir'*. (Marpon & Flammarion. 1879.)

Les idée morales du temps présent. (Lausanne. Payot. 1891.)

Rosny, J.-H., aîné *Torches et Lumignons*. Souvenirs de la vie littéraire. (Editions 'La Force Francaise'. 1921.)

Mémoires de la vie littéraires. L'Académie Goncourt. Les Salons. Quelques Éditeurs. (Crès. 1927.)

Rothenstein, William *Men and Memories*. Recollections, 1872–1900. Vol. I. (Faber. 1931.)

Roux, Marius *Évariste Planchu*. Mœurs vraies du Quartier Latin. (Dentu. 1869.)

Rufener, Helen La Rue *Biography of a War Novel*. *Zola's 'La Débâcle'*. (New York. King's Crown Press. 1946.)

Sackville-West, Edward *Inclinations*. (Secker & Warburg. 1949.)

Sala, G. A. *Paris herself again in 1878–9.* 2 volumes. (Remington. 1880.)

Salvan, Albert J. *Zola aux États-Unis.* (Providence, Rhode Island. Brown University, 1943.)

[Sardou, Victorien] *Les Papiers de Victorien Sardou.* Notes et Souvenirs rassemblés et annotés par Georges Mouly. (Albin Michel. 1934.)

Saurat, Denis *Perspectives.* (Stock. 1938.)

Schwarz, Martin *Octave Mirbeau.* Vie et Œuvre. (Mouton. 1966.)

Seillière, Ernest *Émile Zola.* (Grasset. 1923.)

Sévérine *Affaire Dreyfus. Vers la lumière.* Impressions vécues. (Stock. 1900.)

Sherard, R. H. *Émile Zola.* A biographical and critical study. (Chatto & Windus. 1893.)

Twenty Years in Paris. Being some recollections of a literary life. (Hutchinson. 1905.)

Modern Paris. Some sidelights on its inner life. (Werner Laurie. 1911.)

Silvestre, Armand *Au pays des Souvenirs.* Mes Maîtres et mes Maîtresses. (Librairie illustrée. 1893.)

Ternois, René *Zola et son temps.* Lourdes–Rome–Paris. (Société 'Les Belles Lettres'. 1961.)

Thalasso, Adolphe *Le Théâtre libre.* (Mercure de France. 1909.)

Thomas, Louis *La Maladie et la Mort de Maupassant.* (Messein. 1912.)

Tieghem, Philippe Van *Introduction à l'étude d'Émile Zola. 'Germinal'.* (Documents inédits de la Bibliothèque Nationale.) (Centre de Documentation Universitaire. 1954.)

Tison-Braun, Micheline *La Crise de l'humanisme.* 2 tomes. (Nizet. 1958, 1967.)

Topin, Marius *Romanciers contemporains.* (Charpentier. 1876.)

Toulouse, Dr E. *Émile Zola.* Enquête medico-psychologique sur la supériorité intellectuelle. (Flammarion. n.d.)

Trilling, Lionel *A Gathering of Fugitives.* (Secker & Warburg. 1957.)

Troubat, Jules *Plume et Pinceau.* Études de littérature et d'art. (Lisieux. 1878.)

Turnell, Martin *The Art of French Fiction.* (Hamish Hamilton. 1959.)

Tyssandier, Léon *Figures parisiennes.* Préface par Arsène Houssaye. (Ollendorff. 1887.)

Vandam, Albert *An Englishman in Paris.* (Chapman & Hall. 1893.)

Vizetelly, E. A. *With Zola in England.* A Story of Exile. (Chatto & Windus. 1889.)

Émile Zola. Novelist and Reformer. An account of his life and work. (John Lane. The Bodley Head. 1904.)

Republican France, 1870–1912. Her Presidents, statesmen, vicissitudes and social life. (Holden & Hardingham. 1912.)

Paris and her people under the Third Republic. (Chatto & Windus. 1919.)

Voguë, Vicomte E.-M. de *Heures d'histoire.* (Armand Colin. 1893.)

Walker, Philip D. *Émile Zola.* (Routledge & Keegan Paul. 1968.)

Zakarian, Richard H. *Zola's 'Germinal'.* A Critical Study of its Primary Sources. (Genève. Droz. 1972.)

Zévaès, Alexandre *À la gloire de . . . Zola.* (Nouvelle Revue Critique. 1945.)

Zola, Émile

LETTERS

Correspondance (1858–1871). Notes et Commentaires de Maurice Le Blond. (Typographie François Bernouard. 1928.)

Correspondance (1872–1902). Notes et Commentaires de Maurice Le Blond. (Bernouard. 1929.)

Correspondance. Lettres à Maître Labori (1898–1902). Notes et Commentaires de Maurice Le Blond. (Bernouard. 1929.)

Lettres inédites à Henry Céard. Publiées et annotées par Albert J. Salvan. (Providence, R. I. Brown University Press. 1959.)

Letters to J. Van Santen Kolff. Edited by Robert Judson Niess. (St. Louis. Washington University Studies. 1940.)

EARLY WORKS

Contes à Ninon et Nouveaux Contes à Ninon. Précédés d'une Vie de l'Auteur par Denise Le Blond-Zola. Texte de l'édition Eugène Fasquelle. (Bernouard. 1927.)

La Confession de Claude suivi de Le Vœu d'une Morte. Notes et Commentaires de Maurice Le Blond. Texte de l'édition Eugène Fasquelle. (Bernouard. 1928.)

Les Mystères de Marseille. Notes et Commentaires de Maurice Le Blond. Texte de l'édition Eugène Fasquelle. (Bernouard. 1928.)

Thérèse Raquin suivi de Madeleine Férat. Notes et Commentaires de Maurice Le Blond. Texte de l'édition Eugène Fasquelle. (Bernouard. 1928.)

Contes et Nouvelles. Notes et Commentaires de Maurice Le Blond. Texte de l'édition Eugène Fasquelle. 2 tomes. (Bernouard. 1928.)

LES ROUGON-MACQUART

Les Rougon-Macquart. Texte intégral établi, annoté et présenté par Armand Lanoux et Henry Mitterand. 5 tomes. (N.R.F. Bibliothèque de la Pléiade. 1960–7.)

La Fortune des Rougon. Texte de l'édition Eugène Fasquelle. Notes et Commentaires de Maurice Le Blond. (Bernouard. 1927.)

La Curée. Texte de l'édition Eugène Fasquelle. Notes et Commentaires de Maurice Le Blond. (Bernouard. 1927.)

Le Ventre de Paris. Texte de l'édition Eugène Fasquelle. Notes et Commentaires de Maurice Le Blond. (Bernouard. 1927.)

La Conquête de Plassans. Texte de l'édition Eugène Fasquelle. Notes et Commentaires de Maurice Le Blond. (Bernouard. 1927.)

La Faute de l'Abbé Mouret. Texte de l'édition Eugène Fasquelle. Notes et Commentaires de Maurice Le Blond. (Bernouard. 1927.)

Son Excellence Eugène Rougon. Texte de l'édition Eugène Fasquelle. Notes et Commentaires de Maurice Le Blond. (Bernouard. 1928.)

L'Assommoir. Texte de l'édition Eugène Fasquelle. Notes et Commentaires de Maurice Le Blond. (Bernouard. 1928.)

L'Assommoir. Translated from the French and with an Introduction by Arthur Symons. (Werner Laurie. 1928.)

Une Page d'Amour. Texte de l'édition Eugène Fasquelle. Notes et Commentaires de Maurice Le Blond. (Bernouard. 1928.)

Nana. Texte de l'édition Eugène Fasquelle. Notes et Commentaires de Maurice Le Blond. (Bernouard. 1928.)

Pot-Bouille. Texte de l'édition Eugène Fasquelle. Notes et Commentaires de Maurice Le Blond. (Bernouard. 1928.)

Piping Hot! (Pot-Bouille). Translated from the 63rd French edition. With a preface by George Moore. (Vizetelly & Co. 1887.)

Au Bonheur des Dames. Texte de l'édition Eugène Fasquelle. Notes et Commentaires de Maurice Le Blond. (Bernouard. 1928.)

La Joie de Vivre Texte de l'édition Eugène Fasquelle. Notes et Commentaires de Maurice Le Blond. (Bernouard, 1928.)

Germinal. Texte de l'édition Eugène Fasquelle. Notes et Commentaires de Maurice Le Blond. (Bernouard. 1928.)

L'Œuvre. Texte de l'édition Eugène Fasquelle. Notes et Commentaires de Maurice Le Blond. (Bernouard. 1928.)

La Terre. Texte de l'edition Eugène Fasquelle. Notes et Commentaires de Maurice Le Blond. (Bernouard. 1929.)

Le Rêve. Texte de l'édition Eugène Fasquelle. Notes et Commentaires de Maurice Le Blond. (Bernouard. 1928.)

La Bête Humaine. Texte de l'édition Eugène Fasquelle. Notes et Commentaires de Maurice Le Blond. (Bernouard. 1928.)

L'Argent. Texte de l'édition Eugène Fasquelle. Notes et Commentaires de Maurice Le Blond. (Bernouard. 1928.)
La Débâcle. Texte de l'édition Eugène Fasquelle. Notes et Commentaires de Maurice Le Blond. (Bernouard. 1928.)
The Downfall (La Débâcle). A story of the horrors of war. Translated by Ernest A. Vizetelly. (Chatto & Windus. 1892.)
Le Docteur Pascal. Texte de l'édition Eugène Fasquelle. Notes et Commentaires de Maurice Le Blond. (Bernouard. 1928.)
Doctor Pascal or, Life and Heredity. Translated by Ernest A. Vizetelly (Chatto & Windus. 1894.)

LES TROIS VILLES

Lourdes. Texte de l'édition Eugène Fasquelle. Notes et Commentaires de Maurice Le Blond. (Bernouard. 1929.)
Lourdes. Translated by Ernest A. Vizetelly. (Chatto & Windus. 1894.)
Rome. 2 tomes. Texte de l'édition Eugène Fasquelle. Notes et Commentaires de Maurice Le Blond. (Bernouard. 1928, 1929.)
Paris. Texte de l'édition Eugène Fasquelle. Notes et Commentaires de Maurice Le Blond. (Bernouard. 1929.)
Paris. Translated by Ernest Alfred Vizetelly. (Chatto & Windus. 1898.)

LES QUATRE ÉVANGILES

Fécondité. 2 tomes. Texte de l'édition Eugène Fasquelle. Notes et Commentaires de Maurice Le Blond. (Bernouard. 1928.)
Travail. 2 tomes. Texte de l'édition Eugène Fasquelle. Notes et Commentaires de Maurice Le Blond. (Bernouard. 1928.)
Vérité. 2 tomes. Texte de l'édition Eugène Fasquelle. Notes et Commentaires de Maurice Le Blond. (Bernouard. 1928.)
Truth (Vérité). Translated by Ernest Alfred Vizetelly. (Chatto & Windus. 1903.)

THEATRE

Théâtre, I, II. Texte de l'édition Eugène Fasquelle. Notes et Commentaires de Maurice Le Blond. (Bernouard. 1927.)
Poèmes lyriques. (Charpentier. 1921.)

ŒUVRES COMPLETES

Œuvres complètes
Édition établie sous la direction de Henri Mitterand. 15 tomes.
(Cercle du Livre précieux. Hachette, 1962–9).

CRITICAL WORKS

Mes Haines. Texte de l'édition Eugène Fasquelle. Notes et Commentaires de Maurice Le Blond. (Bernouard. 1928.)
Le Roman expérimental. Texte de l'édition Eugène Fasquelle. Notes et Commentaires de Maurice Le Blond. (Bernouard. 1928.)
Nos Auteurs Dramatiques. Texte de l'édition Eugène Fasquelle. Notes et Commentaires de Maurice Le Blond. (Bernouard. 1928.)
Le Naturalisme au Théâtre. Texte de l'édition Eugène Fasquelle. Notes et Commentaires de Maurice Le Blond. (Bernouard. 1928.)
Documents littéraires. Études et Portraits. Texte de l'édition Eugène Fasquelle. Notes et Commentaires de Maurice Le Blond, Bernouard. 1928.)
Les Romanciers naturalistes. Texte de l'édition Eugène Fasquelle. Notes et Commentaires de Maurice Le Blond. (Bernouard. 1928.)
Une Campagne (1880–1881). Texte de l'édition Eugène Fasquelle. Notes et Commentaires de Maurice Le Blond. (Bernouard. 1928.)
La Vérité en Marche suivi de *Nouvelle Campagne.* Texte de l'édition Eugène Fasquelle. Notes et Commentaires de Maurice Le Blond. (Bernouard. 1928.)
Salons. Recueillis, annotés et présentés par F. W. J. Hemmings et Robert J. Niess et précédés d'une étude sur Émile Zola critique d'art de F. W. J. Hemmings. (Minard. 1959.)

MISCELLANEOUS

Mélanges. Préfaces et Discours. Notes et Commentaires de Maurice Le Blond. (Bernouard. 1929.)
Mes Voyages, Lourdes. Rome. Journaux inédits présentés et annotés par René Ternois. (Fasquelle. 1958.)
The Attack on the Mill and other Sketches of War, with an essay on the short stories of M. Zola by Edmund Gosse. (Heinemann. 1892.)
Lettres de Paris. Choix d'articles traduits de russe et présentés par Philip A. Duncan et Vera Erdely. (Minard. 1963.)
L'Atelier. Textes de journaux, 1865–1870, présentés et annotés par Martin Kanes. (Droz. Genève. 1963.)

La République en marche. Chroniques parlementaires. 13 février 1871–
16 septembre 1871. Texte présenté par Jacques Kayser. 2
tomes. (Fasquelle. 1956.)

PAMPHLETS

La République et la littérature. (Charpentier. 1879.)
L'Affaire Dreyfus, Lettre à la jeunesse. (Fasquelle. 1897.)
L'Affaire Dreyfus. Lettre à la France. (Fasquelle. 1898.)
Pages d'exil. Publiées et annotées par Colin Burns. (*Nottingham French Studies*, Vol. III, Nos. 1 and 2, May and October 1964.)

BOOKS WITH PREFACES OR CONTRIBUTIONS
BY ZOLA

Blavet, Émile *La Vie Parisienne* (*1888*) par Parisis. (Ollendorff. 1889.)
Chincholle, Charles *Les Mémoires de Paris.* (Librairie modarne. 1889.)
Fouquier, Henry *Au siècle dernier.* (Bruxelles. Kistemaeckers. 1884.)
Hyenne, R. [*et al.*] *La Morasse.* (Marpon & Flammarion. 1889.)
Marès, G. *Lourdes et ses environs.* (Bordeaux. Gounouilhou. 1894.)
Villas Belz de *Un Amour avorté.* Roman naturaliste. (Chez tous les libraires. 1883.)
Zola, Émile [*et al.*] *Bagatelles.* (Dentu. 1892.)
[Zola, Émile] *Livre d'Hommage des Lettres Françaises à Émile Zola.* (Société Libre d' Édition des Gens de Lettres. 1898.)
[Zola, Émile] *Exposition organisée pour la cinquantième anniversaire de sa mort.* Catalogue. (Bibliothèque Nationale. 1952.)
Zola, François *Lignes stratégiques pour la défense de la capitale du royaume, du territoire français et de l'Algérie.* (Imprimerie d'Ad. Blondeau. 1840.)

ARTICLES AND PAMPHLETS

Adhémar, Jean 'La Myopie d'Émile Zola' (*Æsculape*, 1952.)
Albert, Charles *À M. Émile Zola.* (Bruxelles. Bibliothèque des Temps Nouveaux. 1898.)
Arrighi, Paul 'Zola à Rome (1894)' (*Revue de Littérature comparée*, July–September 1928.)
'Zola en Italie. Zola et de Sanctis' (*Revue de Littérature comparée*, December 1953.)
Artinian, Artine et Maynial, Édouard 'Lettres inédites de Guy de Maupassant à Émile Zola' (*Bulletin du Bibliophile*, 1950.)
Aubéry, Pierre 'Quelques sources du thème de l'action directe dans

Germinal' (Syracuse, N.Y. *Symposium*, Vol. XIII, No. 1, Spring 1959.)

Auriant 'Quelques sources ignorées de *Nana*' (*Mercure de France*, 15 May 1934.)

'Une autre source ignorée de *Nana*' (*Mercure de France*, 15 August 1934.)

'*Venise sauvée* ou les débiteurs découverts' (*Mercure de France*, 1 March 1935.)

'Émile Zola et les deux Houssaye' (*Mercure de France*, 1 June 1940.)

'*Nana* et ses illustrateurs' (*Æsculape*, 1952.)

Baffier, Jean *Les marges d'un carnet d'ouvrier*. Objections à la médaille à Monsieur Zola offerte à propos de l'affaire Dreyfus. (No publisher given. 1898.)

Baguley, David 'Émile Zola en décembre 1870. Une lettre inédite à Glais-Bizoin' (*Les Cahiers Naturalistes*, No. 34, 1967.)

'Image et symbole: la tache rouge dans l'œuvre de Zola' (*Les Cahiers Naturalistes*, No. 39, 1970.)

Bakker, B. H. 'Vingt-cinq lettres inédites de Paul Alexis à Émile Zola et à Jeanne Rozerot (1890–1900)' (*Les Cahiers Naturalistes*, 1975.)

Bandy, W. T. 'Quelques pages retrouvées de Zola' (*Mercure de France*, 1 October 1954.)

Bouvier, Jean '*L'Argent*: Roman et réalité' (*Europe*, April–May 1968.)

Brady, Patrick 'Claude Lantier' (*Les Cahiers Naturalistes*, No. 17, 1961.)

'Sources littéraires de *L'Œuvre* de Zola (1885)' (Bruxelles. *Revue de l'Université de Bruxelles*, August–September 1964.)

Brown, Calvin S. 'Music in Zola's fiction, especially Wagner's music' (*PMLA*, Vol. LXXI, 1956.)

Burns, C. A. 'Henry Céard and his relations with Flaubert and Zola' (*French Studies*, October 1952.)

Butor, Michel 'Émile Zola, romancier expérimental, et la flamme bleue' (*Critique*, April 1967.)

Carel, Alfred *Biographies contemporaines. Émile Zola*. (Capiomont. 1880.)

Carias, Léon 'Anatole France et Zola avant l'Affaire' (*La Grande Revue*, September 1927.)

Carrère, Jean *Affaire Dreyfus. Réponse à Émile Zola*. (Rouam. 1898.)

Cazaux, Michèle 'Zola en Suède' (*Revue de Littérature comparée*, December 1953.)

Céard, Henry 'Zola intime' (*Revue Illustrée*, Vol. 3 No. 29, 15 February 1887.)

Chabaud, Alfred 'Un épisode inconnu de l'enfance d'Émile Zola' (*Mercure de France*, 1 March 1929.)

Chambron, Jacqueline 'Réalisme et épopée chez Zola. De *L'Assommoir* à *Germinal*' (*La Pensée*. September–October 1952.)

Chemel, Henri 'Zola collaborateur du *Sémaphore* de Marseille (1871–1877)'. II. La Vie parisienne. (*Les Cahiers Naturalistes*, No. 18, 1961.)

Chennevière, Georges 'Émile Zola' (*Europe*, 15 December 1927.)

Christie, John 'Zola, Labori and 'La Grande Revue' (1900): an unpublished correspondence' (Nottingham. *Renaissance and Modern Studies*, Vol. IV, 1960.)

'Deux manuscrits inédits de Saint-Georges de Bouhélier (1876–1947)' (*Les Cahiers Naturalistes*, No. 37, 1969.)

Claretie, Jules 'La Mort de Zola' (*Revue de France*, 15 October 1922.) 'Souvenirs d'un Académicien' (*Les Œuvres Libres*, January 1934.)

Clark, Roger J. B. '*Nana* ou l'envers du rideau' (*Les Cahiers Naturalistes*, No. 45, 1973.)

Claverie, Michel 'La fête impériale' (*Les Cahiers Naturalistes*, No. 45, 1973.)

Cornell, Kenneth 'Zola's City' (*Yale French Studies*, No. 32, October 1964.)

Deffoux, Léon 'Émile Zola pendant la Commune'. (*Mercure de France*, 1 August 1924.)

'Émile Zola et la sous-préfecture de Castelsarrasin en 1871' (*Mercure de France*, 15 October 1926.)

'Émile Zola et l'édition illustrée allemande de *La Débâcle*' (*Mercure de France*, 1 January 1929.)

Descaves, Lucien 'Autour du Grenier. Souvenirs' (*Les Œuvres Libres*, 1946.)

Descotes, Maurice 'Le personnage de Napoléon III dans les Rougon-Macquart' (*Archives des Lettres Modernes*, No. 114, 1970.)

Duclaux, E. *Avant le procès*. (Stock. 1898.)

Duncan, Phillip A. 'Genesis of the Longchamp Scene in Zola's *Nana*' (*Modern Language Notes*, December 1960.)

Ebin, Ima N. 'Manet and Zola' (N.Y. *Gazette des Beaux-Arts*, June 1945.)

Europe. Numero spécial. November–December 1952. Numéro spécial. April–May 1968.

Fournier, Albert 'Itinéraire des logis de Zola' (*Europe*, April–May 1968.)

Franc, Christian *À refaire 'La Débâcle'!* (Dentu. 1892.)

Frandon, Ida-Muriel *La pensée politique d'Émile Zola*. (Librairie ancienne Honoré Champion. 1959.)

Gauthier, E. Paul 'Zola as Imitator of Flaubert's Style' (*Modern Language Notes*, May 1960.)

'New Light on Zola and Physiognomy' (*PMLA*, Vol. LXXV, 1960.)

George, A. J. 'Some Unpublished Correspondence of Émile Zola' (Syracuse, N.Y. *Symposium*, Vol. X, No. 2. Fall, 1956.)

Girard, Marcel 'Positions politiques d'Émile Zola jusqu'à l'affaire Dreyfus' (*Revue Française de science politique*, No. 3.)

'Émile Zola ou la joie de vivre' (*Æsculape*, 1952.)

'L'univers de *Germinal*' (*Revue des Sciences Humaines*, January–March 1953.)

'Émile Zola et Louise Solari' (*Revue d'Histoire Littéraire de la France*, 1958.)

'Deux lettres inédites de Zola à Huysmans' (*Revue d'Histoire Littéraire de la France*, 1958.)

Gohier, Urbain *Zola au Panthéon*. (Chez l'auteur. 1907.)

Grant, Elliott M. 'Studies on Zola's *Son Excellence Eugène Rougon*' (N.Y. *The Romanic Review*, Vol. XLIV, February 1953.)

'The Composition of *La Curée*' (N.Y. *The Romanic Review*, Vol. XLV, 1954.)

'The Political Scene in Zola's '*Pot-Bouille*' (*French Studies*, October 1954.)

'Concerning the sources of *Germinal*' (N.Y. *The Romanic Review*, Vol. XLIX, October 1958.)

'The Newspapers of *Germinal*: Their Identity and Significance' (*The Modern Language Review*, January 1960.)

'Marriage or Murder: Zola's Hesitations concerning Cécile Grégoire. (*French Studies*, January 1961.)

'The Bishop's Rôle in Zola's *Le Rêve*' (N.Y. *The Romanic Review*, Vol. LIII, April 1962, No. 2.)

'Zola and the Sacré-Cœur' (*French Studies*, July 1966.)

Grant, Richard B. 'The Jewish Question in Zola's *L'Argent*' (*PMLA*, Vol. LXX, December 1955.)

'Confusion of Meaning in Zola's *La Faute de l'Abbé Mouret*' (Syracuse, N.Y. *Symposium*, Vol. XIII, No. 2, Fall, 1959.)

'The Problem of Zola's Character Creation in *L'Argent*' (Lexington. *Kentucky Foreign Language Quarterly*, Vol. VIII, No. 2, 1961.)

Gustave-Toudouze, Georges 'Quelques souvenirs' (*Les Cahiers Naturalistes*, No. 1, 1955).

Halévy, Ludovic 'Mes Carnets. I. 1878–9, II. 1879–1880. III. 1880–1882. IV. 1882–1883' (*Revue des Deux Mondes*, 15 December 1937, 1, 15 January, 1 February 1938.)

Harvey, Lawrence E. 'The Cycle Myth in *La Terre* of Zola' (Iowa City. *Philological Quarterly*, Vol. XXXVIII, October 1959.)

Hemmings, F. W. J. 'The Genesis of Zola's *Joie de Vivre*' (*French Studies*, April 1952.)

'The origin of the terms Naturalisme, Naturaliste' (*French Studies*, April 1954.)

'Zola on the staff of *Le Gaulois*' (*The Modern Language Review*, Vol. L, No.1, January 1955.)

'Zola, *Le Bien Public* and *Le Voltaire*' (N.Y. *The Romanic Review*, Vol. XLVII, No. 2, April 1956.)

'Zola's apprenticeship to journalism (1865–70)' (*PMLA*, Vol. LXXI, 1956.)

'The Present Position in Zola Studies' (*French Studies*, April 1956.)

'Zola, Manet and the Impressionists (1875–80)' (*PMLA*, Vol. LXXIII, 1958.)

'Zola et *L'Éducation Sentimentale*' (N.Y. *The Romanic Review*, Vol. L, No. 1, February 1959.)

'The Secret Sources of *La Faute de l'Abbé Mouret*' (*French Studies*. July 1959.)

'The Elaboration of Character in the *ébauches* of Zola's Rougon-Macquart Novels' (*PMLA*, Vol. LXXXI, June 1966.)

'La critique d'un créateur: Zola et Malot' (*Revue d'Histoire Littéraire de la France*, January–March 1967.)

'Émile Zola romancier innovateur' (*Les Cahiers Naturalistes*, No. 33, 1967.)

'Zola et la religion' (*Europe*, April–May 1968.)

Hemmings, F. W. J., et Niess, Robert J. 'Un *Salon* inconnu d'Émile Zola' (*Revue des Sciences Humaines*, fasc. 92, 1958.)

Hertz, Henri 'Émile Zola, témoin de la vérité' (*Europe*, November–December 1952.)

Hoche, Jules 'Le premier roman d'Émile Zola' (*La Revue Illustrée*, tome IV, 1887.)

Hubert, Constant 'Paul Brulat nous parle d'Émile Zola' (*Les Cahiers Naturalistes*, No. 7, 1957.)

Jourdain, Francis 'Zola calomnié' (*La Pensée*. January–February 1953.)

Kahn, Maurice 'Anatole France et Émile Zola' (*La Grande Revue*, July 1926.)

Kanes, Martin 'Zola and Busnach: The Temptation of the Stage' (*PMLA*, Vol. LXXVII, 1962.)

'*Germinal*: Drama and Dramatic Structure' (Chicago. *Modern Philosophy*, Vol. LXI, No. 1, August 1963.)

'Zola, Pelletan and *La Tribune*' (*PMLA*, Vol. LXXIX, 1964.)

'Zola, Balzac and *La Fortune des Rogron*' (*French Studies*, July 1964.)

'Zola, Flaubert et Tourguéniev: autour d'une correspondance' (*Les Cahiers Naturalistes*, No. 36, 1968.)

Kayser, Jacques 'J'accuse!' (*Europe*, January 1948.)

Laborde, Albert 'Laissons parler Zola' (*Les Cahiers Naturalistes*, No. 36, 1968.)

'Émile Zola à Médan: un entretien avec Albert Laborde' (*Les Cahiers Naturalistes*, No. 38, 1969.)

Lalo, Charles 'Taine et Zola. L'esthétique naturaliste et l'esthétique réaliste' (*Revue Bleue*, 12, 19 August 1911.)

Lanoux, Armand 'Cézanne et Zola' (*Revue de Paris*, October 1966.)

Laporte, A. *Émile Zola et les Dreyfus ou, La Débâcle des traîtres*. Lettre ouverte à l'Italien *Zola* ... (Vente en gros. 35 *bis*, rue des Saints-Pères. 1898.)

Lapp, John C. 'The Critical Reception of Zola's *Confession de Claude*' (*Modern Language Notes*, November 1953.)

'Zola et Maurice de Fleury' (*Revue des Sciences Humaines*, January–March 1954.)

'Zola et la Tentation de Saint-Antoine' (*Revue des Sciences Humaines*, fasc. 92, 1958.)

'On Zola's Habits of Revision' (*Modern Language Notes*, December 1958.)

'The Watcher Betrayed and the Fatal Woman: Some Recurring Patterns in Zola' (*PMLA*, Vol. LXXIV, 1959)

'The Play *Germinal*: an Unpublished Letter of Zola' (*French Studies*, January 1961.)

'The jealous window-watcher in Zola and Proust' (*French Studies*, April 1975.)

Le Blond, Maurice *Émile Zola devant les Jeunes*. (Bibliothèque de la Plume. 1898.)

'Sur Émile Zola' (*Mercure de France*, November–December 1913.)

'Les Projets littéraires d'Émile Zola au moment de sa mort' (*Mercure de France*, 1 October 1927.)

Le Blond-Zola, Denise 'Émile Zola et l'amour des bêtes' (*Les Cahiers Naturalistes*, No. 6, 1958.)

Le Blond, J.-C. 'Le Centenaire d'Alfred Bruneau' (*Les Cahiers Naturalistes*. No. 7, 1957.)

'Zola acquéreur de biens' (*Europe*, April–May 1968.)

Lecercle, Jean-Louis 'De l'art impassible à la littérature militante: 'Les Trois Villes' d'Émile Zola' (*La Pensée*, January–February 1953.)

Lefrancq, Paul 'La vie et la mort d'Émile Zola vues par un sénateur du nord' (*Les Cahiers Naturalistes*, 1976.)

Legouis, Émile '*La Terre* de Zola et le Roi Lear' (*Revue de Littérature Comparée*, December 1953.)

Libens *L'Affaire Dreyfus. Lettre à Émile Zola* (Bruxelles. Agence de publicité N. Bertoux. 1898.)

Loquet, Francis 'La documentation géographique dans *Germinal*' (*Revue des Sciences Humaines*, fasc. 79, 1955.)

Lote, Georges 'Zola historien du Second Empire' (*Revue des Études Napoléoniennes*, July–August 1918.)

Macdonald, Arthur *Émile Zola. A study of his personality, with illustrations*. (Washington, D.C. No publisher given. 1898.)

Mann, Heinrich *Zola*. Traduction française de Yves Le Lay. Préface de G. Gruau. (*Nouvelle Revue Critique*. 1937.)

Les Marges [January–March 1930]. Numéro spécial: *Le Naturalisme et les Soirées de Médan*.

Matthews, J. H. 'Note sur la méthode de Zola. (Documents inédits)' (*Revue des Sciences Humaines*, fasc. 83, 1956.)

'Zola's 'Le Rêve' as an Experimental Novel' (*Modern Language Review*, April 1957.)

'Émile Zola et Gustave Le Bon' (*Modern Language Review*, February 1958.)

'The Railway in Zola's *La Bête Humaine*' (Syracuse, N.Y. *Symposium*, Vol. XIV, No. 1, Spring 1960.)

'L'impressionisme chez Zola: *Le Ventre de Paris*' (*Le Français Moderne*. Tome 29, 1961.)

'The Art of Description in Zola's *Germinal*' (Syracuse, N.Y. *Symposium*, Vol. XVI, No. 4, Winter 1962.)

Maublanc, René 'Actualité de Zola' (*La Pensée*, January–February 1949.)

Maupassant, Guy de 'Romanciers contemporains. M. Émile Zola' (*La Revue Politique et Littéraire*, 10 March 1883.)

Mitterand, Henri 'Un projet inédit d'Émile Zola en 1884–85: Le roman des villes d'eaux' ('*Notes sur le Mont-Dore*') (*Les Cahiers Naturalistes*, No. 10, 1958.)

'La jeunesse de Zola et de Cézanne; observations nouvelles' (*Mercure de France*, February 1959.)

'La publication en feuilleton de *La FortunedesRougon* d'Émile Zola. (Lettres inédites.)' (*Mercure de France*, November 1959.)

'Émile Zola à Marseille et à Bordeaux de septembre à décembre 1870. (Lettres et documents inédits.)' (*Revue des Sciences Humaines*, April–September 1960.)

'La genèse et la publication de *Son Excellence Eugène Rougon* d'Émile Zola' (*Mercure de France*, August 1961.)

'La correspondance (inédite) entre Émile Zola et Michel Stassulevitch, directeur du *Messager de l'Europe* (1875–1881)' (*Les Cahiers Naturalistes*, No. 22, 1962.)

'Souvenir de Maurice Le Blond (1877–1944)' (*Les Cahiers Naturalistes*, No. 27. 1964.)

'Le Regard de Zola' (*Europe*, April–May 1968.)

Moncoq, Dr 'Réponse au *Lourdes* de M. Zola' (Caen. Typographie-Lithographie A. Le Boyteux. 1894.)

Montrenaud, Florence 'Un journaliste russe chez Zola, ou les étonnements de Boborykine' (*Les Cahiers Naturalistes*, 1975.)

Moore, George 'My Impressions of Zola' (*English Illustrated Magazine*, Vol. XI, 1894.)

Moreau, Pierre 'Le *Germinal* d'Yves Guyot' (*Revue d'Histoire Littéraire de la France*, 1954.)

Morel, le Général 'A propos de *La Débâcle*' (Charles-Lavauzelle. 1893.)

Newton, Joy 'Émile Zola impressioniste (I, II)' (*Les Cahiers Naturalistes*, Nos. 33, 34, 1967.)

'Zola et l'expressionisme: le point de vue hallucinatoire' (*Les Cahiers Naturalistes*, No. 41, 1971.)

Niess, Robert J. 'Henry James and Zola: a parallel' (*Revue de Littérture Comparée*, tome XXX, 1936.)

'Zola's *La Joie de Vivre* and the Opera *Lazare*' (N.Y. *The Romanic Review*, XXXIV, No. 3, October 1943.)

'Zola's final revisions of *La Joie de Vivre*' (*Modern Language Notes*, November 1943.)

'Another View of Zola's *L'Œuvre*' (N.Y. *The Romanic Review*, Vol. XXXIX, December 1948.)

'Hawthorne and Zola – an influence?' (*Revue de Littérature Comparée*, December 1953.)

'Antithesis and *reprise* in Zola's *L'Œuvre*' (*L'Esprit Créateur*, Summer 1964.)

'George Moore and Émile Zola again' (Syracuse, N.Y. *Symposium*, Vol. XX, No. 1, Spring 1966.)

Pelletier, Jacques 'Zola évangeliste' (*Les Cahiers Naturalistes*, No. 48, 1974.)

Peter, René 'Zola et l'Académie' (*Mercure de France*, 1 March 1940.)

Picon, Gaétan 'Le *réalisme* d'Émile Zola: du *tel quel* à l'œuvre-objet' (*Les Cahiers Naturalistes*, No. 22, 1962.)

Place, David 'Zola and the working class: the meaning of *L'Assommoir*' (*French Studies*, January 1974.)

Pryme, Eileen E. 'Zola's Plays in England, 1870–1900' (*French Studies*, January 1959.)

Psichari, Henriette 'Le rôle social d'Émile Zola' (*Les Cahiers Naturalistes*, No. 12, 1959.)

Zola et la misère humaine. (Cercle Parisien de la Ligue Française de l'enseignement. No. 75. May–June 1963.)

Randal, Georges 'Émile Zola et l'Académie-Française' (*Æsculape*. 1953.)

Raphaël, Paul 'La Fortune des Rougon et la vérité historique' (Mercure de France, 1 October 1923.)

Reynaud, Georges 'Zola et compagnie à Marseille' (Les Cahiers Naturalistes, 1975.)

Rhodes, S. A. 'The Source of Zola's medical references in La Débâcle' (Modern Language Notes, February 1930.)

Richardson, Joanna 'Unpublished letters of Flaubert' (The Times Literary Supplement, 13 June 1968.)

'Claudius Popelin and his Correspondents.' I and II (French Studies, Vol. XXIII, 1969, Nos. 2 and 3.)

'J.-M. de Heredia. An Unpublished Correspondence.' (The Modern Language Review, January 1970. Volume 65, No. 1.)

Ripoll, Roger, 'Zola juge de Victor Hugo (1871–1877)' (Les Cahiers Naturalistes, No. 46, 1963.)

Robert, Guy 'Zola et le classicisme' I, II. (Revue des Sciences Humaines, January–March, April–June 1948.)

'Trois textes inédits d'Émile Zola' (Revue des Sciences Humaines, July–December 1948.)

'Lettres inédites à Henry Fèvre (Antoine, Barrès, Daudet, Goncourt, Huysmans et Zola)' (Revue d'Histoire Littéraire de la France. January–March 1950.)

Robert, Louis de 'Les Paroles d'un Solitaire. Souvenirs' (Les Œuvres Libres, August 1923.)

Rod, Édouard 'The place of Émile Zola in literature' (The Contemporary Review, December 1902.)

Romains, Jules Zola et son exemple. Discours de Médan. (Flammarion 1935.)

Rostand, Edmond Deux romanciers de Provence. Honoré d'Urfé et Émile Zola. (Champion. 1921.)

Saint-Georges de Bouhélier Affaire Dreyfus. La Révolution en marche. (Stock. 1898.)

'La Fatalité dans la mort d'Émile Zola' (Revue Bleue, 28 March 1908.)

Salvan, Albert J. 'Vingt messages inédits de Zola à Céard' (Les Cahiers Naturalistes, No. 19, 1961.)

'Vingt-deux lettres et billets d'Émile Zola' (Les Cahiers Naturalistes, No. 37, 1969.)

'Quatre lettres de Zola à sa femme (1895)' (Les Cahiers Naturalistes, No. 41, 1971.)

Scott, J. W. 'Réalisme et réalité dans La Bête humaine' (Revue d'Histoire Littéraire de la France, October–December 1963.)

Sigaux, Gilbert 'Les Rougon-Macquart en 1962' (Les Cahiers Naturalistes, No. 22, 1962.)

Solari, Émile 'Circonstances dans lesquelles Zola composa ses œuvres' (*La Grande Revue*, June 1924.)

Suffel, Jacques 'L'Odorat de Zola' (*Æsculape*. 1952.)

Sutton, Geneviève 'Au pays de La Terre' (*French Review*, vol. xli, 1967.)

Tancock, L. W. 'Some Early Critical Work of Émile Zola: *Livres d'aujourd'hui et de demain*' (1866)'. (*The Modern Language Review*, January 1947.)

Ternois, René 'Les amitiés romaines d'Émile Zola' (*Revue de Littérature Comparée*, October–December 1947.)

'La naissance de *L'Œuvre*' (*Les Cahiers Naturalistes*, No. 17, 1961.)

'Les Zola. Histoire d'une famille vénitienne' (*Les Cahiers Naturalistes*, No. 18, 1961.)

'En marge de *Nana*' (*Les Cahiers Naturalistes*, No. 21, 1962.)

'Ce que Zola n'avait pas osé dire' (*Les Cahiers Naturalistes*, No. 36, 1968.)

Thibaudet, Albert 'Sur Zola' (*Nouvelle Revue Française*, 1 December 1935.)

Thomas, Marcel 'Zola et *L'Affaire*' (*Æsculape*, 1952.)

Triomphe, Jean 'Zola collaborateur du *Messager de l'Europe*' (*Revue de Littérature Comparée*, October–December 1937.)

Vanwelkenhuyzen, Gustave *Camille Lemonnier et Émile Zola*. (Bruxelles. Académie Royale de Langue et de Littérature Françaises de Belgique, 1955.)

Varloot, Jean 'Zola vivant ou le procès du naturalisme, I.' (*La Pensée*, September–October 1952.)

'Zola vivant. II. Le réalisme de Zola' (*La Pensée*, January–February 1953.)

Vauzat, Guy '*Nana* et Blanche d'Antigny' (*La Grande Revue*, January 1933.)

Vicaire, Gabriel 'L'Esthétique d'Émile Zola' (*Revue des Deux Mondes*, 15 June 1924.)

Vinchon, Dr Jean 'Zola dîne avec les Goncourt' (*Æsculape*, 1953.)

Vizetelly, E. A. 'Émile Zola at Wimbledon' (*The Wimbledon and Merton Annual*, 1903.)

Some recollections of Émile Zola. With a number of Photographic Illustrations taken by the late Novelist during his Residence in England. (*Pall Mall Magazine*, Vol. XXIX, January–April 1903.)

Vizetelly, Henry *Extracts principally from the English Classics showing that the legal suppression of M. Zola's novels would logically involve the bowdlerising of some of the greatest works in English literature*. (No publisher given. 1888.)

Walker, Philip 'Prophetic Myths in Zola' (*PMLA*, Vol. LXXIV, 1959.)

'Zola's use of Color Imagery in *Germinal*' (*PMLA*, Vol. LXXVII, 1962.)

'Zola's Art of Characterization in *Germinal*' (*L'Esprit Créateur*, Summer 1964.)

'The Ébauche of *Germinal*' (*PMLA*, Vol. LXXX, December 1965.)

Walter, Rodolphe 'Zola à Bennecourt en 1867. *Thérèse Raquin* vingt ans avant *La Terre*' (*Les Cahiers Naturalistes*, No. 33, 1967.)

Weinberg, Henry H. 'Some Observations on the Early Development of Zola's Style' (N.Y. *The Romanic Review*, Vol. LXII, No. 4, December 1971.)

Weinstein, Sophie R. 'The Genesis of Zola's *La Confession de Claude*' (*Modern Language Notes*, March 1938.)

Wenger, Jared 'Character-Types of Scott, Balzac, Dickens, Zola' (*PMLA*, March 1947.)

Zola, Émile 'Tolstoi et la question sexuelle' (*Les Cahiers Naturalistes*, No. 20, 1962.)

Zola, Émile, et Le Blond, Maurice 'Une enquête sur l'éducation (textes retrouvés)' (*Les Cahiers Naturalistes*, No. 21, 1962.)

Xau, Fernand 'Émile Zola' (Marpon & Flammarion. 1880.)

INDEX

EZ=Émile Zola